THE BLUE NILE

Merry Christmas — 1989/
Enjoy the Journey!

Keith E. Ruterman

THE
BLUE NILE

ALAN MOOREHEAD

—

Vintage Books
A Division of Random House
New York

FIRST VINTAGE BOOKS EDITION, April 1983
Reprinted 1986
Copyright © 1962, 1972 by Alan Moorehead

All rights reserved under International and Pan-American
Copyright Conventions. Published in the United States
by Random House, Inc., New York. Originally published
by Hamish Hamilton, London, in 1962; revised edition
published in 1972. Originally published in the United
States of America by Harper & Row, Publishers, Inc.,
in 1962; revised edition published in 1972.

This book was designed and produced by
George Rainbird Ltd, 40 Park Street, London W1Y 4DE

Library of Congress Cataloging in Publication Data

Moorehead, Alan, 1910–
The Blue Nile.

Reprint. Originally published: Rev. ed. London:
Hamilton, 1972.
Bibliography: p.
Includes index.
1. Nile Valley – History.   I. Title.
[DT115.M6 1983]   962   82-48895
ISBN 0-394-71449-0

This edition printed and bound by
Toppan Printing Co. (S) PTE. Ltd, Singapore

TO SIDNEY BERNSTEIN

N O T E. This book, first published in England in 1962, deals with events from 1798 to 1869 on the Blue Nile and the main stream that descends from Ethiopia through the Sudan and Egypt to the sea. Thus it complements *The White Nile*, which is concerned with the years between 1856 and 1900, and completes my study of the history of the river in the nineteenth century.

This new illustrated and revised edition has been planned to enable the reader to see the Blue Nile and its countries and peoples as they were revealed to eighteenth- and nineteenth-century Western explorers, scholars and soldiers: most of the illustrations have been chosen from contemporary sources. The work of selecting and assembling these pictures has been carried out with great insight and imagination by Mrs Joy Law, to whom I wish to express my gratitude.

A C K N O W L E D G M E N T S. The first and almost the last person I consulted about this book was Colonel R.E. Cheesman, whose work on the Blue Nile in the 1920s and 1930s secured for him an honoured place among the remarkable men who explored the river; indeed at the age of 84 he was almost the last of the original African explorers to survive. He advised me about my journeys, he set me right on several controversial points, he read the proofs, and he wrote me a number of lively and charming letters just before he died early in 1962. I wish he could have known how grateful I am to him.

I am also much indebted to Mr Richard Hill of Durham University and Mr Felix Markham, the Dean of Hertford College, Oxford, who also read the proofs.

In Khartoum Sir Edwin Chapman-Andrews and Professor and Mrs Alexander Potter helped me greatly by their encouragement, their advice and their hospitality. Then again when things were at a low ebb for me in Ethiopia – a revolution had just occurred and I despaired of getting down to the Blue Nile gorge and out to the source of the river – Mr Donald Barnes came to the rescue with no other motive than disinterested kindness; he provided the helicopter and accompanied me on the journey described in the Epilogue. I was also fortunate in obtaining the advice of Mr Wilfred Thesiger, the authority on Ethiopian travels.

I am greatly indebted to Madame Coural in Paris, Dr John R. Baker, Mr Rodney Searight, Mr D.H. Simpson, Librarian of the Royal Commonwealth Society, and the National Army Museum, London, for generous help with the illustrations.

I also wish to thank Routledge & Kegan Paul, Ltd for permission to quote from Professor Toynbee's preface to *The Beginnings of the Egyptian Question and the Rise of Mehemet Ali*, by Shafik Ghorbal. Finally, there was no possibility of my even attempting this book without the assistance of the London Library, which, over a period of two years, supplied me with almost every volume mentioned in the Bibliography.

———

Extracts from this book have appeared in *The New Yorker* and the *Sunday Times*.

Contents

Colour Plates

Maps

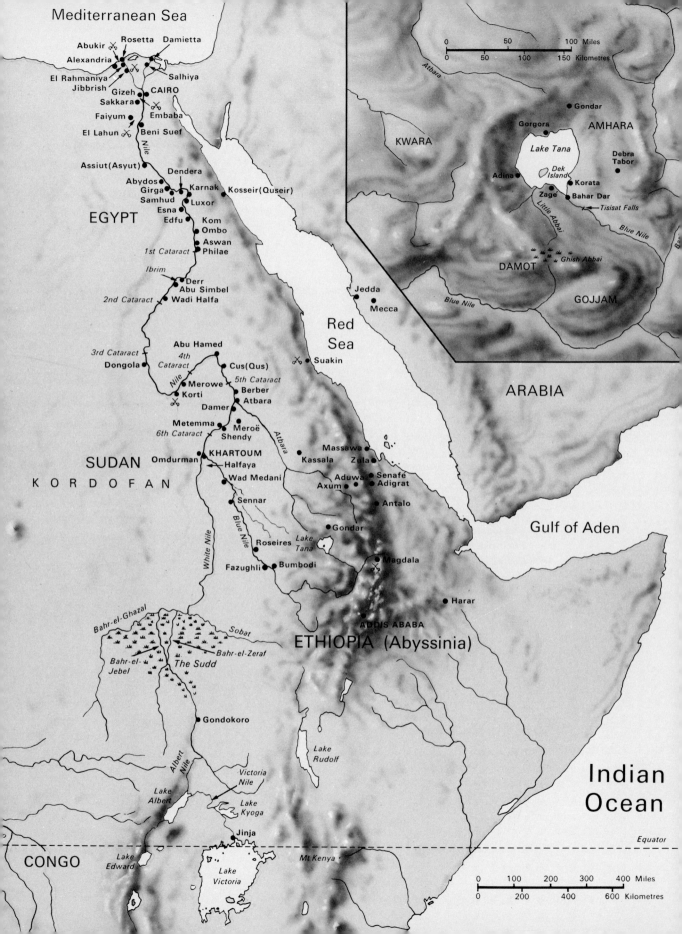

Mediterranean Sea

Abukir Rosetta Damietta
Alexandria
El Rahmaniya Salhiya
Jibbrish
Gizeh CAIRO
Sakkara
Faiyum Embaba
El Lahun Beni Suef

Nile

Assiut (Asyut)
Dendera
Abydos
Girga Karnak Kosseir (Quseir)
Samhud Luxor
Esna
Edfu Kom
Ombo
Aswan
1st Cataract Philae

Ibrim
Derr
Abu Simbel
2nd Cataract Wadi Halfa

EGYPT

3rd Cataract Abu Hamed
4th
Cataract
Dongola Cus (Qus)
5th Cataract
Nile Merowe Berber
Korti Atbara
Damer
Metemma Meroë
6th Cataract Shendy

SUDAN

KHARTOUM
Omdurman Halfaya
Wad Medani

KORDOFAN

Sennar

White Nile *Blue Nile*

Roseires Lake
Tana
Fazughli Bumbodi
Gondar

Bahr-el-Ghazal
Sobat
Bahr-el-Zeraf
Bahr-el-
Jebel The Sudd

Gondokoro

Albert Nile
Lake
Rudolf

*Victoria
Nile*
Lake
Albert Lake
Kyoga

Jinja

CONGO
Lake
Edward Mt Kenya

Lake
Victoria

Red
Sea

Jedda
Mecca

Suakin

Massawa
Kassala Zula
Aduwa Senafé
Axum Adigrat
Antalo

Magdala

Harar

ADDIS ABABA
ETHIOPIA (Abyssinia)

ARABIA

Gulf of Aden

Indian
Ocean

Equator

Atbara

Gondar
Gorgora AMHARA
KWARA Lake Tana
Dek
Island Debra
Tabor
Adina Korata
Zage Bahar Dar
Tisisat Falls
Little Abbai *Blue Nile*

DAMOT Ghish Abbai

Blue Nile GOJJAM

0 50 100 Miles
0 50 100 150 Kilometres

0 100 200 300 400 Miles
0 200 400 600 Kilometres

PART ONE

——

THE
RECONNAISSANCE

The Course of the Nile; the inset shows the area around Lake Tana, Ethiopia.

1
The Blue Nile

━━━

The Blue Nile pours very quietly and uneventfully out of Lake Tana in the northern highlands of Ethiopia. There is no waterfall or cataract, no definite current, nothing in fact to indicate that a part at least of this gently moving flow is embarked upon a momentous journey to the Mediterranean, 2,750 miles away. The actual outlet lies in a bay at the southern end of the lake, and it would be quite possible for a traveller to miss it altogether. The shore line unobtrusively divides into low islands fringed with black lava boulders and overgrown with jungle, and the grey-green water slips in between. There are no villages here, and except for a few fishermen paddling about on their papyrus rafts like water-boatmen in a pond, no sign of civilization at all. The silence is absolute. One sees a few spry grey monkeys on the rocks, and the black and white kingfisher, fluttering ten feet above the water before he makes his dead-straight drop upon a fish. Pythons are said to live in these regions, and they grow to a length of twenty feet or more and are adorned in patterns of black and many colours. If you are very lucky you might catch sight of one of them swimming to new hunting grounds along the shore, but more often they are to be found in the low branches of trees, and from that safe hiding place among the leaves they lash out to grab and demolish a monkey or a small unsuspecting antelope coming down to the river to drink.

We are here 6,000 feet above the level of the sea, and the equatorial sunshine is immensely hot and bright. Towards midday, however, a breeze gets up on the lake, and it continues until evening when, in an instant, the sun vanishes in an explosion of lurid colour, and it can be very cold if you are sleeping out at night. The river is full of these contrasts and surprises. At the source you may feel yourself to be at the extremity of isolation and loneliness, but you can be pretty sure that some dark Ethiopian hidden in the trees is watching every move you make, and the township of Bahar Dar lies just around a headland to the south. Hardly half an hour away across the lake there are Coptic monasteries that have survived since the Middle Ages, and they are inhabited by priests who in the morning and again in the evening walk slowly round their circular thatch-roofed churches with the cross in one hand and the smoking censer in the other. In the wall-paintings in the sanctuary, overrun by rats, peeling with damp and decay, Christ and his Ethiopian disciples are depicted as white men, and they are attended by the half-naked figures of female saints. Only the devil is black.

In these surroundings where it can be blazing hot one minute and freezing the next, where the bronze church bell rings in a wilderness, one soon learns to come to terms with anachronisms and apparent contradictions. It is even denied that Lake Tana is the source of the river. There is an argument – indeed, it is more than an argument, it is an established and accepted belief – that the river really rises in a swamp called Ghish Abbai, some seventy miles away to the south. From this swamp the Little Abbai river courses down through the Ethiopian plateau to the south-western corner of the lake, and its waters are said to proceed through the lake itself to the opening near Bahar Dar which has just been described. All the early maps show the line of the river drawn firmly through the lake. All the latest maps give Ghish Abbai as the source.

But this is a little puzzling. Tana is a very big lake covering a thousand square miles, with a drainage area five times as large. The Little Abbai, though admittedly the largest tributary, is only one of a number of others, and except for a few months during the rainy season there is no perceptible current from its mouth to the outlet at Bahar Dar; its waters become lost in the vast reservoir of the lake. (A somewhat similar situation exists at the source of the White Nile in Uganda, where the Kagera River flowing into Lake Victoria from the west *does* have a fairly well defined flow across the lake to the outlet at Jinja. But the Kagera is not regarded as the source of the White Nile; the source is at Jinja, or, in other words, Lake Victoria itself.)

This is, of course, an academic controversy, and the traveller on the Blue Nile (called here the Big Abbai) will be well advised to leave it behind him and instead proceed down the river from its quiet outlet near Bahar Dar. He will be blocked almost at once. A few miles downstream from the lake the water begins to boil turbulently over rocks and shallows which are impossible to navigate with any safety; and so he must take to mules and follow the river as close to its banks as the thick scrub will allow him.

The landscape is delightful, a combination of tropical and mountainous Africa: acacia trees and the lotus, the banyan and the alien eucalyptus, palms and delicate water-ferns. The baobab in these rain forests is not the smooth bald barrel of a tree which the river will meet far down below in the Sudanese deserts: it puts out broad shady leaves. We are as yet a little too far upstream for the crocodile, but there is an exuberance of birds; the fish eagle calling from the treetop in the morning, white storks with a delicate fringe of black on the wings, starlings that look like anything but starlings since their feathers gleam with iridescent blue, the black ibis with its scimitar beak, pelicans, darters, hoopoes, rollers and kites; and the giant hornbill which is the size of a young ostrich and rather more ungainly until it lumbers into the air, and then reveals the great sweep of its wings, each tipped with white.

The eastern bank is a succession of rough hills, but on the west black cotton-soil plains spread away to distant mountains which are very strange: their tops are the granite cores of extinct volcanoes and they sprout like vast grey cactuses in the sky.

After about twenty miles of this one is aware of some sort of commotion ahead. The murmur of the water grows into a roar, and a low wet cloud hangs over the valley. This is the great object of this stage of your journey, the Tisisat Falls, and it is an extraordinary thing that they should be so little known, for they are, by some way, the grandest spectacle that either the Blue or the White Nile has to offer; in all Africa they are only to be compared with the Victoria Falls on the Zambezi. As with the Victoria Falls, there is the same calm approach past small wooded islands and smooth rocks, and then abruptly the stream vanishes in a tremendous white downpour that thunders as it falls. Looking down from the top one sees far below a narrow gorge filled with racing water, and it twists and turns until it is finally lost to sight in the surrounding cliffs. The spray flung up from this gorge creates a perpetual soft rain which is blown upon the hillside opposite, and here a forest of wet green reeds keeps waving from side to side like seaweed at the bottom of the sea. To stand there just for five minutes means that you will be wet to the skin. For the newcomer it is an alarming sort of place, and he will see with surprise flocks of little black birds with pointed pinkish wings flying directly into the spray and landing on the slippery rocks at the very lip where the water makes its frightful downward plunge. Unconcerned they fly off again through a rainbow which is nearly circular and which hangs in the spray like a whirling firework.

The Tisisat Falls are the end of all peace on the Blue Nile. The river now begins to make its great gash through the Ethiopian plateau. For over four hundred miles it continues in an immense curve, at first in a southerly direction, then west, then north, until it pours itself out of the mountains into the hot plains of the south Sudan. The further it goes the deeper it cuts; by the time it reaches central Ethiopia the gorge is a mile deep and at places fifteen miles wide, yet still, even at the height of the dry season, it tears and boils along too fast for any ordinary boat to live upon the surface. No one succeeded in making the boat journey down the Blue Nile from Lake Tana until 1968, when members of the Great Abbai expedition used specially modified inflatable craft.

One can, of course, get down to the river at the points where its tributaries come in from the plateau above, and these tributaries occur in scores at every stage of the way. Some, like the Bashilo, which comes in from the highlands of Magdala in the east, and the Guder and the Didessa that join from the south, are great rivers in their own right. Others are mountain brooks that flow only in winter, and provide through the rest of the year a rocky and difficult descent to the gorge. But having once arrived at the main stream you must go back to the plateau above by the path you came and then descend again by another tributary: you cannot make your way along the bank. And so the Blue Nile in Ethiopia is only really known from above, and you can, as Colonel Cheesman has remarked, trace its course in the early morning by a curving line of fleecy clouds that hangs about a thousand feet above the water.

At the places where the river valley temporarily widens out a few native settlements scrape an existence down there, remote from all the world, but apart from these no one lives in the Blue Nile gorge. The Ethiopians who are accustomed to the bright horizons of the plateau fear to go down to that damp and malarial heat, and many of them regard the river with a superstitious awe. Even the wild animals in the gorge are not very numerous, and in the main it has been left to the hippopotamuses and the crocodiles to take possession of the river. It is not, then, until we approach the Sudanese border, 470 miles from Lake Tana and some 4,500 feet below, that villages reappear, and one notices at once how great a change has overtaken the people. In the highlands we have been among the Amharic and the Galla races, who resemble no one else in Africa: thin, lively, good-looking people, with skins ranging from light coffee to the deepest black. They have a certain arrogance which may come perhaps from their highland blood and a religious tradition that dates

Thin, lively, good-looking people from the Highlands: LEFT *an Amharic woman milling wheat;* RIGHT *a Galla woman spinning*

back well over 2,000 years, and their mentality is commonly a good deal higher than that of the East and Central African tribes that surround their mountain stronghold. Christianity here is not an importation brought in by Western missionaries, but an ancient indigenous growth of the Middle East itself. But for this and for their dark skins and white robes it is impossible not to associate these people with the Jews – from whom in fact their kings claim to be descended.

Now, however, as one comes down from the mountains to the Sudanese border, the Christian civilization falls away and pagan Negro settlements take its place. This is a country of conical grass huts and of oppressive heat that creates a sort of woolliness in the mind, and of long, slow, uneventful days that have stunted human ambition from prehistoric times. The river, instead of being a menacing thing, tearing away at the rocks and soil in its forbidding gorge, becomes the reassuring source of life itself and its water more precious than anything. In this primitive world every woman is bound to a daily routine of carrying her gourd of water from the river to the village, and since she needs no clothing to protect her from the cold she decorates her body instead. Tattooing – the raising of scars on their naked shoulders, breasts and torsos – is a common thing, and in some of these border tribes the girls smear their bodies with a paste of grease and red ochre, very messy to touch. Maize is the endless diet of the villagers, but sometimes the men, walking out into the scrub with a bundle of spears, will bring home an antelope or perhaps, with a crude net and inexhaustible patience, get possession of a fish. In the river too they wash for gold brought down from the Ethiopian plateau, and there is an exotic local trade in civet cats: their glands produce a substance like ambergris which fixes scent. The killing of an elephant or a hippo-potamus here is an event which is as important as a birth, a marriage or a death. There is a mad rush to tear the dead animal apart, and men standing up to their waists in the entrails hack away with their swords and knives until nothing but skin and bones is left.

There was never any possibility that these undeveloped people would be left alone in their slow dull round of existence; the Ethiopians from the earliest times came down from their mountains and carried them off as slaves, and the Arabs pushing inland from the Red Sea soon added to the havoc in the villages. But it was the Arabs who remained to settle, and from now on, as we cross the border into the Sudan, we meet them everywhere.

We are not quite in the desert as yet; the river still moves along swiftly over black granite boulders and occasional cataracts with a scrub forest on either bank, and the mountains subside only gradually into the plain. Nevertheless, this is a genuine frontier, and anyone who visits this place will come much closer to an understanding of the history of the river. This is the point of contact between the desert Arabs and the highland Ethiopians, between Islam and Christianity; and the pagan Negroes stand as a kind of buffer between the two. No one crosses this border with impunity. When the Arab invades Ethiopia his camels die in the mountains and he himself soon loses heart in the fearful cold. When the Ethiopian comes down into the desert his mules collapse in the appalling heat, and he is soon driven back into the hills for the lack of water. It is the conflict between two absolutely different ways of life, and even religion seems to be unable to make a bridge since Christianity falters as soon as it reaches the desert and Islam has never been really powerful in the mountains. Nor has there ever been any considerable trade between Ethiopia and the Sudan; the caravan routes remain in the plains and Ethiopia looks to the Red Sea for her outlet to foreign countries. Only the river binds these two conflicting worlds together.

The village of Bumbodi is supposed to mark the actual border between Ethiopia and the Sudan, but it is hardly a village at all, merely a few huts scattered through the scrub along the river bank, and it is not until we move further downstream to Fazughli, where there are gold mines, and to Roseires, where the river passes through its last cataract, that we begin to feel the effect of the hard spaces of the Sudan. All that is now left of the mountains are the jebels, the huge outcrops of isolated rock that stand like sentinels on the empty plain.

The river now runs on into the ancient Kingdom of Sennar, which once pushed out its frontiers across to the White Nile and Kordofan in the west, almost to Egypt in the north, and the Red Sea in the east. This is the heart of the Moslem Sudan and the Blue Nile grows steadily wider and warmer as it advances at a slower pace into the desert. There is still a wet season here, and at the first touch of rain every tree trunk and shrub that looks dead beyond recall bursts into hectic leaf. North of Sennar, however, not even the shrubs remain. A few yards inland from the river bank the desert sand takes control, and it will yield practically nothing unless it is irrigated by canals; then fields of cotton spread away to the far horizon. Two tributaries come in from the east, the Dinder and the Rahad, both of them torrents in the wet season, and these too have found their way across the desert by different routes from the mountains round Lake Tana. The Blue Nile is now a formidable stream, and it flows on with increased force to join the White Nile at Khartoum.

The White Nile is a much longer river than the Blue. Already at Khartoum it has come 2,000 miles from its source in Lake Victoria in Central Africa, and except for its passage through the great swamp of the Sudd in the south Sudan its banks are inhabited nearly all the way. But the fall of the White Nile's water over this vast distance has been barely 2,000 feet (compared to the Blue Nile's tumultuous drop of nearly 5,000 feet), and so it has a quiet and sedate appearance. Steamers and feluccas move about comfortably on its broad expanse of water. It is very much the parent stream. However, the real strength of the two rivers that now unite and lose their separate identity at Khartoum lies in the Blue Nile. It provides six-sevenths of the total volume of water in the combined stream, and for six months of the year it rushes down from the Ethiopian mountains with the effect of a tidal wave. By June the force of this flood is so great that the White Nile is dammed back upon itself at Khartoum; it pauses, as it were, and stands back while the younger, livelier river pushes past, carrying hundreds of thousands of tons of discolouring grit and soil to Egypt. At last in January the tremendous rush subsides, and the White Nile begins to assert itself again. Then at Khartoum you can see the two rivers flowing on quietly side by side, and for a few miles there is a distinct dividing line between them on the surface of the water; the White Nile not precisely white but more nearly muddy grey, the Blue seldom absolutely blue except for certain moments at dawn and in the evening, but more of a brownish-green.

The river still has another 1,750 miles to go before it reaches the Mediterranean, and it will receive only one more tributary, the Atbara – another gift of the Lake Tana highlands – before it plunges into regions where there is no rain at all, nothing but this warm, brown, softly moving flow of water to relieve the endless sameness of the desert. Here at last, in a region where everything would seem to conspire to make life a misery – the heat, the dust-storms, the isolation and the lack of any green thing beyond the confines of the river – we come on the first evidence of ancient civilizations which are a flat denial of the primitiveness of Africa, indeed, they are hardly African at all. The first adumbration of these things occurs about 180 miles downstream from Khartoum, at Meroë, near Shendy, where there are some two hundred ruined pyramids standing in the desert, but then, as the river descends towards the Egyptian border over a series of long but gentle cataracts, more and more temples and fortresses appear. This is the region of Nubia, which is another frontier of a kind, or rather a no-man's-land where in ancient times invading armies came up the Nile in search of slaves, gold and ivory, each conqueror in his turn raising a new dynasty and new monuments to his own glory, only to be driven out again by other conquerors, Egyptians, Persians, Greeks, Romans and the Nubians themselves, and it is strange that so many of them worshipped the sun, which was their enemy, and not the river which was their only hope of life. It is also remarkable that in our own era this wild region which was so eagerly fought for and cultivated in the past should have been so very much abandoned.

The pyramids at Meroë

Such life as has remained fixes itself upon the Nubian settlements on the river bank, where the brightly painted designs on the houses remind one far more of primitive Africa than ancient Egypt, and upon the caravan routes winding from oasis to oasis across the desert, and the pilgrimage to Mecca which continues to cross these wastes year after year with a kind of ant-like fidelity, a determined search for grace through the awful hardships of travelling in the African heat.

At Aswan, which was a great caravan centre in its day, and the most southerly outpost of the Roman Empire, another change overtakes the river valley. For the last few hundred miles all has been stark rock and arid yellow sand, but now as one descends the last cataract past the island temples of Philae plantations of wheat and sugar-cane appear, lines of camels and donkeys move along the river bank among palms and tamarisks, and there is hardly a moment when one is out of sight of a village. On the river itself feluccas slide by with long thin coloured pennants on the masts to show the direction of the wind; and even the wind

Hieroglyphics on a wall at Luxor

which was such a terror on the Upper Nile is now beginning to fail. It is the beginning of the softness and lushness of Egypt, and the end of the wildness of the Nile. The very birds have a tame and unhurried air, whether they be the white egrets feeding in the swamps, the pigeons on every rooftop, or the herons and storks standing in the shallows like decorations on a Japanese screen. Even that murderous thrust of the heron's beak, the quick upward jerk of the head and the swallowing of the fish, is a rhythmical and poetic movement as far removed from the image of death as is the frieze on the temple wall where the Pharaoh, with his raised arm, is about to club his cringing enemies to the ground. The buffalo, released at last in the evening from his monotonous circling round the waterwheel, comes down to the bank and subsides with a groan of satisfaction into the mud. Both crocodiles and hippopotamuses have now vanished from the river.

One after another the great temples next come into view: Kom Ombo dominating a bend in the river, Edfu still intact on the western bank, Luxor and Karnak, Dendera and Abydos.

There is a monumental stillness in the warm air, an intimation of past existence endlessly preserved, and day after day one glides on to the north seeing the same things that every traveller has always seen. It is a process of recognition: the pyramids and the Sphinx are prefigured in the mind long before they meet the eye.

Now finally the Nile begins to drop its Ethiopian mud at Cairo, a hundred miles from the sea. Confused by flatness and its own tame pace, it spreads out through many different canals and waterways into the green fan of the delta. Little by little with its falling silt it has pushed the land out into the Mediterranean and lost itself in swamps and lakes. Of the seven mouths the ancients knew only two remain, one at Rosetta and the other at Damietta, but still at the height of its flood the river stains the sea for many miles out, and in a storm coming from the north russet waves are driven back on to the Egyptian shore.

This, then, is the end of the river, the end of a continuous chain of re-creation by which the Blue Nile brings life down from the mountains to the desert and the delta. Without it the people of Egypt and of a great part of the Sudan could not exist for a single day. Even a 'low Nile' – an annual flood that has been less than average – is a disaster. This has always been so and is likely to continue for ever. It seems astonishing, therefore, that so little was known about the river to the outside world in comparatively recent times. Even as late as the closing years of the eighteenth century hardly any commerce moved along its waters, and apart from the caravan routes there were no roads. Above Cairo there were no bridges, and no city of any consequence, no government that looked beyond its own parochial affairs – and this in an area almost the size of Europe. Lake Tana was placed with fair accuracy on the map, and so was the general course of the Blue Nile to central Sudan. But the White Nile was an utter mystery, and it was not even generally accepted that the river had not one source but two. Most of the great temples on the Lower Nile were buried in sand, and in the ramshackle mud-hut villages that perched on the river bank life went by in a torpor of ignorance and monotony. For well over a thousand years the great civiliza-tion of ancient Egypt had been forgotten and its writings were a closed book; nor did there appear to be any bright prospects for the future. The Mamelukes had made Egypt almost as inaccessible to travellers as Tibet is today, the Sudan was virtually unknown, and Ethiopia, locked away in its remote mountains, was still the land of Prester John, a region of horrendous legends and medieval myths.

Just a few indomitable men had made their way into this wilderness. In the early seven-teenth century a group of Portuguese priests had penetrated Ethiopia from the Indian Ocean, and had actually converted the court to Roman Catholicism, but they were soon expelled. Nearly a century later a French doctor, Jacques Charles Poncet, an engaging character who is described as 'an adventurer, a great talker and a great drinker', had travelled up the Blue Nile with a Jesuit priest as far as Gondar, where he treated the emperor of Ethiopia for a 'distemper'; and in the next few years he was followed by other priests, Jesuits and Franciscans, but they too soon lost heart and died or came away.

In the winter of 1737 a Danish sea-captain named Frederick Lewis Norden and an English churchman named Richard Pococke, travelling separately, got up the river from Cairo as far as Philae and a little beyond. Norden produced a remarkably fine collection of drawings and engravings – the first real attempt to depict the Nile monuments – but

Detail of a temple at Karnak

Norden. From the frontispiece to his book Travels in Egypt and Nubia

neither of these two explorers could do much more than throw the light of their own personal adventurers upon the darkness. Norden's editor put the matter very well in the preface to the English edition of his book when he wrote, 'Ruins, monuments, magnificent buildings, cataracts, deserts, haunts of wild beasts, or men as they, everything that can attract the eye, or affect the imagination, is exposed to view. In short the reader seems to accompany the author in his voyage, and to share all his pleasures without undergoing the fatigue and dangers.' The Nile, in other words, was regarded very much as are the jungles of the Upper Amazon at the present time: as the exotic background of an adventure story, closer to fiction than to the normal affairs of human life.

After this there were a few others who wandered for a time over the unmapped spaces of the Nile valley and managed to return to Europe, but by the 1770s a great silence had again closed over the river, and no one, not even the Mamelukes in Cairo, who were strange enough in themselves, could say what was happening there.

Clearly this detachment and stagnation could not last. It could only be a short time before the aggressive curiosity of Europe was drawn irresistibly towards Africa: before Egypt, the Sudan and Ethiopia were each in turn invaded by foreign armies, and the river and its tremendous past were reopened to the outside world. But there were still a few more years of isolation to run out, and it was at this moment that news arrived from the most unexpected and least accessible quarter of all – from the heart of Ethiopia itself. James Bruce declared that he had been to the very source of the Blue Nile and had traced its course from Lake Tana to the sea. It was a kind of reconnaissance for the great upheaval that lay ahead.

A decorative chapter heading from Norden's book

2

Don Quixote at the Source

———

Even the briefest glance at Bruce's life reveals the great gulf that divides us from the privileged classes of eighteenth-century England. He belongs to a world that seems to us now as dead as the dodo: the ancestral arms and the entailed estate, the classical education and the emphasis on manners, the patronage and the violent prejudices. Bruce hated the Papists as some people hate snakes, and if he did not actually believe in the divine right of kings he was certainly monarchist to the core.

Unlike the Victorian explorers who were soon to follow him to Africa, he never takes a moral attitude about such matters as the slave trade or the benefits that civilization could confer on the benighted blacks. He does not even make the pretence of being a reformer or an educator. He accepts the world as it is. Quite simply he is out to do the best he can for himself, and he explores purely for the sake of curiosity and personal adventure.

Even by the standards of his time and his class he was a formidable man. He was six foot four in height and strong in proportion, and he had dark red hair and a very loud voice. He had a reputation as a horseman and a marksman, and wherever he went he seems to have dispensed an air of confident superiority. He felt superior. Even Arabic and the Ethiopian dialects did not defeat his natural fluency in languages, he was an enthusiastic amateur of such subjects as astronomy, he was socially at ease and he was rich. If he was quick to take offence (he describes himself as of 'a sanguine, passionate disposition, very sensible of injuries'), and was often childishly vain and boastful, he was also a man of imagination, and there is no doubt whatever that he was very brave and very determined.

It is strange that with all his obvious merits one does not like Bruce very much, and stranger still that his own contemporaries should have been so brutal with him. Some vital ingredient was missing in his nature, perhaps it was humanity, and when all his hardships and misfortunes are related one is still left with the cold impression of an intensely self-reliant man, one of the kind who repels sympathy by his own conceit.

He was born on the family estates at Kinnaird in Scotland in 1730, and within three years his mother had died. His father soon married again and had three daughters and six sons by his second wife. Thus from the first Bruce remained a little apart from the rest of the family as the eldest son by another wife, and the heir to property and privileges which dated back, it was claimed, to the ancient kings of Scotland. He was a delicate child who soon outgrew his own strength, yet at the age of 6 he was sent to be educated by tutors in London, a week's journey away by coach to the south. At the age of 12 he was put into Harrow school, where they thought very well of him as a scholar. Education 200 years ago was pushed ahead much more rapidly and thoroughly than it is today, and at 16 Bruce was sent back to Scotland to continue his studies at Edinburgh University. He would have preferred the Church, but his father insisted on the law, and this was a mistake, for Bruce hated it so much that he soon became ill. There followed then several years of idleness and convalescence at Kinnaird, and in the end it was decided that he should go down to London and find a post with the East India Company.

In London, however, he soon fell in love with the daughter of a well-to-do wine merchant, and after the marriage he entered her family's firm. With wealth and good connections he was now installed in English society, and it seemed that his career might follow more or less upon the lines of his near contemporary, James Boswell, who was also destined one day, for all his love of London, to inherit family estates and set himself up as a laird in Scotland. But within nine months of his marriage Bruce's wife died of consumption when she was pregnant, and one has to consider just how far Bruce's toughness and self-sufficiency spring from the sudden disappearance of women from his life, for it was to happen again, and more than once.

They were in Paris on their way to the south of France when the girl died, and there was a grisly scene when Bruce, in a Protestant rage, rejected the attentions of the Roman Catholic priests and at length found a burial ground on the outskirts of the city. She was buried at midnight, and Bruce at once got on his horse and rode all night through a wild storm to the Channel. At Boulogne he collapsed, and it was a day or two before he could continue to England.

He was now 24, and the tragedy appears to have had the effect of revealing himself to himself. From this time forward he never really hesitates. He hungered for solitary travel just as Boswell hungered for social life in London, and he seems to have turned by instinct to Africa and the south. Not even his father's death in 1758 could bring him back.

For the next few years Bruce's life is that of the talented young man making the Grand Tour. He studied Arabic manuscripts in the Escorial in Spain, he sailed down the Rhine, he fought a duel in Brussels, he made drawings of ruins in Italy, and eventually George III's ministers found him a job as British consul among the Barbary pirates in Algiers. It was not an easy post. Ali Pasha, the Bey of Algiers, was a sensual and cruel old man who thought nothing of throwing foreign consuls into gaol and of enslaving the crews of visiting ships. He had disliked the previous British consul very much and had written to 'the English Vizier, Mr Pitt': 'My high friend . . . your consul in Algiers is an obstinate person, and like an animal.' Bruce presumably knew what he was in for but already he had vague plans for getting to the source of the Nile – that mystery which for 2,000 years had been, he declared, 'a defiance of all travellers, and an opprobrium to geography' – and Algiers was a step along the way. In June 1762, aged 32, he arrived at Algiers equipped with two camera obscuras for drawing ruins and a quantity of astronomical instruments to chart his journeys in Africa. He found things much worse than he could have anticipated: the Bey was furious at the seizure of one of his ships by the British and the French and was out for blood. Within the first few months of his consulship Bruce saw the French consul taken away in chains, Forbes, his own assistant, was threatened with 'a thousand bastinadoes' and fled into hiding, and Bruce himself scarcely dared to go out. When he did have an audience with the Bey one of the court officials was strangled in his presence. Bruce

stuck it for two years before the British Government gave him permission to leave his post and continue with his journey to the east. From Algiers he travelled on along the North African coast to the cities and the great ruins of the Near East, and it was a progress in the Byronic manner, brigands, shipwrecks and hand-to-hand skirmishes besetting him all the way.

The year 1768, when he was 38, finds him in Cairo accompanied by a young Italian secretary named Luigi Balugani, and dressed as a dervish. And now at last he has his great design in view: he will travel up the Nile into the unknown fastnesses of Ethiopia.

There are a number of unusual aspects about the tremendous journey upon which Bruce now embarked. It was, in a way, a journey in a vacuum, not only in the sense that the places he visited were virtually unknown to the civilized world, but also in the sense of time as well. Some seventy years had elapsed since Poncet had been in Ethiopia, and after Bruce's visit in 1771 another thirty years were to go by before any other European penetrated far into the country. The secretary Luigi Balugani died at Gondar, and so Bruce is the only eye-witness of what befell the two men there; his account cannot be checked by either collaborators or contemporaries. Like Marco Polo he tells an intensely personal story, and the people he writes about so confidently and familiarly were then as strange to Europe and the civilized world as the denizens of outer space are to us today. On his return, says his biographer, Francis Head, he told the public 'of people who wore rings in their lips instead of their ears – who anointed themselves not with bear's grease or pomatum, but with the blood of cows – who, instead of playing tunes upon them, wore the entrails of animals as ornaments – and who, instead of eating hot putrid meat, licked their lips over bleeding living flesh. He described debauchery dreadfully disgusting, because it was so different from their own. He told of men who hunted each other – of mothers who had not seen ten winters – and he described crowds of human beings and huge animals retreating in terror before an army of little flies! In short, he told them the truth, the whole truth, and nothing but the truth; but . . . the facts he related were too strong.'

There was yet another impediment to the success of Bruce's journey. He was absolutely fixed in the mistaken idea that the Blue Nile was the main stream and that the White Nile was a tributary. However, this scarcely mattered; every journey in Africa at this time added something to human knowledge, and the Blue Nile was every bit as important as the White.

He set out at first on Norden's and Pococke's route up the Nile from Cairo, but at Aswan he found his further progress on the river blocked by local wars, and so he decided to enter Ethiopia by the Red Sea route instead. He turned back to the town of Cus below Luxor, and thence made his way across the desert to Kosseir. Here he embarked on a roundabout trip across the Red Sea to Jedda, where he found a British consul who helped him on his way. In September 1769 he landed at Massawa, which was then in the hands of a piratical gang that was even more rapacious than those he had left behind so long ago in Algiers. It took him two months to extract himself from Massawa, and then in November 1769 he turned towards the interior. Up to this point he had covered ground which was dangerous but fairly well explored. Now he faced the unknown.

There were about twenty men in the little party: Luigi Balugani, a Moor named Yasine,

An Abyssinian at Massawa. From a drawing by Henry Salt in Lord Valentia's Voyages and Travels

The mountains of Aduwa. From a drawing by Henry Salt in his own book Voyage to Abyssinia

who acted as a sort of major-domo, and a gang of porters who were mainly occupied in carrying an enormous quadrant and other scientific instruments. Six asses had also been bought in Massawa, but Bruce himself walked. In three weeks he had crossed the coastal plain and had struggled up the mountain paths to Aduwa, which was then a place of some 300 houses and one of the principal strongholds of the country. Here Bruce had a warning of what lay before him: several hundred miserable wretches were imprisoned in cages awaiting the day when their families could raise enough money to buy their release. He pushed on to Axum, the ancient capital of the country, where he saw forty obelisks and the ruins of a great temple, and then marched on again towards Gondar, which by now, he learned, was the seat of the government. It was on this stage of the journey that the famous incident of the raw beef occurred. Bruce declared that he saw three Ethiopians throw a cow to the ground and cut two steaks off its buttock. The skin was then pinned back over the wound and covered with clay, after which the beast was allowed to get up and was driven off. The three Ethiopians fell on the warm meat.

In mid-February 1770, ninety-five days out of Massawa, the party reached Gondar, and Bruce settled into a house in the Moslem quarter. Addis Ababa at this time had not yet been built, and Gondar was the principal city of the country. It was a settlement of some

One of the forty obelisks at Axum. An aquatint after Henry Salt

10,000 families who lived in clay huts with conical roofs, but the king's palace was a large square building flanked by towers and a surrounding wall. It had a view down to Lake Tana, and its principal reception hall was 120 feet long. For most of the year, however, the court lived in tents and followed the army on its endless meanderings across the Ethiopian plateau.

There is an air of nightmarish fantasy about affairs in Ethiopia at this moment, and in the pages of Bruce's book they never really achieve coherence or sanity from the day he arrived in the country to the day he left. This is the atmosphere of *Grand Guignol*, and of medieval melodrama: of horror piled upon horror until everything dissolves into a meaningless welter of brutality and bloodshed. Bruce describes it all in the minutest detail: the endless marchings and countermarchings of futile little armies, the pitched battles, the savage feasts, the treachery and the rhetoric. It all very much recalls the Chinese, who in their traditional opera handle this sort of thing very well. The General struts on to the stage waving his sword, and you can judge his importance by the number of flags stuck into his costume. His Grand Vizier and his executioner stand at his side and scowl ferociously while he hurls defiance at the enemy. Then with a crash of drums and cymbals he marches off, to be replaced by the rival chieftain, who is an even more terrible fellow with his black moustaches and his dagger, and he too is full of braggadocio. The battle, when it comes, is like the dialogue, a pattern of stylized rhythmic gestures signifying nothing. There is a great deal of noise, a great deal of rushing about, and in the end one side is the victor and the other the vanquished; and then it all begins again.

There may be a certain entertainment to be had from these things when they are treated as an illusion on the stage, but when they are presented as actual happenings the drama is lost, the horror becomes gruesome and tedious, and one begins to hunt about for reasons why human beings should be as dreadful as this. It almost seems from Bruce's account that a death-wish was operating among these people, that they were born expressly to hate and destroy one another, and the fact that they maintained an outward show of Christianity and observed a crude ceremony in their manners only made matters worse.

The young king, Tecla Haimanout, and his vizier Ras Michael, who really ruled the country, were away on one of their punitive raids when Bruce arrived, and so he paid court to the Iteghe, the queen mother. She seems to have been an intelligent woman. 'See! See!' she exclaimed one day to Bruce when he confided to her the object of his journey, 'how every day our life furnishes us with proofs of the perverseness and contradiction of human nature: you are come from Jerusalem, through vile Turkish governments, and hot, unwholesome climates, to see a river and a bog, no part of which can you carry away were it ever so valuable, and of which you have in your own country a thousand larger, better and cleaner. . . . While I, on the other hand, the mother of kings, who have sat upon the throne of this country more than thirty years, have for my only wish, night and day, that, after giving up everything in the world, I could be conveyed to the church of the Holy Sepulchre in Jerusalem, and beg alms for my subsistence all my life after, if I could only be buried at last in the street within sight of the gate of that temple where our blessed Saviour once lay.'

Her daughter, Ozoro Esther, who was married to Ras Michael, also attracted Bruce's sympathy, for she was a beautiful girl and she was driven half mad by the violence around her. Hardly so much could be said for Tecla Haimanout and Ras Michael; when Bruce first met them they were busy putting out the eyes of a dozen captives. Of the king's appearance Bruce tells us very little, but Ras Michael emerges as a fairly well-defined figure, a terrible, white-haired old tyrant in his seventies, who adopted the airs and manners of a medieval baron. He rode into Gondar wearing a cloak of black velvet with a silver fringe, a page marching at his right stirrup carrying a silver wand. Behind him came the army, each soldier who had killed a man bearing on his lance a shred of scarlet cloth and the testicles of his victim.

Bruce was received in audience a day or two later, and he found Michael sitting on a sofa, surrounded by his followers, his hair hanging in short curls, a gaunt, authoritative figure, about six foot in height, with very intelligent eyes. Bruce made the customary obeisance by kissing the ground at his feet and was well received. After warning him of the dangers of moving about the country alone, Michael gave him the command of a troop of the king's horse.

It is wonderful that Bruce should have survived and have even been honoured among these violent men whose first instinct was to kill a stranger and then rob him of his goods.

He had a certain value as an oddity, of course, and he carried with him a formidable portfolio of letters from the Sultans in Constantinople, Cairo and Mecca, but they hardly counted for much in this barbaric Christian world. He tells us that the Ethiopian warriors were greatly impressed by the power of his modern rifle, especially when he galloped about on a black charger potting at the mountain kites. Bruce's skill as a doctor also made him very welcome, since plagues like smallpox were endemic; and it was useful that he had

Ozoro Esther. From Bruce's Travels to Discover the Sources of the Nile

learned to speak both Geez and Arabic. But in the end probably it was his commanding presence and his air of assurance that really saved his life. Explorers in Africa tend to fall into two groups: the sophisticates and romantics who absorbed the protective local colouring of the country, and who went about in disguise pretending to be merchants, couriers or even pilgrims on their way to Mecca; and the practical men who boldly announced their identity and who disarmed opposition by marching ahead to their objectives with a show of perfect confidence. Bruce was no fool in the arts of persuasion, and he tells us that in Ethiopia he got himself up in chainmail, cloaks and bright cummerbunds stuck with pistols like any other chieftain, but he tends on the whole to belong to the practical group. He also possessed a good eighteenth-century knowledge of court intrigue and the soft word that induces patronage. 'Man is the same creature everywhere although different in colour,' he wrote. 'The court in London and that in Abyssinia are in their principles the same.' (The term Abyssinia was in general use at this time; Ethiopia is more correct.)

And so, when he had cleared the queen mother's palace of smallpox and had flirted with Ozoro Esther and had flattered Ras Michael, they were ready enough to take him off on the next expedition at the south of Lake Tana, where a rebel chief named Fasil was raising an army against the throne.

This was precisely the direction in which Bruce wanted to go, and it was a great disappointment to him that Fasil should have surrendered before he could get to the Little Abbai, which he believed to be the true source of the Nile. He did, however, reach the river close to its outflow from Lake Tana, and here he turned south-east to the Tisisat Falls. 'The cataract itself,' he says, 'was the most magnificent sight that I ever beheld. The height has been rather exaggerated. The missionaries say the fall is about sixteen ells, or fifty feet. The measuring is indeed very difficult; but by the position of long sticks, and poles of different lengths, at different heights of the rock, from the water's edge, I may venture to say, that it is nearer forty feet than any other measure. The river had been considerably increased by rains, and fell in one sheet of water, without any interval, above half an English mile in breadth, with a force and noise that was truly terrible, and which stunned, and made me, for a time, perfectly dizzy. A thick fume, or haze, covered the fall all round, and hung over the course of the stream both above and below, marking its track, though the water was not seen. It was a magnificent sight that ages, added to the greatest length of human life, would not efface or eradicate from my memory; it struck me with a kind of stupor, and a total oblivion of where I was, and of every other sublunary concern. It was one of the most magnificent, stupendous sights in the creation, much degraded and vilified by the lies of a grovelling fanatic priest.'

The passage is revealing; in fact, it provides a valuable key, not only to Bruce's nature but also to the account of his journey which he was eventually to publish in England. There is first of all his inaccuracy, and it is very puzzling. One cannot altogether blame him for exalting the scene before him – after all, most of the explorers were guilty of exaggeration, and the Tisisat Falls are indeed very fine. But such phrases as 'one of the most magnificent, stupendous sights in the creation', are perhaps a little too much; they smack of the story-teller and the supernatural. Then when he gets down to facts he makes the Falls much wider than they really are, but less than a third of their true height; the actual drop is not forty feet but a hundred and fifty. The references to the missionaries and the 'grovelling fanatic priest' are even more disturbing.

These were the two Portuguese priests, Pedro Paez and Jerome Lobo, who were in Ethiopia early in the seventeenth century, that is to say about 150 years before Bruce. Paez was the remarkable man who, after being for many years a captive in Arabia, made his way to Ethiopia and (in 1621) converted the emperor Susenyos to Roman Catholicism. The ruins of a large and beautiful church at Gorgora at the north end of Lake Tana are a witness to Paez's ability as an architect and a builder. Father Lobo, who followed Paez to Ethiopia, left an account of a journey to Tisisat. In it he declared that he clambered on to a ledge of rock that was below the falls and between them and the precipice. From this perch he says he looked out through the falling water and saw rainbows in the gorge. Bruce makes great play with this: the whole story, he says, is 'a downright falsehood'. No man could have reached that spot through the thundering, boiling water. 'And, supposing the friar placed in his imaginary seat, under the curve of that immense arch of water, he must have had a portion of firmness more than falls to the share of ordinary man, and which is not likely to be acquired in a monastic life, to philosophize upon optics in such a situation, where everything would seem to his dazzled eyes to be in motion, and the stream, in a noise like the loudest thunder, to make the solid rock (at least as to sense) shake to its very foundation, and threaten to tear every nerve to pieces, and to deprive one of other senses beside that of hearing.'

In this tumble of words Bruce overlooked the fact that while he himself visited the falls when they were in flood Lobo arrived at Christmas, which is the height of the dry season. And in point of fact Colonel Cheesman, the chief geographer of the river in modern times, actually sat under the falls just as Lobo says he did, when he (Cheesman) was prospecting the river in May 1926. On the way down the cliff-face one of Cheesman's men grasped the tail of a python, thinking it was the branch of a tree, and very nearly came to grief.

But Bruce, where his own explorations were concerned, was as jealous and as prickly as a lover, and his hatred of the Jesuits was a special hate. This attack on Lobo was the prelude for another and much stronger onslaught which was to follow shortly afterwards.

For the moment, however, he was thwarted in his attempt to reach his main objective, the source of the Little Abbai, and he returned with the army to the intrigues at Gondar and the mutilation and massacre of the prisoners there. For a while he was ill with fever (no doubt malaria), and it was not until October 1770 that he was able to set out again. This time he travelled with his own small party, which included Balugani and a Greek named Strates, and porters carrying the quadrant as before. For the moment the country was at peace, and Bruce had so far got himself into the good graces of the king and Ras Michael that he had been nominated governor of Ghish, the territory around the source of the Little Abbai. It was hardly more than a nominal appointment, since Bruce had neither the means nor the intention of residing there, but it provided a sort of passport for his journey, and it enabled him to impress the local chieftains he met along the way. He passed around the west side of Lake Tana and then moved up the valley of the Little Abbai towards Ghish mountain, which is about seventy miles south of the lake. The final march was made on November 4, 1770, through charming country filled with flowering shrubs and tropical birds and with a view of vast mountains in the distance. Late in the afternoon, when they had climbed to 9,500 feet, they came on a rustic church, and the guide, pointing beyond it, indicated a little swamp with a hillock rising from the centre; that, he declared, was the source of the Nile.

'Throwing my shoes off,' Bruce says, 'I ran down the hill, towards the little island of green sods, which was about two hundred yards distant; the whole side of the hill was thick overgrown with flowers, the large bulbous roots of which appearing over the surface of the ground, and their skins coming off on treading upon them, occasioned me two very severe falls before I reached the brink of the marsh; I after this came to the island of green turf, which was in the form of an altar . . . and I stood in rapture. . . .'

There was no actual flow to be seen – the water merely appeared to seep through the swamp from several springs to a point on its downward side where it combined into a tiny brook – but there was clear, cold water in the well and to Bruce at that moment it was sacred.

'It is easier to guess than to describe the situation of my mind at the moment,' he says, 'standing in that spot which had baffled the genius, industry and inquiry of both ancients and moderns, for the course of near three thousand years. . . . Though a mere private Briton, I triumphed here in my own mind, over kings and their armies.'

But then, almost at once, he tells us, a reaction set in. For well over a year through tremendous hardships and dangers he had struggled to reach this goal, and now suddenly, having won the battle, having achieved what had so often seemed impossible, the impetus and the inspiration of his journey were gone; now he faced the long way home. 'I found,' he says, 'a despondency gaining ground fast upon me, and blasting the crown of laurels I had woven for myself. I resolved, therefore, to divert myself till I could, on more solid reflection, overcome its progress. I saw Strates expecting me on the side of the hill. "Strates," said I, "faithful squire! Come and triumph with your Don Quixote, at that island of Barataria where we have most wisely and fortunately brought ourselves! Come, and triumph with me over all the kings of the earth, all their armies, all their philosophers, and all their heroes!"

'"Sir," says Strates, "I do not understand a word of what you say, and as little what you mean; you very well know that I am no scholar. But you had much better leave that bog . . ."'

Determined to be merry, Bruce picked up a half coconut shell he used as a drinking cup. Filling it from the spring he obliged Strates to drink a toast to 'His Majesty King George III and a long line of princes,' and another to 'Catherine, Empress of all the Russias' – this last was a gesture to Strates's Greek origin, since Catherine just then was attacking the Turks in the Aegean. There was still another toast. 'Now, friend,' Bruce said, 'here is to a more humble name, but still a sacred name, here is to – Maria!' Strates asked if that was the Virgin Mary and Bruce answered, 'In faith, I believe so, Strates.' We are to hear more of this lady later, on Bruce's return to Europe.

It was a strange scene, full of delusions, more to be likened to Lear and the Fool on the blasted heath than to Don Quixote and Sancho Panza. If Bruce was looking for the source of the Nile he was on the wrong river. The true source was in Lake Victoria, a thousand miles away. He was even on the wrong part of the wrong river, since, as Cheesman says, from an engineer's point of view, the overflow from Lake Tana near Bahar Dar should be considered as the source of the Blue Nile.

There was an even more serious delusion than this: Bruce was utterly mistaken in thinking that he was the first European to reach this spot. Pedro Paez had been here in 1618, and his account of his experiences is very clear and very similar to Bruce's: 'On April 21 in the year 1618,' Paez says, 'being here, together with the king and his army, I ascended the place, and observed everything with great attention; I discovered first two round fountains, each about four palms in diameter, and saw, with the greatest delight, what neither Cyrus, the king of the Persians, nor Cambyses, nor Alexander the Great, nor the famous Julius Caesar, could ever discover. The two openings of these fountains have no issue in the plain at the top of the mountain, but flow from the foot of it. The second fountain lies about a stone-cast west from the first. . . .'

And he goes on to give a detailed and accurate description of the swamp and the surrounding country. It is useless for Bruce to claim that all Paez's distances and place-names are wrong, and that Paez's whole account is based upon hearsay. There can be no doubt whatever that Paez had been here 150 years earlier, and Bruce's attack was both spiteful and ungenerous. This was a pity, because Bruce was to make a tremendous contribution to the knowledge of the Nile and of north-east Africa, he was a genuine pioneer, and he had no need to filch others' spoils or discredit their reputation. He in his turn was soon to know the full bitterness of such unfairness when it was directed upon himself.

The whole argument, of course, is very trivial – who really cared about this discovery of a remote spring in Ethiopia? – and yet it was true that from Cyrus to Julius Caesar the kings of the ancient world had occupied themselves with this matter in vain; and it is also true that the history of the river is compounded not out of calm deductions and wise decisions but out of just such petty disputes and jealousies as this. It is a story that unfolds through rivalry, pride, greed and finally bloodshed. 'Peace', Richard Burton says somewhere, quoting an old proverb, 'is the dream of the wise, war is the history of man.'

Kefla Abay, high priest of the Nile
A fanciful illustration from Bruce's
Travels to Discover the Source of the Nile

3

The Way Back

———

After spending four days at Ghish to complete his observations Bruce returned to Gondar, to find that during his absence the whole country had abandoned itself to civil war. There was no possibility of his returning home while the hostilities were going on, and so, like Gulliver among the Lilliputians, he threw himself into the fray with the others and helped his friends where he could. It was a valuable period: as month after month went by he was able to observe the Ethiopians more closely than any contemporary European had ever done. He went to great pains over the study of their history, and his list of the kings of Ethiopia is one of the few authentic documents on the subject that we have. He made collections of original manuscripts and of plants and minerals, he kept daily meteorological recordings ('Smart showers in the evening and night; inches ·342', runs a typical entry: it was always raining), and his general notes are full of interest. He relates that the fish in the Lake Tana waters were caught by being drugged with a substance like *nux vomica*, and that in the Lake itself there were forty-five inhabited islands – 'if you believe the Abyssinians, who, in everything are very great liars . . . dissimulation in all ranks of these people is as natural as breathing'. Bruce himself thought there were eleven islands. (Cheesman's map shows over thirty but many are only rocks.) He says that the lake was too cold for crocodiles, but that he observed many 'river-horses' in addition to deer, buffaloes, boars and hyenas so ferocious that they would drag a donkey down in the night and even attack a man.

He visited the Coptic churches but did not think highly of the traditional Ethiopian frescoes – 'a daubing much inferior to the worst of our sign-painters'. He speaks of the tremendous consumption of raw beef and of the local beer, and of the fear in every man's heart that he would be taken in battle and have his testicles cut off. Mutilation, blinding, the cutting off of ears, nose, hands and feet – these were the aftermath of every battle, and in the end Bruce found himself sinking into a daze of apathy and disgust. 'I at last scarce ever went out, and nothing occupied my thoughts but how to escape from this bloody country.' Balugani died of dysentery, Ras Michael was driven out in disgrace, and one after another the corpses of his followers were laid out on the flat hilltop of Gondar to be picked clean by the hyenas. The weather itself seemed to be part of this holocaust: lightning 'ran on the ground like water', and the sky was dark as in an eclipse.

It was during these dark days, when campaigning was impossible, that the Ethiopians liked to engage in their drunken feasts. The guests assembled in a large hut, a cow or a bull was led in, tightly secured, and with a scarcely credible brutality steaks were hacked from its living flesh. 'The prodigious noise the animal makes,' Bruce says, 'is a signal for the company to sit down to table.'

Women as well as men took part in the orgy of eating and drinking that followed and it was not long, Bruce continues, before all were very much elevated: 'Love lights all its fires, and everything is permitted with absolute freedom. There is no coyness, no delays, no need of appointments or retirement to gratify their wishes: there are no rooms but one, in which they sacrifice both to Bacchus and Venus. The two men nearest the vacuum a pair have made on the bench by leaving their seats, hold their upper garment like a screen before the two that have left the bench; and, if we may judge by sound, they seem to think it as great a shame to make love in silence as to eat. Replaced in their seats again, the company drink the happy couple's health; and their example is followed at different ends of the table, as each couple is disposed. All this passes without remark or scandal, not a licentious word is uttered, nor the most distant joke upon the transaction.'

At last in December 1771, a full year after he had returned from the Little Abbai, and over two years since his first arrival in the country, Bruce got permission to go. He was determined not to trust himself once more to the bandits on the Red Sea at Massawa, but chose instead the long inland route that led down from the mountains to Metemma and the deserts of the Sudan and thence along the valley of the Nile to Cairo. Thus he was taking Poncet's route in reverse, and would not see the Blue Nile again until he reached it at Sennar.

He left in surprisingly good order with three Greeks and a gang of porters, well mounted on horses and baggage animals, and he carried with him in addition to his quadrant and his collections a gold chain given him by the court, and a quantity of cloth and other goods with which to buy off the predatory local chieftains along the way. He was now 41, and a diet of raw meat and honey had not impaired his strength in the least. On the way down to Metemma he delayed for a while to go off elephant hunting, but the hot malarial foothills and the empty desert were very nearly his undoing: he came down with fever for two months and some of his followers died of thirst. With the end of the wet season the tsetse fly, which was fatal to domestic animals, was driving everything before it, and Bruce's

Ethiopians killing a cow. From an eighteenth-century Ethiopian manuscript

small party was a very easy prey for the warlike sheikhs along the route; more than once he was very nearly murdered. Eventually, at the end of April 1772, four months after leaving Gondar, the little band crossed the Rahad and Dinder rivers and struggled into Sennar.

Sennar, though hardly flourishing, had not greatly altered since Poncet's day, but it was the worst time of the year, and Bruce's description of it is depressing: 'No horse, mule, ass, or any beast of burden, will breed, or even live at Sennar, or many miles around it. Poultry

Sennar in 1837. From Joseph Russegger's Reisen in Europa, Asien und Afrika

does not live there. Neither dog nor cat, sheep nor bullock, can be preserved a season there. . . . Two greyhounds which I brought from Atbara, and the mules which I had brought from Abyssinia, lived only a few weeks after I arrived.' As for the temperature at Sennar, Bruce says, 'I call it *hot*, when a man sweats at rest, and excessively on moderate motion. I call it *very hot*, when a man, with thin or little clothing, sweats much, though at rest. I call it *excessive hot*, when a man in his shirt, at rest, sweats excessively, when all motion is painful, and the knees feel feeble as if after a fever. I call it *extreme hot*, when the strength fails, a disposition to faint comes on, a straitness is found round the temples, as if a small cord was drawn round the head, the voice impaired, the skin dry, and the head seems more than ordinary large and light. This, I apprehend, denotes death at hand. . . .' Apparently he suffered all these degrees of heat during his four months' stay at Sennar.

He was now among the desert Moslems and could reasonably expect to find a more cultivated way of life than he had seen in Christian Ethiopia. But the declining empire of Sennar was hardly the best recommendation for Islam. The king, Ismail, like Tecla

Haimanout in Ethiopia, was scarcely more than the puppet of his vizier, the Sheikh Adlan. He was a derelict young man, aged about 34, with an Arab, rather than a Negro complexion, and he seems to have had a weak and fretful disposition. He received Bruce while he was being rubbed down copiously with elephant's grease, which was supposed to give him strength, and in the background there lurked a harem of fat and repulsive wives. Being caught in the web of his own indolence, it astonished Ismail that Bruce, with a home of his own, should risk his life and ruin his comfort, by making hazardous journeys in Africa. Bruce replied that he was a sort of dervish who had renounced the good things of the world in order to atone for his sins. 'And how long have you been travelling about?' he was asked.

'Near twenty years.'

'You must have been very young,' the king said, 'to have committed so many sins, and so early; they must all have been with women?'

Modestly Bruce admitted that a part of them were.

Next he called upon the Sheikh Adlan, who lived in a healthier spot some distance out of Sennar. Here he found a very different man, a genuine desert leader, with a clear eye and a direct approach. Adlan was dressed in crimson satin with a gold-mounted dagger in his sash, and a huge amethyst ring on his finger. In many ways he reminds one of the Mamelukes in Egypt, with his warlike slaves, his elaborate trappings and his famous troop of 400 Arab stallions, the Black Horse of Sennar. He ruled through his cavalry, and it is surprising that he did not achieve more than he did, for it was the strongest striking force on the Upper Nile and it was kept in a state of remarkable efficiency.

Bruce observed that 'a steel shirt of mail hung upon each man's quarters, opposite to his horse, and by it an antelope's skin, made soft like shamoy, with which it was covered from the dew at night. A head-piece of copper, without crest or plumage, was suspended by a lace above the shirt of mail, and was the most picturesque part of the trophy. To these was added an enormous broad-sword, in a red leather scabbard; and upon the pummel hung two thick gloves, not divided into fingers like ours, but like hedgers' gloves, their fingers in one poke.'

With such men Adlan should have been able to bestride his little world on the Blue Nile, but the Moslems were if anything even more divided into warring tribal groups than the Ethiopians, and the decay at the court at Sennar was a growth that spread outward like a wasting disease. More than any other place on the Nile this little medieval state was unprepared for the devastating shock of the nineteenth century that was about to fall upon it. Like the Mamelukes, Adlan and his Black Horse were ideal targets for modern cannon.

Bruce hated Sennar and fled from it as soon as he could get away, but before that happened, in September 1772, he was mulcted of nearly all the goods he had brought with him from Ethiopia. Even his gold chain was taken away from him, and but six links of it remained to him to pay his way down 2,000 miles of the river to Cairo. Within a week or two he arrived on camels at the junction of the two Niles at Halfaya, 'a large handsome and pleasant town, although built with clay'. It stood further back from the river than the present city of Khartoum, and he noted that the inhabitants ate cats, crocodiles and river-horses. Of the White Nile, however, he says barely a word. One can almost see him turning his head away from it; how unbearable after so many years of danger and hardship to admit the thought that his own stream, the Blue Nile in Ethiopia, could have a rival. He allows that the White Nile is larger than the Blue, but he refuses to call it the Nile at all – he refers to it by its native name, the Abiad. One sympathizes.

He was now growing very tired, and to add to his discomfort he contracted the Nilotic disease of guinea worm, which is a parasite that eats into the flesh. However, on October 4 he reached Shendy and now at last he was in touch with the outside world. From this point caravans set out fairly regularly for Cairo. The village at this time had been reduced to a bare twenty-five houses but the market was flourishing – goods were much cheaper and better than they were at Sennar – and Bruce was aware that he had reached a very ancient settlement on the Nile. For the first time since he had been in Axum in Ethiopia three years before he came upon the relics of ruined temples. Outside Shendy 'heaps of broken pedestals and pieces of obelisks' covered with hieroglyphics were strewn in the desert. His route did not take him past the pyramids that lay nearby but he noted in his journal: 'It is impossible to avoid risking a guess that this is the ancient city of Meroë'; and his guess was perfectly right.

Curiously he does not mention Shendy castle but during his two weeks' stay he paid court to the Sittina, the queen of the province who lived about half a mile outside the town.

She sat behind a screen when she first received Bruce but he induced her to emerge on his second visit and he beheld a tall beautiful woman of 40 with very red lips and the finest teeth and eyes he had ever seen. She was dressed in a purple stole with a magnificent gold crown on her head and her plaited hair fell below her waist; and to Bruce she seemed a living reincarnation of the legendary Queen Candace who had ruled Meroë and all the Nile north to Egypt in Pharaonic times. He kissed her hand and the Queen, starting back, exclaimed that such a thing had never happened to her before. These Rider Haggard-like effects were increased by the fact that all through this month – October 1772 – a strange light glowed in the sky. 'The planet Venus,' Bruce says, 'appeared shining with undiminished light all day, in defiance of the brightest sun' – a statement that seems hardly credible although indeed Venus did, that year, approach very close to the earth.

At the end of October he moved on again. He crossed the Atbara, the Nile's last tributary, which he found at this season to be a quarter of a mile wide and very deep, and at Berber he paused to rest and buy more camels before setting out on the fearsome caravan route that ran directly across the desert to Aswan. This was a journey of some four hundred miles, but it was infinitely shorter than the alternative route that followed the river on its great loop around to the west.

There was a final visit to the river bank – 'I bathed myself with infinite pleasure for a long half hour in the Nile; and thus took leave of my old acquaintance, very doubtful if we should ever meet again' – and on November 11, 1772, Bruce and eight men 'committed themselves to the desert'. It was said by later travellers that Bruce greatly exaggerated the horrors of this crossing, especially in his account of the 'simoon', the blasting wind that gathers up the sand in columns like waterspouts in the sky. 'Silence,' he says, 'and a desperate kind of indifference about life, were the immediate effect upon us.' Yet it is only fair to remember that he had only recently come from the mountains, and that quite possibly he may have struck a particularly severe heat-wave. One of his men went mad and was abandoned. His camels died, and the quadrant, along with the rest of his baggage, had to be left behind.

Bruce's quadrant, telescope and compass

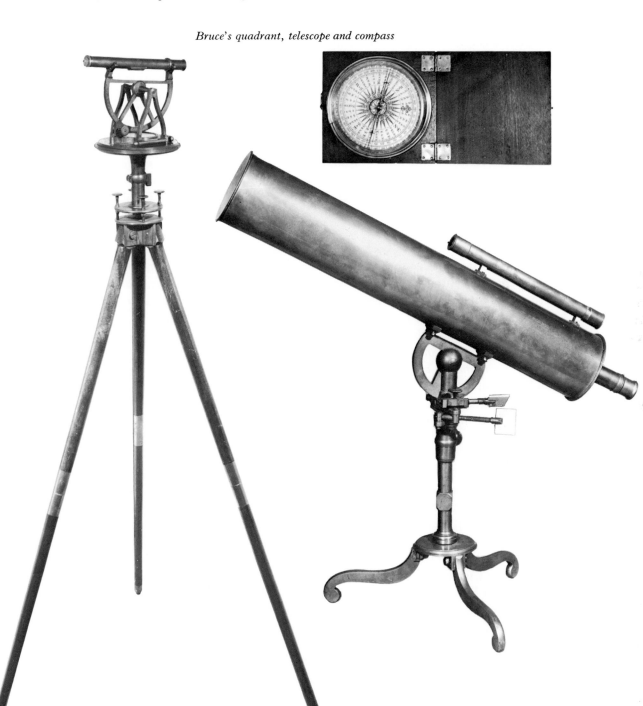

He himself went lame with blistered and suppurating feet, and in addition they were constantly fighting off marauding Arabs around the water wells. At last on November 28, like sailors who know from the appearance of floating driftwood that land is near, they saw river-birds in the sky, and the following morning they dragged themselves into Aswan. The crossing had taken eighteen days.

Bruce was now virtually back in civilization, since from here on the Mameluke government of Egypt was in control, and he still carried his *firman* from the Bey in Cairo. The governor of Aswan was helpful: Bruce recovered his abandoned baggage from the desert, and on December 11 he set sail down the river to Cairo. A month later, dressed like a beggar, feeling ill and exhausted and suffering great pain from his feet, he arrived in Cairo. Here he recuperated for two months, and by the time he sailed for Europe in March 1773 only the guinea worm was troubling him; on being drawn out of his knee it had broken off and had retreated into his leg again. He landed in Marseilles after a three weeks' voyage.

It was just ten years since the traveller had seen Europe, and at this point his behaviour, which had been extraordinary enough, became bizarre. One would naturally have expected him to hurry home, at first to London to meet his friends and give them his news, and then to Scotland. In the normal course of events Bruce should then have sat down to classify his collections and to write his book on his adventures. He did nothing of the kind. He spent a month in Marseilles getting treatment for his leg, and here he was befriended by Buffon, the celebrated naturalist. The two men travelled up to Paris together, and for two months Bruce was entertained very agreeably in the capital. He was received by Louis XVI, and later sent some seeds of rare Ethiopian plants to the king's garden.

Next he turned south to Italy. The ostensible reason for this new journey was that his knee was still troubling him, and that he intended to try the medicinal baths at Porretta, in the Apennines. The real reason, however, was that he had discovered, like so many soldiers returning from the wars, that his girl had abandoned him for another man. This was the Maria whom he had toasted at the source of the Little Abbai. She was a Scotswoman to whom he had become engaged before setting out on his journeys, and it seems that Bruce seriously expected her to wait for him – without letters or news of any kind, and for twelve years. But she had not waited; she was now the wife of an Italian aristocrat, the Marchese Filippo d'Accoramboni, and she was living in Rome. Bruce, on arriving there, burst in on the astonished husband with an effect that might have been devastating if it had not been so near to French farce; one must remember his six foot four inches, and he was now a gaunt, weatherbeaten figure and very angry. He wanted an apology, and failing an apology a duel. The Italian, aghast, wrote out a letter saying that he had never even heard of Bruce until this moment, and that he now hastened to offer his apologies if he had done him any wrong. With this Bruce retired, and settled down to a winter season in Rome, calling upon Pope Clement XIV, and getting treatment for his leg.

In the spring of 1774 he turned north again. But still he lingered, and it was not until June that he crossed from Paris to London. At first things went well. The fact that George III kindly received his drawings, or rather Balugani's drawings, of the ruins and cities of the Near East and Africa perhaps did not mean very much, since His Majesty, in that scintillating age of Burke, Gibbon, Johnson and Walpole, was always receiving books and portfolios of one kind or another, and was not the best appreciator of them. But the learned societies and the salons of fashionable London were very ready to hear what Bruce had to say. It was soon apparent, however, that they were listening, not with respect, but with amusement: the sort of amusement one reserves for marvellous story-tellers such as Baron Munchausen. What on earth was all this about cutting steaks from cows? And how droll the good man was about his barbarous emperors and sheikhs, his girl-brides, his black slaves and his river-horses.

There can hardly have been a time when London could produce so many wits to deal with this sort of thing. Peter Pindar, the fashionable satirist of the day, was soon to compose a couplet:

> *Nor have I been where men (what loss alas!)*
> *Kill half a cow and turn the rest to grass.*

It was all too good to be true. The land of Prester John had turned out to be the land of Prestidigitator Bruce.

The explorer's fate was finally sealed when Dr Johnson turned upon him. Johnson, now an old man, was deeply interested in Ethiopia. Some forty years before he himself had

One of Luigi Balugani's drawings: the temple at Sufetula (modern Sbeitla), in Tunisia

translated Father Lobo's *A Voyage to Abyssinia* into English. It was his first literary work, and in his preface to the book he produced, in its full power, the following Johnsonian style: 'He [Father Lobo] appears, by his modest and disaffected narration, to have described things as he saw them; to have copied nature from life; and to have consulted his senses, not his imagination. He meets with no basilisks, that destroy his eyes; his crocodiles devour their prey without tears; and his cataracts fall from the rock without deafening their neighbouring inhabitants . . . he [the reader] will discover, what will always be discovered by a diligent and impartial inquirer, that, wherever human nature is to be found, there is a mixture of vice and virtue, a contest of passion and reason. . . .'

Holding as he did these views about Father Lobo, Johnson did not at all welcome Bruce's description of the man as a liar. On the contrary, he found Bruce himself very unreliable, a man who consulted his imagination rather than his senses, and who was not at all modest. On the authority of one of his biographers we have it that Johnson said, 'that when he first conversed with Mr Bruce, the Abyssinian traveller, he was very much inclined to believe he had been there, but that he had afterwards altered his opinion.'

There is even a slight note of derision from Fanny Burney, who also met Bruce about this time. She wrote: 'Mr Bruce's grand air, gigantic height, and forbidding brow awed everybody. He is the tallest man you ever saw *gratis*.'

Bruce was affronted and disgusted. 'As soon as Bruce found,' his biographer says, 'that in England public opinion was against him, in sullen indignation, he determined to retire into his own country . . . his spirit too proud to accept a smile as an atonement for a barbarous prejudice and an unjustifiable insult.'

Edinburgh received him better, and so did Bruce's own estates at Kinnaird which, though badly in need of attention, now included a number of valuable coal-mines. Within two years he had married Mary Dundas, who was a grand-daughter of the Earl of Lauderdale and a charming girl who had been born in the same year that Bruce's first wife had died; she was thus twenty-four years younger than her husband. They had several children, and Bruce, a rich man with a fine house (which he rebuilt), was happy enough dispensing patronage and hospitality. He went through his collections. He indulged his passion for astronomy by erecting an observatory on the top of his house, and there he could often be found dressed in a turban and Ethiopian costume, observing those same stars which had looked down on him so long ago in the Ethiopian mountains. He continued to be an active horseman, but he grew so fat that his carriage was observed to bend sideways when he got into it. He was a laird in the grand manner, still with his eccentricities, and gracefully growing old.

Yet still the sullen indignation burned on. He would not publish. He arranged his journals, he made translations of Ethiopian documents, but resolutely he refused to commit anything to print. It well could have been that things would have gone on like this, but one more tragedy awaited him. In 1788, when he was 58, his young wife died. Bruce felt this blow very deeply, and in an effort to rouse him from his apathy and melancholy friends urged him to bring out an account of his travels; and at last he gave way. After all, the critics had had their moment of malice fourteen years before and were hardly likely to return to the attack a second time. The book was to be his final justification.

Bruce was not the first traveller to find that writing can be, in its own way, as irksome a business as the most arduous journey, and he began his task with great difficulty and very slowly. However, an amanuensis was found for him, a Mr B. H. Latrobe, who was a pastor of the Moravian church in Fetter Lane, and in May 1788 Bruce went down to London to work with him. He took rooms in Buckingham Street off the Strand.

Latrobe has left an account of his collaboration with the great traveller. He says that he called on Bruce, 'and was immediately set to work by him; he dictated to me his ideas,

Kinnaird House, Stirlingshire. A drawing from J. S. Fleming's Ancient Castles and Mansions of the Stirling Nobility

leaving it to my own judgment, in a great measure, in what words I was to express them. This was a task that required the most persevering attention, as well as a great quickness of pen, as he himself, seated in an easy chair, had nothing to do but crowd his ideas upon me, and he was very impatient if I did not keep pace with him. In this manner I attended him every morning before eight o'clock and was frequently detained until nine at night, during which time I had no intermission of labour unless when he was under the necessity of devoting some time to a friend that called upon him, or he chanced to fall asleep in the midst of his dictating, or during the time of dinner, for breakfast and tea were expected to make no interruption to the business. I believe that during the whole time of my attendance I did not miss about four or five days without doing more or less for him.'

Latrobe says that in addition he edited nine folio volumes of the manuscript, 'a very tedious and disagreeable task. . . . I had once or twice the misfortune to offend him in endeavouring to expunge a few grammatical errors.'

By June 1789, a year after its commencement, the work was finished, and Latrobe goes on: 'He said that he was much embarrassed how to recompense the labour and assiduity and the assistance I had given him, as he wished to *remunerate* me as a *friend*, not as a clerk: I told him I was under the same embarrassment, especially as I wished to serve him as a friend, and not as a *clerk*. He then told me he should be in town, and want my assistance the following November, he would postpone his *remunerations* till then, to which I agreed.'

Thereafter Latrobe continued to supply Bruce with information and books that he wanted, but he received no answer. At length he decided that Bruce was no longer treating him as a friend, and that he now wanted his money: 'I wrote to him in the capacity of his *clerk*, a letter in terms as polite as I was master of reminding him of his *remuneration*.' There was no answer from Scotland and Latrobe wrote again. At last, after a further two months' delay, the following letter arrived:

Mr Latrobe.
Sir,
    I have received your letter and really never thought you put yourself on the footing of payment, nor do I well know for what, for it has been of no use to me. . . . As for your reading of the book, I never understood it was to be material to me indeed it is so little so that I have quite changed and new modelled it and wrote it fair since you saw it, nor has your reading the manuscript save[d] me an hour's work. Elmsley [Bruce's London agent] has an account with me. . . . If he will advance you such a thing as five guineas for me I will repay him and he may draw upon the whole, but I never really though[t] I had another debt in London.
    I am, Sir,
                    your most obedient Servant,
                            James Bruce.

All this bears a strong resemblance to Bruce's treatment of Balugani, the Italian artist who died in Ethiopia. Bruce never in his book or elsewhere acknowledged that Balugani had been with him to the Little Abbai – indeed, he hardly mentions the artist at all – and when he first returned to London he presented Balugani's drawings to George III as his own. In short, Bruce lived in a private world of egomania and he could not bear either a partner or a rival.

The book, when it appeared in 1790, seventeen years after Bruce's return from Ethiopia, was a handsome affair of five large quarto volumes entitled, 'Travels to discover the Sources of the Nile, in the years 1768, 1769, 1770, 1771, 1772, and 1773, by James Bruce of Kinnaird Esq., F.R.S.', and it was dedicated to George III. In his preface Bruce declares that he will not deign to reply to 'any cavills, captious or idle objections' which the critics might raise: 'What I have written I have written.'

'His enemies,' says his biographer, 'with pens in their hands had impatiently waited for his book, like Shylock, whetting his knife, and it was no sooner published, than Bruce was

Benjamin Latrobe. Engraving by William Bromley after a painting by John Astley

deprived of what was actually nearest to his heart – his honour and his reputation. It was useless to stand against the storm that assailed him; it was impossible to swim against the current that overwhelmed him. His volumes were universally disbelieved. . . .'

Once again the old outcry against such stories as the eating of raw beef cut from living cattle was raised; meticulously, wittily and maliciously the book was reviled and taken to pieces. Walpole found the five volumes 'dull and dear'. It seemed that there was no length to which literary London would not go to turn Bruce into a laughing-stock. A new edition of Baron Munchausen was brought out and it was entitled 'Gulliver Reviv'd: the Singular Travels, Campaigns, Voyages, and Sporting Adventures of Baron Munnikhouson, commonly pronounced Munchausen; as he relates them over a bottle when surrounded by his friends. Or the Vice of Lying properly exposed.' It was dedicated to James Bruce.

Morose and enraged, Bruce retired into his shell in Scotland. Occasionally he made brief visits to London, but he remained for the most part with his family at Kinnaird, entertaining his neighbours. The news of the French revolution and of the execution of his old patron Louis XVI increased his disgust with the outside world. Just occasionally he flared up, as when a guest at a country house-party was rash enough to say that it was impossible that the Ethiopians could eat uncooked meat. Bruce went out to the kitchen and returned with a piece of raw beef which he had peppered and salted in the Ethiopian manner. 'You will either eat that, sir, or fight me,' he said. When the unfortunate guest had consumed the whole steak Bruce said, 'Now, sir, you will never again say it is impossible.'

The last act was tragic. Bruce had been entertaining a large party at Kinnaird, and having seen off one of his guests was hurrying up the great staircase of his house to fetch another when he tripped and fell. He pitched on to his head. He lived for a few hours but never regained consciousness. He was just 64.

It is still a little difficult to assess Bruce's place in African travels. Long after his death – for forty years at least – his book was believed by many people to be romantic fiction, and critics continued to attack it. Yet almost from the first it had a popular success, and in the last 150 years it has been repeatedly reprinted and read all over the world. Copies of the first edition, which were once burned as wastepaper in Dublin, are now valuable items in the shops that sell rare books. There are of course innumerable weaknesses and inaccuracies in the text: the author is a vain and intolerant man, he embroiders and exaggerates, and it is hardly likely that the grandiose speeches he so confidently puts into the mouths of his wild characters were really made in just that way. Yet all this does not explain why his contemporaries should have failed to see here a work of major originality and importance which stuck to the truth in all its more serious facts, and which was far in advance of the scientific and geographical knowledge of Ethiopia at that time. No one doubted Captain Cook, a contemporary of Bruce's, who brought back accounts of equally marvellous things from the South Pacific. It seems that Bruce's contemporaries may have disbelieved him because they wanted to disbelieve him. They disliked his style, and when they attacked his facts they were in reality attacking his ungenerosity to his companions, his boastfulness, his snobbery and his aggressive pride, in short his bumptiousness. It may also have been that the privileged members of the London clubs did not particularly want to be reminded of the barbarous and menacing outer world any more than Louis XVI wanted to be reminded of the mob: their own safe and amusing coterie was good enough, and interlopers like Bruce were a natural target for sophisticated wit.

But Bruce's place may be even more complicated than this. He was disbelieved but he was not ignored. He gave life to a legend, he stirred up people's imaginations; at a time when European politics and ambitions were moving outward he turned people's attention to the Nile. A new and more scientific generation of explorers and men of action was being born, and it was not long before the more serious among them, men like Browne and Burckhardt, began to discover that Bruce, far from being a romancer, was a most reliable guide. Little by little they got through the embroideries of his book to the heart of the story he had to tell, and they found it astonishingly sound.

These effects were even more important in France than they were in England, for the French had never scouted Bruce's achievements. They took him very seriously. They added his information to their own African archives, and to the work being produced by such men as their geographer d'Anville, who had already published a map of the Nile valley which was far superior to any other in existence. And so an attraction towards Africa that was both geographical and political was building itself up in France towards the end of the eighteenth century, and it needed only some dominant figure to give it direction and force. Now at last the long Egyptian sleep was ending, and the great eruption into the Nile valley was ready to begin.

Engravings from the title-page of Bruce's
Travels to Discover the Sources of the Nile

PART TWO

——

THE FRENCH IN
EGYPT

Double caricature of Bonaparte by De Vinck

4

Bonaparte Sets Out

Bonaparte's admiring biographer, Thiers, describes the French invasion of Egypt as 'the rashest attempt that history records: rasher even than Moscow'. But was it really so? In the year 1798 French arms were everywhere victorious; the Dutch were allies, the central European states were contained along the Rhine, Spain was helpless, and by his defeat of Austria Bonaparte had not only conquered northern and central Italy but had made himself virtually director of the Papacy as well. It was really a matter of finding fresh battlefields for the revolutionary army, since it was filled with confidence and eager for more victories.

It was true that England was still in the field, but what could England do? The Royal Navy might be very strong, but its morale had recently been damaged by two mutinies, and for some time past England had withdrawn her fleet from the Mediterranean, merely contenting herself with the blockade of Cadiz. Her best ships were needed nearer at home, since she herself was in imminent danger of invasion, and it was by no means certain that the French army would not manage to get ashore, either in Ireland or in the vicinity of Folkestone, on the south coast. The French, in fact, were actively planning just such an expedition.

Nor was the Egyptian campaign a hastily conceived project or a mere pretext for continuing the war. Bonaparte had been preparing for it for a long time. He had very carefully studied affairs in the Near East: in 1797 Milan's celebrated library was removed by the French as part of their booty; when the books arrived in Paris it was found that nearly every volume relating to the East was annotated by marginal notes in Bonaparte's handwriting. He had every reason to believe that the Ottoman Empire was far too weak to defend its distant province in Egypt, and that in Egypt itself the Mamelukes were a worn-out military clique of medieval backwardness; how could their cavalry hope to contend with the new infantry tactics and modern artillery? Bonaparte's friend Volney had travelled widely through the Sultan's dominions, and had provided him with very full information on this score. 'The forces of the Mamelukes,' Volney had written, 'are a rabble, their way of fighting a duel, their war merely brigandage.'

As for Alexandria, the port at which presumably the French would land, it was defenceless: 'One sees there no fortifications of any kind: the lighthouse, even with its high towers, is no bastion. There are not four cannon in order, and not a single gunner who knows how to aim them. The five hundred Janissaries who are supposed to form the garrison have been reduced in numbers by a half, and are common workmen who hardly know how to light a pipe.'

Once conquered, Egypt would not be difficult to govern. 'There is no country in the world,' Bonaparte was to write later, 'where the government controls more closely, by means of the Nile, the life of the people. Under a good administration the Nile gains on the desert: under a bad one, the desert gains on the Nile.'

Then too, it has to be remembered that Bonaparte was no northern Frenchman; he was a Corsican, he felt at home in the Mediterranean. He believed, with some confidence, that he had an understanding of the devious politics of the Moslems and the East. The Mamelukes were hated as foreign tyrants in Egypt, and had all but thrown off their allegiance to Constantinople. Why should it not be possible to go to the Sultan and offer to regain for him his lost province? Why should not the French invade and proclaim themselves as liberators who had no quarrel with Islam or with the Egyptian people, but only with their oppressors, the Mamelukes?

And surely this was the most effective way to injure England. She had seized the Cape of Good Hope to open up a new safe route to the east. Well then, the French would have Egypt, and from that base they would be able to menace the British in India, perhaps even land in India itself. A canal cut through the isthmus at Suez would give the French immediate access to the Red Sea, and not all the British ships labouring round the Cape could hold her back. From Egypt, too, the French could strike north into the Ottoman Empire, and if the Sultan could not be coerced or cowed he might very well be conquered. Egypt in fact could be made to fill a new role in the world, as a kind of outlying fortress threatening both the east and the west, and once it was made secure it would be time enough to turn directly upon England herself. And suppose all these dreams came to nothing, suppose the French succeeded in taking Egypt and nothing more, the possession of the country would be a very useful bargaining point in making peace with England.

Since early in 1797 Bonaparte had had all these matters in mind. He had discussed them with Desaix, whom he was already beginning to single out as one of the ablest of the revolutionary generals. He had pressed the idea in his correspondence with Talleyrand in Paris. And in making peace with Austria in Italy he had taken good care to get possession not only of the Venetian fleet but also of the Ionian Islands at the mouth of the Adriatic. Admiral Brueys, with a French squadron, was already at Corfu, and it simply remained now to seize Malta as well. With Malta in French hands the Mediterranean would be well on the way to becoming a French lake. While he was still in Italy Bonaparte sent an agent to spy on the island, and this man had returned with the very good news that the Knights of St John were quite unable to defend the place. The fervour which had once taken them on crusades to Jerusalem had long since gone, and now in Malta, their last refuge, they had sunk into the futile daze that overtakes an aimless garrison life. The French knights in particular would never resist an invasion.

Malta, Corfu and now Egypt: the way lay open to the French and the strategy practically declared itself upon the map.

There were visions of glory in all this, dreams of Alexandrian conquests in the fabulous East, but even the most superficial study of Bonaparte's actions at this time shows that he was very far from being carried away by his own enthusiasm. He was very cool and very practical. He was not a Hitler making impassioned speeches; he was a newly-arrived young general of incredible confidence, quietly and precisely imposing his will upon the men who held the power in Paris. He had conquered Italy, not to enjoy a popular success, but to prepare himself for the next jump forward.

Now at the age of 28 he was very well aware that he was the idol of all France; indeed, this was made evident to him every day in Paris. The street where he had bought his little house had been renamed Rue de la Victoire, and he could not emerge from it without exuberant crowds pressing round him. He had but to enter a theatre for the audience to rise and applaud. But no man ever had fewer delusions about himself than Bonaparte. When his secretary, Bourrienne, remarked upon his popularity one day he replied, 'Bah, the crowd would flock to see me just as eagerly if I were going to the scaffold.' It was true, of course. It was also true that he could not continue for long as the national hero unless he consolidated his reputation with new victories. The important thing at this stage, however, is that Bonaparte saw all this very clearly – just as clearly as he saw that the Directory feared him and therefore hated him and wanted to get rid of him. He on his side despised the Directors: 'Do you imagine,' he asked Miot, 'that I triumph in Italy in order to aggrandize a pack of lawyers who form the Directory, and men like Carnot and Barras? What an idea!' – but he was also aware that the time to strike had not quite arrived as yet.

And so he affects to fall in with the government's plans. He accepts the command of the expedition to invade England, he even makes a tour of the Channel ports, detaches privateers to reconnoitre the English coast between Rye and Folkestone, and places orders for cannon of an English type that can be loaded with captured ammunition once the French army is ashore.

One cannot say that Bonaparte was absolutely opposed to the direct invasion of England, but it was obvious from the first that he did not like it, and he cannot have been too displeased when Brueys reported from the Mediterranean that his ships were not ready and could not join the rest of the French fleet at Brest. It was also significant that although the hatred of England in France was very great at this time (the early spring of 1798), a government appeal for a loan of eighty million francs to finance the expedition failed miserably. Now was the moment to manœuvre the attention of the Directory away from the English Channel and back to the Mediterranean. Bonaparte declared his plan: 'To go to Egypt, to establish myself there and found a French colony, will require some months. But as soon as I have made England tremble for the safety of India, I shall return to Paris, and give the enemy its death-blow. There is nothing to fear in the interval. Europe is calm. Austria cannot move, England is occupied with preparing her defence against invasion, and Turkey will welcome the expulsion of the Mamelukes.' Elsewhere he said that if he sailed in May he thought he might be back in October, but he was by no means certain about this. When Josephine later asked him when he would return, he is said to have answered: 'Six months, six years, perhaps never.' But this reply may perhaps have been induced by the momentary despondence of parting from her; on all occasions, now and later, Bonaparte had his eye firmly placed upon France. To the Directory, however, the time element hardly mattered; long or short, the main thing was to get him out of the way, and so by March 1798 we find them coming around to the Egyptian plan.

One pauses here to glance once again at the phenomenon of how the young man had got himself into such a commanding position. Granted that he was a prodigy from birth, granted that the revolution had opened for him opportunities that would never have come his way under Louis XVI, it is still a fact that a bare four years earlier his name was nothing in the world; he was then actually under arrest in Paris, charged with disloyalty, and he had contemplated offering his services as an artillery officer to the Sultan in Turkey. His support

Bonaparte – a gauche figure, long uncombed hair straggling to his shoulders
From a drawing by Antoine Jean Gros

of Barras in the coup of October 1795 had brought him into notice at last, and this in a revolutionary atmosphere when youth was everything and a reputation could be made in a day. Yet he was still a gauche figure in the Parisian salons, long uncombed hair straggling down to his shoulders, a sallow complexion, sombre blue eyes, an air of fatigue and dull restlessness, a short, thin, ugly body covered with clothes that were ill-kept and too big for him. His sword draggled ineffectually at his side. Perhaps these outward effects might not have counted for much among intelligent people, but he was generally silent, and when he did speak it was with an ungainly Corsican accent. In brief, he is the intense young genius who is perfectly conscious of his own superior powers and just as perfectly unable to see how he will ever manage to express them.

Josephine, with her lush background of Martinique and her love affairs under the shadow of the guillotine, seems to have been astonished and perhaps even a little frightened when the full force of Bonaparte's passion was turned upon her. Whatever it was she felt for this gloomy and egocentric young soldier, it was not the blind rapture of love, and she had naturally hesitated before committing herself. However, Barras, with the disinterested patronage of a former lover, was able to assure her that Bonaparte was to have the command

Bonaparte and Josephine at the time of their marriage. From a drawing by an officer wounded in Bonaparte's army

in Italy, and so one supposes that she thought it would all be worth while – especially if she did not have to accompany her husband on the campaign. An odd little bourgeois note was struck at their marriage in March 1796: Josephine's age (she was six years older than Napoleon) appears to have weighed on their social consciences, for he put himself down in the register as eighteen months older than he actually was, and she four years younger. This does not sound like Bonaparte at all, but then Bonaparte infatuated with Josephine is one thing, and Bonaparte himself another.

Now, however, in 1798, two tremendous years in Italy had intervened, and General Bonaparte at 28 was an unrecognized genius no longer. His appearance may have been as uncompromising as ever, but now his face has the stamp of a man in authority. He exerts authority as naturally as he breathes, and it is wonderful to see how he has inspired the devotion of such men as the ex-aristocrat Menou, and the artist Vivant Denon, of the mathematician Monge and of others like Berthier, Davout, Lannes, Junot and Murat, whose names are presently to strike terror all over Europe. Of his more talented colleagues only Kléber dislikes him, and Talleyrand, in his bland, episcopal way, has his reservations, but these two also are quite unable to resist him. 'A charming personality,' Talleyrand permits himself to comment, 'a handsome eye, a pale complexion, a hint of fatigue.'

Desaix might easily have been jealous of this spectacular rival, for he was a year older than Bonaparte and his career hardly less successful. At the age of 28 he had risen to the command of the army on the Rhine, and he was the prototype of everything a revolutionary general ought to be, an utterly concentrated soldier, full of courage and shrewd decisions, who lived in the field with his men and had no affectations of any kind. It was said that in the thick of a battle Desaix's little figure seemed to increase in height and his voice took on a note of absolute command; and so his troops would follow him anywhere. But Desaix

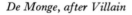
De Monge, after Villain   *Berthollet, after Dutertre*

had no thought of making his own independent way in the world. He instantly recognized Bonaparte as his superior, and offered his services. 'I am persuaded,' he declared about this time, 'that Bonaparte will achieve so immense a glory that it is impossible that it will not reflect on his lieutenants. . . . He is proud, hidden, never forgives. He follows his enemy to the end of the world.' The new commander-in-chief liked Desaix very much.

Bonaparte's influence upon the intellectuals of the *Institut de France* seems even more remarkable. Success, of course, is infectious, and in every age intellectuals have always been charmed by literate men of action, but Bonaparte appears to have roused the *Institut* as though it were a corps of cadets about to follow him into battle. They invite him to become a member, and they are delighted by the modest air with which he reads his papers, astonished at his knowledge and flattered by his interest in their work. All at once respectable men of science and letters, men like Monge and Berthollet who are many years his senior, find themselves becoming young again, and they can think of nothing so exciting as to go

Murat, by Gérard

Kléber

off on a military expedition to Egypt. The young commander is more than welcoming. He wants them all on his staff, engineers, geologists, mathematicians, chemists, zoologists, astronomers, geographers, mineralogists, archaeologists, Arabists, poets and painters; and in the end, almost without realizing what was happening to them, these sedentary and studious men really do become another corps of cadets following young Caesar into battle.

Meanwhile the plans for the campaign went forward with the same sure touch. From the first it was almost a private expedition; once he had got his credit from the Directory (a sum of some nine million francs), Bonaparte rendered no accounts, spent the money as he wished, and it was certainly not the Ministry of War which was the operational head-

Marmont, by Rouget

Davout, by Dutertre

Lannes, after Bonneville

Berthier, after Gros

quarters: it was the little house in the Rue de la Victoire. He absolutely rejected the Directory's demand that they should send commissars on the expedition to watch his movements, and the general outline of the plan seems to have been entirely of his own making. He estimated that he needed a force of something over thirty thousand infantry and three thousand cavalry, supported by a hundred guns. These in the main were to be drawn from the soldiers he had so successfully commanded in Italy, and his generals of brigade and division were to be the men he himself had promoted or appointed: Desaix and Kléber, Berthier, Murat, Marmont, Lannes, Davout and Junot. Josephine's son Eugène de Beauharnais was added to the staff as his aide-de-camp. Most of these men were as young as

Beauharnais, by Gros

Junot, by Raverat

Bonaparte himself, many had been wounded in his service; and thus they followed him with the *esprit de corps* that belongs only to young men who have already risked themselves in battle and have survived to enjoy the intoxication of power. This, perhaps more than any other single factor, ensured the success of the expedition.

Next the ships had to be assembled, thirteen sail of the line with their accompanying frigates, and two hundred or more transports for the troops. Toulon was to be the main port of embarkation, and other contingents were to join from Marseilles, Genoa, Corsica and Civitavecchia. Malta was to be the first objective, and once the island was secured the entire fleet was to sail in company for Alexandria.

Bonaparte is said to have feared the sea and to have never understood it. Yet nothing in his career is more astonishing than the speed and precision with which this complicated and dangerous amphibious operation was set up in Paris in a few short months in the spring of 1798. From the Rue de la Victoire a stream of orders go out, and are obeyed with an alacrity that no modern general could ever hope to achieve with all the aids of aircraft, the telegraph and the telephone. It is a conspiracy in the grand manner, and nothing is forgotten. Monge is sent off to obtain maps, and Arabic and Greek printing presses, Talleyrand is induced to put on foot a scheme for placating Constantinople (the Sultan shall have the Ionian Islands and an annual tribute from the French if he connives at the invasion of Egypt), a line of propaganda is devised (Malta has been hostile to the Republic and has

Toulon harbour. Gouache by Balzac

sheltered *émigrés*, and French citizens have been maltreated by the Mamelukes in Egypt – thus the French have a legitimate reason for war), a library is collected for the expedition (the Koran and the Hindu Vedas being lumped together under the section marked 'Politics'), a French soldier who had served against the British in India is enlisted in the intelligence corps, the annual rise and fall of the Nile is studied and it is agreed that the army must arrive in Egypt before the flood begins in August; sappers, miners and a medical staff are appointed, and a letter goes off to Admiral Brueys asking for a berth on a ship 'suitable for a commander-in-chief who expects to be seasick the entire voyage'.

A fresh wind of hope and excitement blows through all this. It was certainly true that not all the soldiers were eager for the adventure – there were dissensions both in the fleet and the army assembling in Toulon – but nobody seriously questions the plan or raises doubts about the commander-in-chief. Already Bonaparte's name is a guarantee of success, and this in itself was a remarkable thing, since the soldiers and sailors had no inkling of where they were going or of how long they would be away. They were simply told in a vague way that they were to strike a blow against England, and this inevitably meant that many of them would never see their homes again.

One still finds it hard to understand how the secret of the expedition's destination was so well kept; many people knew the plan in Paris, couriers were travelling all over France and Italy, regiments were on the move and the ships assembling in the ports were there for all

to see. The British knew well enough that an expedition was being prepared, but the fact remains that long after the French fleet had sailed they still believed that either a descent was to be made on Naples or that Bonaparte, turning west through the Straits of Gibraltar, would head for England or Ireland.

It might also be wondered how Brueys could so confidently set out with his large unwieldy convoy of small transports, when he knew that at any moment the British fleet could put in an appearance in the western Mediterranean – indeed, already in early May there were reports of British frigates cruising off Corsica and Toulon. But the sheer size of the Mediterranean was greatly to the French advantage, and these were still the days of sail. It was a full month's voyage from Toulon to Alexandria, and even so large an expedition as this could reasonably hope to conceal its movements in that great expanse of sea. Nor can it be assumed that in 1798 the French acknowledged the superiority of the British fleet. Nelson had still to fight his greatest battles, and the Mediterranean for the French was a familiar sea. They might not have welcomed a conflict when they were impeded by their convoy, but it cannot be asserted that their captains were afraid to fight. Given the right conditions they may even have been eager for a contest; after all, that was what their thirteen ships of the line and their fourteen frigates were designed for.

And so as the day of embarkation drew near there was a growing confidence in the expedition. The size of the force (with the addition of the sailors it now numbered about 40,000), was an assurance in itself, and as usually happens on these occasions both soldiers and sailors took heart from the fact that together they were committed irrevocably to a great adventure.

There was a hitch at the last moment over the treaty negotiations with Austria, and for a week or two it looked as though the war might be renewed in Europe itself, but by May 4, 1798, the crisis was over and Bonaparte slipped quietly out of Paris. He travelled with Josephine in the first of two carriages, and the luggage and the aides-de-camp followed on behind. They took the route through Auxerre, Châlon, Lyons, Valence and Avignon, and reached Toulon in the excellent time of five days. The port was alive with the stir and movement of the embarkation, and soldiers were everywhere, the infantry in their black, knee-length gaiters, tight white breeches, coats faced with scarlet and the revolutionary cockade in their hats, the officers in their shakos and epaulettes. Bonaparte took rooms with Josephine in the Hôtel de l'Intendant and issued the customary exhortation to the troops. They were, he declared, 'a wing of the Army of England', and at the successful conclusion of the expedition each man was to be given six acres of land.

By May 12 the embarkation was complete, but a storm had blown up and Brueys waited until May 18 for it to abate. Then at last he gave the word to sail. Bonaparte seems to have hoped almost to the end that Josephine would come with him, but she had good reasons (quite apart from her lovers) for remaining behind; she was not well, and if she was to have a child by Bonaparte she must follow the doctors' advice and take the waters at Plombières, she must look after her house and family in Paris, she would join him in a month or two. . . . In the end Bonaparte gave in and they parted on the quay. On May 19 he went on board *l'Orient*, a ship of the line with 120 guns, with Berthier and his personal staff, and followed the rest of the fleet out to sea.

The capture of Malta. After a drawing by Nodet

Who in this present age can ever hope to know the lift and excitement of an armada of
sailing ships setting out on an invasion? Through two world wars we have grown used to
dark embarkations in the night and the sinister secret shapes of destroyers and submarines,
the ominous aircraft overhead. But here it was all bulging canvas, flags flying, the bands
playing, the soldiers in bright uniforms on the decks, and the rolling natural movement
of the sea. It was a lovely day. In this same year *The Ancient Mariner* had been published
in England, and now in actual fact the white foam flew, the furrow followed free, and there
were many on board who really did feel, like Coleridge's hero, that they were to be the first
who ever burst into a new undiscovered world over the horizon. The frigates led the way,
followed by the ships of the line and then the smaller transports in their scores, bobbing
about for miles astern on the bright blue water. Brueys before sailing had received a report
that a squadron of thirty British ships had been sighted off Majorca heading north-east,
but today the sea was empty, and without incident the fleet sailed on to Genoa and Ajaccio
to pick up the reinforcements. Turning east again to the Italian coast they hove to off
Civitavecchia, but word was sent out to them from the shore that Desaix, who had been
assembling his division there, had sailed a day or two earlier for Malta, and so they went

on again. On June 9 they arrived off the island to find that Desaix was already engaged in parleying with the Knights of St John.

Shafik Ghorbal, the Egyptian historian, recounts succinctly that 'one day's skirmishes and another of negotiations sufficed to bring about the fall of Malta', and the event really does appear to have happened as simply as this. Moribund, terrified and ruined by the treachery of their own people – that treachery Bonaparte had so carefully schemed for over a year before – the garrison collapsed under the first assault.

Bonaparte stayed six days in the Palazzo Parisio, and in that time he demolished forever the rule of the Knights and set up his own government in the image of the French Republic. Nothing was spared. Stores, money and arms were ferried out to the fleet, and even the smallest ships in the harbour were seized. A new constitution was written, and a French High Commissioner was set up on the island with 4,000 soldiers to support him. Henceforth the schools were to be non-clerical and teaching was to be done in French. A batch of sixty Maltese children, got up in light blue trousers and red caps, was dispatched to Paris to be educated at the expense of France. Slavery was abolished by decree – a convenient manœuvre since most of the Knights' slaves were Moslems, and Bonaparte hoped to ingratiate himself with the Sultan by sending them off to Constantinople. Now the tricolour floated over the Palazzo Parisio, the cockade was in everybody's hat, and Malta was a part of France. Bonaparte sent off this splendid news to the Directory, together with a letter to Talleyrand urging him to make haste with his negotiations with Constantinople.

On June 19, the commander-in-chief was ready to sail again. There was still no sign of the English, and the French fleet, now swollen to over three hundred vessels, headed east in perfect weather with a following north-west breeze.

Twelve days' sailing lay before them, and it appears to have been a pleasant voyage; not even Bonaparte was seasick. He spent his days aboard *l'Orient* dictating to Bourrienne, reading a good deal from the 287 improving books in the expedition's library, and watching comedies improvised by the soldiers and the crew. One of the favourite themes was concerned with a lovely Circassian girl, a young revolutionary hero and a fat and lecherous pasha who was the villain. The soldiers were kept active by climbing the masts and by daily gun drill, and there were frequent alerts to prepare them for the appearance of the English ships. But still the English did not come, and for the moment, on this calm summer sea, the expedition was locked away entirely from the world. The intellectuals who had enlisted – the famous 'penseurs', the 'living encyclopedia' – numbered about 150, and were distributed in different ships, and one can imagine how, in this strange martial atmosphere, they paced in earnest conversation round the decks. For some at least there was already work to do. Bonaparte had now prepared his first proclamation to the Egyptians, and it was ready for translation into Arabic and the printing press.

According to Ghorbal, Bonaparte's original version in French came nearer to the style and spirit of the Koran than the Arabic translation given by his interpreters, but in any event it is a remarkable case of that holier-than-thou duplicity which has become so familiar in the propaganda of this present century.

'*Gloire au sultan!*' he cries, '*Gloire à l'armée française! Malédiction aux Mamelucks et bonheur au peuple d'Égypte!*' He had come, he declared, as the friend and ally of the Sultan in Constantinople, and the Turkish and French flags were to fly together in every village once the usurping Mamelukes had been ejected. 'Too long have the Mameluke beys who govern Egypt insulted the French nation, and loaded her merchants with vexations; the hour of their chastisement is arrived. Too long has this horde of slaves, purchased from the Caucasus and Georgia, tyrannized over the fairest part of the world; but God, upon whom everything depends, has ordered its empire to end. People of Egypt! You will be told that I come to destroy your religion. Do not believe it. Reply that I come to restore your rights and punish the usurpers, and that I venerate more than the Mamelukes, God, his prophet and the Koran.

'All men are equal before God; but it is wisdom, talents and virtues that make differences between men. Now what wisdom, what talents, what virtues distinguish the Mamelukes that they exclusively should possess all that is lovely and sweet in life? Is there a beautiful estate? It belongs to the Mamelukes. Is there a beautiful slave, a beautiful horse, a beautiful house? They belong to the Mamelukes. If Egypt be their private estate let them show the lease that God has granted.

'But God is just and bountiful to all mankind. The Egyptians are now called upon to rule themselves: let the most wise, the best informed, the most virtuous govern and the people will be happy. There formerly existed in Egypt great cities, great canals, great commerce; by what means have they all been destroyed if not by the avarice, the injustice and the tyranny of the Mamelukes? Cadis! Sheikhs! Imams! Tell the people that we are the friends of true Moslems. Is it not we who have destroyed the Pope who preached that war must be made on Moslems? Is it not we who have destroyed the Knights of Malta because the madmen believed that God willed them to make war on Moslems? Is it not we who have long been the friends of the Sultan (whose wishes may God accomplish!) and the enemies of his enemies? Are not the Mamelukes on the other hand in continual rebellion against the Sultan whom they still refuse to acknowledge? They execute only their own schemes.

'Thrice happy those who are for us; they shall prosper in their rank and fortune. Happy are those who are neutral: they will have time to become acquainted with us and in the end they will come over to our side. But wretched, thrice wretched, are those that arm for the Mamelukes and fight against us: there shall be no hope for them, they shall perish.'

There was at least a grain of truth beneath this chicanery. At this stage Bonaparte still believed that the Sultan might be won over, and it was certainly true that a great part of the French revolutionary army was atheist, or at any rate equally indifferent to both Pope and Prophet; they were creating their own millennium in the world. Bonaparte himself, when he later dressed in Moslem clothes in Cairo and attempted to set up a kind of self-government among the imams and notables there, may really have deluded himself briefly that he might be accepted by the Egyptians as one of themselves. At all events, this was the public role he designed for himself at this critical moment of landing, and he put the matter very forcibly to his own troops. No mosques were to be violated, no Moslem priests were to be disturbed, no plunder was to be taken, and no woman was to be molested – the Frenchman who did that was a scoundrel. In every unit officers were instructed to enforce the strictest discipline in the soldiers' treatment of the civilians. As they came up to the Egyptian coast

بسم الله الرحمن الرحيم لا اله الا الله لا ولد له ولا شريك فى ملكه

من طرف للجمهور الفرنساوى المبنى على اساس الحرية والتسوية السرعسكر الكبير بوناپارته امير الجيوش الفرنساويه يعرف اهالى مصر جميعهم ان من زمان مديد السناجق الذين يتسلطنوا فى البلاد المصرية يتعاملوا بالذل والاحتقار فى حق الملة الفرنساويه ويظلموا تجارها بانواع البلس والتعدى فحضر الان ساعة عقوبتهم

وحسرنا من مدة عصور طويلة هذه الزمرة المماليك المجلوبين من جبال الاباازا والكرجستمان يفسدوا فى الاقليم الاحسن الذى يوجد فى كرة الارض كلها فاما رب العالمين القادر على كل شى قد حتم على انقضا دولتهم

يا ايها المصريين قد يقولوا لكم انى ما نزلت فى هذا الطرف الا بقصد ازالة دينكم فذلك كذب صريح فلا تصدقوه وقولوا للمفترين انى ما قدمت اليكم الا لكيما احلص حقكم من يد الظالمين وانى اكثر من المماليك اعبد الله سبحانه وتعالى واحترم نبيه محمد والقران العظيم

وقولوا ايضا لهم ان جميع الناس متساويين عند الله وان الشى الذى يفرقهم من بعضهم بعضا فهو العقل والفضايل والعلوم فقط وبين المماليك ما العقل والفضايل والمعرفة التى تميزهم عن الاخرين وستوجب انهم يتملكرا وحدهم كلما يميل به حيسات الدنيا

حيثما يوجد ارض مخصمة فى مختصة للمماليك والجوارى الاجمل والخيل الاحسن والمساكن الاشهى فهذا كله لهم خاصا ان كانت الارض المصرية العزام للمماليك فليميزون الحجت التى كتبها لهم الله فلكن رب العالمين هو روؤفا وعادل على المشر بعونه تعالى من اليوم فصاعدا لا يستثنى احدا من اهالى مصر عن الدخول فى المناصب السامية وعن اكتساب المراتب العالية فالعقلا والفضلا والعلما بينهم سيدبروا الامور وبذلك يصلح حسال الامة كلها

سابقا فى الاراضى المصرية كانت المدن المعظمة والخليجات الواسعة والمتجر المتكاثر وما ازال ذلك كله الا الطمع وظلم المماليك

ايها القضاة والمشايخ والايمة وياايها الشورباجيه واعيان البلد قولوا لامتكم ان الفرنساويه هم ايضا مسلمين خالصين واثباتا لذلك قد نزلوا فى رومية الكبرى وخربوا فيها كرسى البابا الذى كان يحث دايما النصارى على محاربة الاسلام ثم قصدوا جزيرة مالطه وطردوا منها الكوالليرية الذين كانوا يزعموا ان الله تعالى يطلب منهم مقاتلة

المسلمين ومع ذلك الفرنساويه فى كل وقت من الاوقات صاروا المحبين الاخلصين لحضرة السلطان العثمانلى واعدا اعدايه ادلم الله ملكه وبالقلوب المماليك امتنعوا من اطاعة السلطان غير ممتثلين لامره فما طاعوا اصلا الا الطمع الا انفسهم

طوبى ثم الطوبى لاهالى مصر الذين يتفقوا معنا بلا تاخير فيصلح حالهم ويعلى مراتبهم طوبى ايضا للذين يقعدوا فى مساكنهم غير مايلين لاحد من الفريقين المحاربين فاذا يعرفونا بالاكثر يتسارعوا اليها بكل قلب

لكن الويل ثم الويل للذين يتحدوا مع المماليك ويساعدوهم فى الحرب عليهما فما يجدى طرق الخلاص ولا يبقى منهم اثر

المادة الاولى

جميع القرى الواقعة فى داير قريبة بثلثة ساعات عن المواضع التى يمر بها العسكر الفرنساوى فواجب عليها انها ترسل للسرعسكر بعض وكلا من عندها لكيما يعرفوا المشار اليه انهم طاعوا وانهم نصبوا السنجاق الفرنساوى الذى هو ابيض وكحلى واحمر

المادة الثانية

كل قرية التى تقوم على العسكر الفرنساوى تحرق بالنار

المادة الثالثة

كل قرية التى تطيع للعسكر الفرنساوى الواجب عليها نصب السنجاق الفرنساوى وايضا نصب سنجاق السلطان العثمانلى محبنا دام بقاه

المادة الرابعة

المشايخ فى كل بلد ليختموا حال جميع الارزاق والبيوت والاملاك بتاع المماليك وعليهم الاجتهاد الزايد لكيلا يضيع ادنى شى منها

المادة الخامسة

الواجب على المشايخ والقضات والايمة انهم يلازموا وظايفهم وعلى كل واحد من اهالى البلد انه يبقى فى مسكنه مطمان وكذلك تكون الصلوات قايمة فى الجوامع على العادة والمصريين باجمعهم ليشكروا فضل الله سبحانه وتعالى من انقراض دولت المماليك قايلين بصوت عالى ادام الله اجلال السلطان العثمانلى ادام الله اجلال العسكر الفرنساوى لعن الله المماليك واصلح حال الامة المصرية

تحرير بمعسكر اسكندريه فى ٣ من شهر مسيدور

سنة من اقامة الجمهور الفرنساوى يعنى فى اواخر شهر محرم

سنة ١٢١٣ هجرية

many of the men may have wondered just what rewards they *were* to have in this distant eldorado. 'There you are,' cried some wit on Denon's ship, pointing to the flat and gloomy shoreline, 'There are the six acres that have been promised you.'

Up to this point – it was now July 1 – Bonaparte had been exceptionally lucky. For the past six weeks Nelson with fourteen ships had been fruitlessly chasing him up and down the Mediterranean, and had in fact called in at Alexandria only two days before. Finding no sign of the French the British had sailed away again at the very moment when the leading French frigates were approaching the coast. It had been Bonaparte's original intention to

The arrival of the French fleet at Alexandria

sail directly into Alexandria harbour and, if possible, take the town by surprise. But now word reached him that the Egyptian garrison was already forewarned, and thus the landing would have to be made on the open beaches to the west of the city. This was a serious setback, since a storm had blown up and heavy waves were breaking on the shore.

Denon has left a lively account of these proceedings. He says that his frigate, the *Juno*, had been ordered a day or two earlier to run on ahead of the fleet and make contact with Bracevitch, the French consul in Alexandria. The *Juno* arrived off the town on June 29 and Bracevitch, rowing out from the shore, was taken on board. Next morning he was delivered to Bonaparte in *l'Orient*. The consul's report, says Denon, was 'perplexing; the English had been seen, and might come up the next moment; the wind was strong; the convoy was

One of Bonaparte's proclamations printed in Arabic on board l'Orient

mingled with the fleet, and in a degree of confusion that, in the event of the enemy's appearance, threatened the most disastrous defeat. Bonaparte caused the particulars he had heard to be repeated over again; and after a silence of a few minutes, gave orders for disembarkation. Dispositions were made to bring the convoy as near to land as the danger of running ashore, during a high wind, would permit. The ships of war formed an outer circle of defence. All their sails were furled and their anchors cast.'

But still the sea continued to rise, and all day went by before the first troops were got ashore.

'The boats', Denon continues, 'received one by one and at random the soldiers descending from the vessels; when they were filled the waves appeared every instant to be on the point of swallowing them; or, at the mercy of the wind, they were forced upon others; and after escaping all this, on gaining the shore, they knew not where to touch without bilging on the breakers.' And so things continued through the night.

Bonaparte himself got ashore shortly before midnight, and he slept briefly on the sand among the soldiers. At dawn he rose and immediately took command of the four thousand odd men who had struggled on to the beach. A small Bedouin fort named Marabou was assaulted and taken. Four miles away across the desert the French could see the walls and minarets of Alexandria. Forming his men into three columns, one heading for Pompey's Pillar, another for the catacombs and the third for the Rosetta Gate, Bonaparte led the way on foot across the sand.

A squadron commander and a captain

5

The Long Egyptian Night

Egypt was not easy to defend. The great deserts to the west of the Nile offered a formidable barrier, and no one attempted to penetrate the country that way, but a landing could be made at any place on the low flat shoreline of the delta, and there was a safe anchorage at Alexandria. Once Alexandria fell and the Rosetta mouth of the Nile was taken, no mountains impeded the advance of the invader inland, and he was certain to find food and water nearly all the way to Cairo, over one hundred miles to the south. Two other routes had been successfully exploited since prehistoric times – the one that came down the Nile itself from central Africa, and the other that led in from the east across the isthmus of Suez – but these were not available to an invader from the west.

The delta was a great prize. Here in this artificial garden where rain hardly ever fell but where fresh water was plentiful, two or even three crops were gathered every year, and the annual flooding of the Nile provided a rich layer of silt several inches deep. With comparatively little labour every good thing in life sprang up in abundance, rice and sugar-cane, coffee and tobacco, cotton and flax, lentils and dates, flowers and vines. So long as the water was distributed through the flat land by canals there was no limit to this fertility. Frosts and storms were almost unknown, and most plagues and pests succumbed eventually in the dry antiseptic air of the desert. Except for occasional sandstorms and a muggy, soporific quality in the air during the floods in September, the heat was not excessive, and the winter months were very nearly perfect.

At the time of Bonaparte's landing the population of Egypt was about two and a half million, which was a third of what it was estimated to have been in the days of the Pharaohs and hardly more than a tenth of what it is at present. The people were a mixed lot. Far away in Upper Egypt the Nubian tribes clung to their strips of vegetation along the river bank and in the cultivated oases. Provincial governors sent out from Cairo gathered taxes from them and maintained a rough and ready sort of administration, but for the most part life went by on the Upper Nile in ignorance and solitude. The Bedouin who roamed the intervening deserts that formed fourteen-fifteenths of Egypt were also very largely a law unto themselves, and cannot have numbered more than a few tens of thousands. By far the largest part of the population was huddled into the delta. Apart from the Mamelukes, whom we must consider in a moment, the delta population consisted of about 1,750,000 fellaheen, the indigenous natives who cultivated the soil and formed the labouring population of the cities; about 150,000 Copts – Egyptians who worshipped Christ and fulfilled more or less the role of the Parsees in India, as money-lenders, traders and government officials – and finally the foreigners. These last numbered perhaps 200,000 and lived almost entirely in the cities. They included Turks (the great majority), Greeks, Armenians, Jews, Syrians and a handful of French traders who, at the first news of Bonaparte's landing, were interned.

The only two cities of any consequence were Cairo and Alexandria, and Alexandria at this time had sunk to the nadir of its fortunes. Of its ancient glory – of its reputed 4,000 palaces, its theatres, temples and monuments that had once made it second only to Rome in the Roman Empire - hardly anything remained. Pompey's Pillar still stood, and the walls still rose to a height of forty feet in some places, but for the rest all had sunk into dust and rubble, the canal from the Nile had silted up, and the inhabitants, decimated by repeated plagues, had dwindled to less than 10,000. Browne, the English traveller who visited the city in 1792, says, 'Heaps of rubbish are on all sides visible, whence every shower of rain, not to mention the industry of the natives in digging, discovers pieces of precious marble, and sometimes ancient coins and fragments of sculpture.' Denon, who got into the city on the heels of the French assault, says he found the houses shut up, the streets deserted except for a few ragged women trailing about like ghosts among the ruins, and a universal silence broken only by the cries of the kites. Even Pompey's Pillar seen from close to was not very impressive.

Cairo, on the other hand, was a flourishing place; after Constantinople it was the most important city in the Near East, with a population of about 250,000 people. Since it was first founded over a thousand years before it had been rebuilt several times, and the present city (variously known as Masr, Misr, El-Kahira or Grand Cairo) stood on the site of an ancient Roman fortress. It lay a little distance from the right bank of the river under the

The harbour at Alexandria. From Description de l'Égypte

cover of the Mokattam Hills, and was ringed by high walls and dominated by a citadel.

The skyline, seen from a distance, had romantic aspects: the domes and minarets of 300 mosques rose from the smoke of cooking fires, and the palm trees and cultivated fields along the river bank gave the place a placid and rather rural air. The citadel, built by Saladin in the twelfth century, was a fine complex of dun-coloured battlements, and in the desert beyond, on the opposite side of the river, one descried the pyramids. Seen from closer at hand, however, these noble prospects disintegrated. Except for the large open squares such as the Esbekiah, which were flooded and thronged with boats during the annual inundation of the Nile, the city was a warren of narrow unpaved streets and non-descript Turkish houses covering about three square miles. Rubbish lay about on every side, the haunt of scavenging dogs and cats, and in the worst slums it was hard to say which were the ruins of fallen buildings and which the hovels of the present generation. 'Not a single fine street,' Denon cries in despair, 'not a single beautiful building. . . . They build as little as they can help; they never repair anything.'

The mosques, crowded with pilgrims living in their outer courtyards, cannot have been very sanitary places, and the bazaars, roofed over with canopies of straw or linen, were both hot and smelly. Browne speaks of 'the polluted dust'.

Yet no one with any love for oriental life could resist this place. The day began before dawn when the mueddins (many of them chosen because they were blind and thus unable to see down into the private houses) roused the people with their first call to the mosques: 'Come to prayer. Come to security. God is most great.' Within an hour – that first fresh

El Rumeila and the citadel, Cairo. From Description de l'Égypte

hour of the Egyptian morning – the life of the city spilled itself out into the streets, the bazaars and the coffee-houses, and at every turn the passer-by was bound to come on a spectacle of some kind: a marriage or a funeral, an impromptu performance of strolling players in the square, a well-to-do merchant trotting along on his ass with a slave running in front to clear the way, a string of camels thrusting through the crowds with their heads held high and disdainfully in the air. There was a constant passage of street-vendors shouting up to the balconies overhead, and of water-carriers with goatskins slung round their shoulders, and a hullabaloo of shouts and cries filled the air: '*Ya bint; dahrak*,' 'Watch thy back, daughter,' '*Ya efendee*,' 'Take care,' 'O consoler of the embarrassed, my supper must be thy gift' – this last from the innumerable beggars whom one refused by replying with some such phrase as 'God will sustain'.

Craftsmen did their work in their shops under the customer's eye; there was one street for gold- and silversmiths and jewellers, another for leatherworkers and brass-founders, others for potters, silk-spinners, makers of weapons, dyers and perfumers. There was no appetite, no refinement of the senses, that could not be satisfied somewhere in the bazaars, and if the city was squalid it was also very much alive.

Nightfall and darkness (there were no street lights) put an end to the hubbub. Soon after the mueddins' fifth and final call the gates of the city were locked, and many of the streets with large wooden doors at either end were shut up for the night as well. 'One might pass through the whole length of the metropolis,' Lane says, 'and scarcely meet more than a dozen or twenty persons, excepting the watchmen and guards, and the porters at the gates of the bye-streets and quarters. The sentinel, or guard, calls out to the approaching passenger in Turkish "Who is that?", and is answered in Arabic, "A citizen". The private watchman, in the same case, exclaims, "Attest the unity of God!" or merely, "Attest the unity!" The reply given to this is, "There is no deity but God!"'

The Nile was the all-provider of this existence. It grew every ounce of food, it supplied water to the wells which were dug in each quarter of the city, and it was the main highway to the outside world. The ceremony of the opening of the canals when the flood rose in August was one of the great occasions of the year. The river at Cairo was about half a mile wide, but it was divided by two islands, Bulaq and Rhoda, where crops were grown and where some of the wealthier people had their pleasure-gardens. Memphis, the ancient capital a little further up the river, had decayed to nothing. In the desert at Gizeh the Sphinx lay buried up to its neck in sand, its nose already broken.

There was one other aspect of the city which gave it a special importance, and which made travellers think of it not simply as Cairo but Grand Cairo: it was the great terminal of the caravan routes that spread out over northern Africa and the Near East. No one dreamed of travelling alone through the desert any more than one would dream of crossing the Atlantic in a canoe. You waited until a caravan was being formed in Cairo, and then applied to the sheikh in command for permission to accompany it. Sometimes months would go by before all was ready, and then on a certain day the order to march would be given, and a long straggling procession of camels, mules, donkeys and men on foot would set off into the desert. Incoming caravans signalled their arrival at the pyramids and were then told where to cross the Nile and encamp. The distances covered were prodigious. One route – and of course there were no clearly defined tracks in the desert, merely a general line of march that led on from one waterhole or oasis to the next – took you north-east to Damascus, where the traveller could join other caravans headed for Aleppo and Baghdad; another carried the pilgrims down to Mecca and the Red Sea; another followed the general course of the Nile to Sennar and Darfur in the Sudan; still another led off to Fezzan in the west. Every journey was an adventure, and the traders, like migratory birds, were controlled by the seasons and beset at every stage by unpredictable hazards such as civil wars, Bedouin raids, drought, floods and sickness. A year, two years on the road – this was nothing to an experienced merchant. Taking with him his wives, his children and his slaves, he would go on and on wherever the markets offered a profit, and in the end nomadism became an object in itself, and many of these men could endure no other way of life. No one knew the extent of this vast, haphazard network. It was quite possible for a man to travel from Egypt to Timbuktu on the other side of Africa, and it is certain that Indian and even Chinese goods appeared in the bazaars in Cairo.

The merchants dealt in kind rather than in money. In Cairo they obtained grain, rice, cotton, flax, and the thousand and one products of the bazaars. These things, increasing in value with every mile they travelled, would be bartered for other goods in the Near East and in the primitive villages in the far interior of Africa. The Sudan trade was particularly profitable. It produced black slaves, gold, ivory, ostrich feathers, rhinoceros horn, gum arabic, ebony, coffee (brought from Ethiopia) and spices (from the Red Sea). Petroleum was also brought in small quantities from the Arabian Gulf; it was either drunk as a medicine or rubbed on the body. Thus there was a continual interchange at Cairo, a constant ebb and flow of strange faces and of strange goods displayed for sale, a commotion of arrivals and departures.

In our time a thousand travellers' books and a spate of illustrated magazines and moving pictures have made a cliché of the East, but in 1798 nothing in Egypt was familiar to the Europeans. Travellers marvelled at everything they saw, and what they did not understand they tended to dismiss as decadent, superstitious and uncouth. It seemed ridiculous, for example, that the Egyptians, on the occasion of a death in the family, should turn their furniture upside down; and that they should believe that, with music, they could charm snakes out of their houses. The music itself was a cacophony to European ears, and the Moslem prayers a grovelling on the ground. The sheikh, sitting cross-legged by the hour on his divan, appeared to be merely apathetic and dull.

Yet the Egyptians were not quite so decadent as the West has liked to imagine, either before or since. The French now, and the English later on, were to exclaim about the lasciviousness of the public dancing girls in Cairo, the prevalence of brothels, the abominations of the slave trade, the shiftlessness and deceit of the orientals, their hopeless indolence. But in fact there were strict rules in the midst of this apparent *laissez-faire*. The majority of Egyptian women were not dancing girls but wives who behaved with much more decorum than women of the West. Divorce was easy, but marriage while it lasted was usually sacrosanct, and family ties were very strong. Drunkenness hardly existed, drug-taking and sodomy were not common vices, and slaves in Cairo were too valuable to be maltreated. As for the sheikhs, they were very far from being apathetic and dull: they were the men of

A caravan preparing to set out from Cairo. From Description de l'Égypte

LEFT *Carpenters;* RIGHT *Ropemakers. From* Description de l'Égypte

Travelling in the desert. From Lane-Poole's Social Life in Egypt

law and religion in the community and they were greatly respected. The Koran which they expounded put the strongest strictures upon everybody's life, and in the main they were obeyed. Lane lists the seven deadly sins in Egypt, and very interesting they are: disobedience to parents, murder, desertion during an expedition against infidels, usury, falsely accusing a woman of adultery, idolatry and the wasting of the property of orphans.

It would be absurd, of course, to make out that the Egyptians were paragons of virtue compared, say, with the invading French – they lied, they stole, they were superstitiously ignorant, they were always lazy when they had the chance, and were probably cowards as well, but they also had a certain dignity in their lives, they knew patience and quietude (which the French did not), and they were graceful, even beautiful, people. Lane describes the women as follows:

'The forms of womenhood begin to develop themselves about the ninth and tenth year; at the age of 15 or 16 they generally attain their highest degree of perfection. . . . They are characterized, like the men, by a fine oval countenance, though in some instances it is rather broad. The eyes, with very few exceptions, are black, large and of a long almond-form, with long and beautiful lashes and an exquisitely soft, bewitching expression – eyes more beautiful can hardly be conceived: their charming effect is heightened by the concealment of the other features (however pleasing the latter may be), and is rendered still more striking by a practice universal among the females of the higher and middle classes, and very common among those of the lower orders, which is that of blackening the edge of the eyelids both above and below the eye, with a black powder called Kohl.'

The other practice of the women – that of tattooing eyelids, lips and chin with a kind of purple ink – was not so pleasant.

The extreme modesty of the respectable women – outside the harem they went swathed from head to foot in black – made a strange contrast to the licence of the dancing girls who were often called in after a banquet. Denon, like most of the European travellers who were soon to follow him up the Nile, affected to be appalled. 'Their dance,' he says, 'began voluptuously and soon became lascivious, displaying nothing but a gross and indecent expression of the ecstasy of the senses; and what rendered these pictures still more disgusting, was that at the moment in which they kept the least bounds, the two (female) musicians, with the bestiality of the lowest women in the streets of Europe disturbed with a coarse laugh the sense of intoxication that terminated the dance.'

Lane makes a distinction between the *almehs*, the singers and musicians who would be admitted into a respectable house, and the *ghazeeyehs*, or common dancing girls. 'Some of them,' he says, 'when they exhibit before a private party of men, wear nothing but the *shinityán* (or trousers) and a *tób* (or very full shirt or gown) of semi-transparent, coloured gauze, open nearly halfway down the front. To extinguish the least spark of modesty which they may yet sometimes affect to retain, they are plentifully supplied with brandy or some other intoxicating liquor. The scenes that ensue cannot be described.' But he adds, rather unexpectedly: 'Upon the whole I think they are the finest women in Egypt. . . . Women, as well as men, take delight in witnessing their performances. . . .'

It was a question of taboos, of course. To the Egyptians of ancient as well as modern times it was quite normal for the sexual act to be sublimated in a dance, and no doubt

'A daughter of the East'. From Lane-Poole's Social Life in Egypt

The Esbekiah square when flooded. From Description de l'Égypte

there were many things about the French, their impiety, their acceptance of adultery, their aggressiveness, which seemed to these conservative people both vulgar and vile. And in the midst of so much apparent looseness of behaviour, of so much materialism and cynical indulgence in the weakness of human nature, the Egyptians were, in fact, extremely conservative, as conservative as only a subject-race can ever be. Mentally they lived in a kind of fatalistic torpor and they had no will for change. There was indeed something about the very nature of the country, the preservative properties of its dry air and dry sand, its absence of strong contrasts in the way of mountains and valleys, storms and high winds, and the unfailing rise and fall of the Nile, that disposed them to think that all change was futile and improvement an impossibility. The Moslem religion, with its absolute rules, suited them perfectly and they never dreamed of questioning it. They never even thought of revolting against their rulers, the Mamelukes.

In this shut-in, hothouse atmosphere, where the people were absorbed to the limit in their own parochial affairs, the energetic proselytizing spirit of the French made no sense at all, and all their revolutionary talk of liberty, equality and fraternity was merely rhetoric. This was a truth Bonaparte had still to learn. The Egyptian imams and sheikhs who were confused about so much else were not taken in for two minutes by his declaration that he had come to rescue them from the Mamelukes. They knew that he wanted the power for

A Mameluke with a sabre

himself and (unlike the Mamelukes) they suspected that it was useless to resist him. He could come to Cairo as a successful general, as a substitute for the Mamelukes, as one more new tyrant (and an infidel at that) to be added to the rest, or not at all; he could never hope to enter into partnership with the Egyptians. It was at the very core of their nature to resist all governments in a passive and dissembling way, to defeat the tax-gatherer, to cheat the magistrates and to avoid military service. Behind the locked doors of their houses and in their mosques they had their own brand of equality, fraternity and liberty, and it had nothing to do with their rulers.

The Mamelukes themselves were hardly less conservative than their subjects; indeed, they were an anachronism only to be compared with the Turkish janissaries in Constantinople or the Manchus in eighteenth-century China. A stranger group of men it is hardly possible to conceive.

The word Mameluke means male slave, more especially a white male slave, but they were slaves of a special kind. They were purchased as children from impoverished peasant families in Georgia and the Caucasus, and then imported into Egypt, where they were brought up by their masters (who had also been slaves in their time) with the express purpose of ruling the country upon the lines of a military oligarchy. War was the Mamelukes' trade. From their earliest years they were trained as horsemen and warriors, as a

A Mameluke with a lance. Drawings by Carle Vernet

military clique, and they went to fantastic lengths to keep their caste intact. The natural instinct of philoprogenitiveness did not apply; the Mameluke boy was taught that marriage and family were fatal to his profession – it was certainly a loss of caste to marry an Egyptian – and in point of fact they produced few male offspring; each new generation of Mamelukes preferred instead to purchase white Christian slave-children from southern Russia, convert them to Islam, and then bring them up as their heirs. Hitler, it will be remembered, had a somewhat similar notion when he proposed to set up a sort of human stud-farm for the creation of perfect men and women in Nazi Germany. The Mamelukes, however, tended not to live very long, and no doubt their addiction to homosexuality was another reason why they had so few children of their own.

Through the years the Mamelukes had steadily increased in numbers. When Browne was in Egypt in 1792 he was told that 16,000 had been imported in the preceding eleven years, and the total Mameluke population with its dependants now in 1798 numbered nearly 100,000. The great majority of them lived in Cairo.

These supermen saw to it that they looked and behaved like supermen. Many of them were tall and strikingly handsome, and their costume was a wonder to behold: a green cap wreathed with a large yellow turban, a coat of chain-mail beneath a long robe that was bound at the waist by an embroidered shawl, voluminous red pantaloons, leather gauntlets and red, pointed slippers. Each man's armament consisted of a brace of pistols, a mace, a long curved sword, a sheaf of arrows and an English carbine, all with handles and blades chased in silver and copper designs of fine workmanship and sometimes studded with precious stones. Thus encumbered they were mounted upon an enormous saddle of wood and iron – each of the copper stirrups alone weighed thirteen pounds – and it was nothing for a man to pay the equivalent of several hundred pounds for a mount. Their horses were the finest Arabs, and probably as cavalry the Mamelukes had no equal in the world; they charged with utter recklessness and fought with a ferocity that was a byword in the East. 'They start,' says one observer, 'like lightning and arrive like thunder.' Once unhorsed, however, they were heavily encumbered by their arms, and it was left to their irregular Bedouin infantry to save the day.

Lane describes the Mamelukes thus: 'A band of lawless adventurers, slaves in origin, butchers by choice, turbulent, bloodthirsty and too often treacherous, these slave-kings had a keen appreciation of the arts . . . a taste and refinement which would have been hard to parallel in western countries. . . .' One can observe something of this even at the present time. The Ibn Tulun mosque in Cairo, the first pure mosque to be built in the world, and possibly the most beautiful building in Africa, was the work of a Tartar Mameluke. The huge domed and minareted tombs of the Mameluke beys, standing in the desert outside the walls of Cairo, are also an architectural triumph of their kind, and not even the dust and squalor of the slums that now surround them, or the hordes of ragged children who haunt this city of the dead, can quite obscure the revelation that there was a vision here that rose above a barbarous and material life.

As for the houses which the Mamelukes inhabited within the city walls, they were rather disappointing on the outside: rickety-looking structures of wood and stone with balconies that projected so far they almost formed a roof over the narrow streets below. But inside

Rickety-looking structures in the Esbekiah square. From Lane-Poole's Social Life in Egypt

their houses the wealthier men indulged themselves in great splendour: a fountain playing in the courtyard fell into a pool lined with black and white marble, mosaics and wooden lattice-work decorated the walls, and Persian carpets were spread upon the floor. In place of chairs there were divans with silken cushions and coverings. No room, not even the harem upstairs, was specifically designed as a bedroom – the bedding was put away in a cupboard by day and laid out at any convenient place at night; very often, in hot weather, one slept on the roof. The general object inside the house was to exclude the hot sunlight, and thus the Mameluke sat with his friends in a fine cool gloom eating his three daily meals (one before dawn, another at 10 a.m. and a third at 5 p.m.), sipping his coffee and sherbet, or puffing at the carved and jewelled ivory mouthpiece of his water-pipe while, sometimes, he watched a performance of musicians and dancers. Some of the leading men maintained pleasure boats on the Nile, and in their country estates they lived in kiosks surrounded by gardens of sycamore, jasmine and orange. Needless to say, their retinues of slaves were very large: one man to guard the door, another to carry water, a third to run before his master and clear a way through the crowded streets, and many others to staff the house. The establishments of the more powerful men were tremendous; it was nothing for a bey

to have several hundred Circassian slaves, all armed and mounted, and each of these slaves would be attended by two or three Egyptian servants of his own.

Ghorbal says of the Mamelukes: 'Without relations, without children, their past was a blank. . . . Power had no other end than procuring women, horses, jewels and retainers.' Yet they were abstemious; their meals were reasonably simple, no wine was served, and the fast of Ramadan was strictly observed.

Their wealth came mostly from customs dues. The merchant caravans that picked up goods from the Red Sea ships and transported them to the Mediterranean were charged enormous sums. £10,000 worth of Indian spices would pay up to £8,000 or £9,000 on the passage through Egypt (which was one reason why the British had developed the trade round the Cape of Good Hope), and the desert caravans were taxed as well. Upon the income from this trade, as well as upon plunder and the ruthless exploitation of the Egyptians, the Mamelukes lived the full, rich life.

To rule, if not by the sword, then by bribery and treachery – this was the mainspring of their existence. And despite murderous quarrels among themselves, endless intrigues and a morality that made a virtue of broken faith, they had succeeded in ruling for something over five hundred years at the time of Bonaparte's arrival. Generation after generation of Egyptians had succumbed to these gorgeous butchers, and between pogroms, invasions and civil wars, the fellaheen tried to eke out some sort of living by remaining inconspicuous and servile. 'Obscurity,' says Browne, 'under the falcon eye of power always a blessing, is here [in Egypt] sought with peculiar avidity.' In short, the Mamelukes lorded it over the land very much as the Pharaohs had done in ancient times.

In theory the Mamelukes were still subject to the Sultan in Constantinople; they were bound to pay him an annual bounty and to accept a Viceroy appointed by the Porte. In fact, it was many years since the bounty had been paid, and the present Viceroy, Abu Bekir Pasha, was hardly more than a puppet of the twenty-three Mameluke beys who composed the government. In recent years two of these beys, Ibrahim and Murad, had formed an uneasy and mutually suspicious partnership in Cairo, and it was they who exercised the real power. In 1798 Ibrahim, a tall, thin figure with an aquiline nose and a reputation for meanness, had reached his sixties, and Murad, the man with whom we are chiefly concerned, was gaining the ascendancy. Browne tells us that Murad Bey could neither read nor write; the engravings made of him at the time reveal a patriarchal figure, rather plump, his face wreathed with a fringe of beard, and he sits complacently on his divan smoking his pipe. Nothing could less reveal the real nature of this formidable man. He was in his late forties at this time, and his life had been one long struggle for power. Eight years before, when he had seemed at the summit of success, a Turkish army had landed and driven him into Upper Egypt. But he had returned and had been reinstated, and it was no small part of his powers of survival that he had married a woman named Fatima who was older than himself (she was about 50), and the daughter of Ali Bey, the leading Mameluke of the previous reign. She had great wealth, intelligence and influence – all very valuable attributes for a man who was by nature an impetuous and ambitious soldier, an adventurer who was physically tough and energetic even by the standards of the Mamelukes. Murad Bey had a flotilla of boats on the Nile, a pleasure garden at Gizeh close to the pyramids, and a

Murad Bey. From Description de l'Égypte

personal bodyguard of about four hundred men. It was accepted that in a crisis he was the general who would lead the Mamelukes into battle, and at this moment very few of his followers doubted that he would succeed.

He felt strong. With his 10,000 cavalry and his 30,000 irregular infantry he believed that he was more than equal to any invasion of 'Franks', however numerous they might be. We are told by a Turkish observer that when the news of the landing first reached Murad in Cairo 'his eyes became red and fire devoured his entrails'. He summoned Carlo Rossetti,

Murad Bey's pleasure garden. From Description de l'Égypte

the Venetian consul, and sounded him out about the French. It was in vain that Rossetti tried to make Murad realize who Bonaparte was, and to explain the power of modern arms; Murad ridiculed the French, calling them 'donkey-boys' whom he did not wish to hurt; they should be given a present and sent away; it was absurd to think that they might conquer Egypt.

Murad was not alone in suffering delusions; for centuries, ever since the Crusades in fact, it had been an article of faith in the Ottoman Empire that the Western Christians were poor soldiers, inexpertly led. Professor Toynbee has summed up the matter very clearly: 'The piquancy of the situation lay in the fact that the French had descended on Egypt before – in the twelfth and thirteenth centuries – at a time when they had been the inferiors of the Orientals in general civilization, not excluding the art of war. The medieval French knight had been a clumsier and less expert version of the Mameluke; and accordingly, when he tried conclusions with the Mameluke, he had been badly beaten and had abandoned the attempt to conquer Egypt as a total failure. For five and a half centuries the Mamelukes remained as they were (except that they abandoned their Central Asian bows for English carbines), and they naturally assumed that the French had changed as little as they had changed themselves. Consequently, when they heard that Napoleon had had the temerity to land at Alexandria, they proposed to deal with him as they had dealt with St Louis. Light-heartedly they rode out to trample his little army under their horses' hoofs. . . .'

And so one finds here all the makings of a major tragedy, a genuine clash of ignorant armies. Cut off from the mainstream of Mediterranean civilization for a thousand years or more, caught up in the long, slow cycle of Moslem life that turned over and over on itself, advancing nowhere, permitting no new ideas, Egypt was absolutely unprepared for the shock of the French landing. She had no means of knowing that this invasion was quite unlike any other invasion in the past, that it meant the collapse at last of the Middle Ages in the Near East – in Ghorbal's phrase, 'the ending of the long Egyptian night'.

And the French on their side had their delusions too, for they had no knowledge of campaigning in the desert, no hope of maintaining their conquest without command of the sea, and no real prospect of consolidating their rule in a country that was hostile to nearly everything they stood for. Once the first devastating clash was over the best that could be hoped for was that each side would learn something from the other, that a bridge of a sort would be established between the East and the West, and that then the French would be willing to depart.

Ibrahim, the older and wiser man of the two reigning beys, may have had an inkling of all this, for he is said to have demurred when resistance was proposed during the Mameluke council of war in Cairo. But he was overruled. The army was called out, and Murad himself rode north, at the head of some four thousand cavalry, to meet the invader on the coast.

6

The March to Cairo

The capture of Alexandria proved exceptionally easy. For a few hours the defenders put up a fight from the city walls, but Volney had been quite right: this was merely an outlying garrison, manned by Arabs and Turkish mercenaries rather than by Mamelukes, and they had no real will to struggle with out-of-date cannon in a hopeless cause. Kléber was hit in the forehead by a fragment during the assault, but there were hardly two hundred French casualties in all, and after a brief parley Bonaparte set up his headquarters in the centre of the town. Here he received the submission of Sheikh Coraim and the other garrison leaders, assuring them that there was to be no vengeance, no tribute, no interference with the local population; they had been liberated, not conquered. On a rapid tour round the town on July 3 Bonaparte ordered the defences to be put in order, and a French garrison under the command of Menou settled into billets around the walls. Soon the transports of the fleet

The French army marching through the desert. From Description de l'Égypte

were sailing in to discharge their stores and the remainder of the soldiers. The ships of the line, uncertain as yet of the depth of the water at the entrance to the harbour, waited in the roadstead outside. Already the printing press, on being landed from *l'Orient*, was striking off copies of Bonaparte's manifesto in Arabic, the first printing ever known in Egypt.

Malta and now Alexandria had fallen at a single blow, and still more important the entire French army, the 30,000 men with a good deal of their equipment, were safely ashore in Egypt. It was a marvellous beginning, and Bonaparte's next move lay clear before him; he must march inland before the Mamelukes had time to realize what he was doing, he must seize the Rosetta mouth of the Nile, and then advance up the river with all possible speed to Cairo.

Two columns were organized: one under Desaix was to march directly towards the Nile and cut it at a place called El Rahmaniya about forty miles from the sea, and the other, commanded by Dugua and accompanied by a flotilla of small boats laden with rice and grain, was to move around the coast to Rosetta. Once the mouth of the Nile was forced the flotilla was to sail upstream and make contact with Desaix at Rahmaniya; the combined army would then advance upon the capital less than one hundred miles away. The men had scarcely time even to see Alexandria, or to accustom their sea-legs to the land, before they were marched away into the desert.

Desaix, with his larger column, had some fifty miles to go before he reached the Nile, and these fifty miles were to reveal to the French as nothing else could, and with brutal suddenness, the real nature of the campaign in which they were now involved. At this time the green fields of the delta did not reach anywhere near Alexandria. The canal linking the city with the Nile had long since filled with sand, and the route (which roughly followed the line of the present railway) provided little food or water. It was now midsummer, and the heat was appalling. Dressed in their thick serge coats, breeches and gaiters, laden with their rifles and packs, the men marched in dense columns over heavy sand and rock, kicking up dust as they went along, and there was no shade anywhere. They carried with them a four-day ration of biscuit, but this was not the ideal food to keep thirst at bay, and at the few meagre wells along the way water was doled out as though it was the most

French military uniforms, about 1790
LEFT *a major-general;* RIGHT *a drummer and a gunner*

precious wine. At the end of the first day men were beginning to fall out with blistered feet, sore eyes, and general exhaustion. But they could not fall out. They were being harassed front and rear by Bedouin tribesmen, and no straggler could hope to rest for ten minutes on the sand without being cut off and attacked. Desaix himself was nearly taken when he was hardly fifty yards away from the column, and another officer, we learn, was assassinated a hundred paces from the advance guard 'in consequence of having failed to pay attention, through a melancholic abstraction of mind, to an invitation to keep up with the rest.'

In a stupor of fatigue the column struggled on, finding every village in its path deserted and empty of food. Occasionally in the oases there were a few water-melons upon which the soldiers fell like wolves, but that was all. On July 9, after a three days' forced march, they reached Rahmaniya and without waiting to take off their uniforms they threw themselves into the Nile.

And now, suddenly, when the French ranks were in disorder and the men could think of nothing but resting and getting cool, Murad appeared. He had made an excellent march down from Cairo with his cavalry, and they had been accompanied by a flotilla of armed feluccas on the river. Couriers had kept him well posted about the French advance, and now he was ready for battle. With some eight hundred picked men he came forward along the river bank and stood for a few minutes to survey the French column. It was one of those moments which are the most dramatic if not the most critical in all campaigns, especially in so bizarre a campaign as this: the moment of first contact when both sides are dealing largely in myths and doubts – the myth of the strange enemy before them and the

French military uniforms, about 1790
LEFT *commanding officer, 1st Regiment of Hussars;* RIGHT *squadron leader, 1st Regiment of Dragoons*

inward inevitable doubt about his own courage that besets every soldier facing the unknown for the first time.

Having by now been a week or more in Egypt the French had heard many stories of the magnificence and the ferocity of the Mamelukes. There was already a rumour in the ranks that Murad led his men into battle mounted on a milk-white camel, his equipment ablaze with gold and precious stones, and that he offered no quarter to his enemies. And so Desaix's weary men were expecting something rather grand and frightening.

The Mamelukes, too, were quite unprepared for this first shock of recognition, since these Frenchmen were unlike any soldiers they had ever seen before. They regarded them as Bonaparte's slaves, and at this first brief glimpse they thought them very poorly uniformed and probably badly equipped as well, though as yet they could not be absolutely sure about this. Thus no one really knew what was going to happen, fear had a place in everybody's mind, and in their uncertainty both sides set about doing what they had been trained to do; Desaix got his artillery into position and formed his infantry into squares, the first ranks kneeling with the bayonets pointing outwards, the second preparing to fire over their shoulders. The Mamelukes charged.

It was all over in a few minutes. Under the blast of the first cannonade the Mamelukes faltered and wheeled aside into the empty desert. Those who did get near the French squares came under the concentrated fire of the muskets and soon turned back, leaving

Rosetta. From Description de l'Égypte

some forty dead and wounded on the field. Only a dozen of the French were hurt. Bonaparte, coming up to the front with reinforcements, found there was no need for his assistance, and having posted his pickets, gave orders for the column to halt for forty-six hours' rest. Neither on the next day nor the day following was there any sign of the Mamelukes returning to the attack. The desert seemed to have swallowed them completely.

Meanwhile Dugua had forced the mouth of the Nile. There had been a tense moment while he got his flotilla of gunboats over the sand bars there – a high wind was blowing and the river was low – but Rosetta had collapsed without a struggle. In the fort guarding the mouth there was a 28-inch calibre gun, but it had long since fallen into disuse; according to Denon its only purpose was 'the procuration of favourable deliveries for those pregnant women by whom, with faith, it was bestrided'. Rosetta itself the French found to be 'the freshest and most verdant of countries', a garden of dates, bananas and sycamores among broken and decaying walls. Dugua had at once pressed on, his soldiers marching on the west bank and keeping pace with the boats on the river, and now he had come up to Raymaniya to join Desaix's column. The plan was working to perfection.

It was now July 12 and Bonaparte was eager to continue the advance, but at dawn the following morning his scouts brought him word that the Mamelukes were standing to meet him in much greater force than before at the village of Jibbrish, a few miles further upstream. Murad, it seemed, had assembled from 3,000 to 4,000 cavalry with which he proposed to block the French approach to the village, while on the Nile itself nine or ten large gunboats were waiting to give battle to the French flotilla.

The French were not quite ready for the encounter – the soldiers were still suffering from fatigue and only 200 of their cavalry were fit for action – but Bonaparte decided to attack at once. He gave orders for his flotilla to sail upstream and thus protect his left flank, while the infantry marched upon Jibbrish, and both were to strike together. He had not, however, calculated the effect of the high north wind; his flotilla was soon driven a good three miles ahead of the army and the French sailors suddenly found themselves confronted with a heavy cannonade both from the banks and the enemy gunboats. In the running battle that followed on the river things went very badly for the French at first: Perrée, their commander, was wounded, and four of their vessels were boarded and seized at the first assault. Hearing the commotion – and something like 1,500 cannon shots were exchanged – Bonaparte hurried his soldiers forward, and they had scarcely time to form their line before the Mamelukes came careering down upon them. Once again the enemy charged directly into the artillery fire, seeking to make a breach in the French squares, at first in front, and then on the flanks, and they came on 'like madmen'. Those who did succeed in reaching the French infantry hacked away briefly with their sabres until they were killed, but the majority in the vanguard were unhorsed or scattered before they could strike a blow. A second and a third charge brought the same result, and in the early afternoon the Mamelukes finally drew off in a dazed and helpless confusion. They had lost about three hundred of their number, and the French soldiers were soon running about looting the bodies. Bonaparte's casualties were barely seventy. Soon, too, better news arrived from the river; the French had recovered their lost vessels and an explosion on board the principal Mameluke gunboat had been the signal for a general enemy retreat.

In contemporary accounts not a great deal has been made of these two brief engagements on the Lower Nile, and historians have concentrated upon the more imposing battle which was soon to follow outside Cairo. Yet in fact the issue was already decided here on July 13. Up to this point all Bonaparte's careful planning had been hardly more than intelligent conjecture. Wars in the main start with text books. But there were no text books here, no European army had campaigned in Egypt since the Crusades, no one could speak with finality about the effects of a Mameluke charge, no one knew what unexpected tactics the enemy might produce. But now, in an instant, a gap in history was closed, and the Mamelukes were revealed as expert horsemen who were both incredibly brave and incredibly out of date. It was their misfortune, of course, in this first contact with the West, that they should have to meet the greatest soldier of the age, but even without Bonaparte the French could hardly have failed to demolish so primitive an enemy. In every department of war, in arms, in training and in organization, they were so immeasurably superior as almost to appear as supernatural beings. To the Mamelukes, war was a matter of personal courage, and there was a certain ferocious chivalry about the headlong charge; you triumphed or you died. Everything depended upon speed and movement, the quick tumultuous clash and the breaking away. But this ruthless machine-like French army obeyed none of the accepted rules, it struck from a distance, its tactics were stationary, and its soldiers fought, not as individuals, but as part of the living fortresses they formed on the battlefield. They overturned entirely the medieval notion that cavalry was always superior to infantry, and war was revealed now to the Mamelukes as anything but a hot-blooded skirmish; it was a calculated plan of mass destruction carried out mainly through intense rifle-fire and cannon balls. The charge instead of being the whole battle was merely a secondary affair.

It was true that Murad did not recognize defeat as yet – his main forces were still waiting to give battle outside Cairo – but it was the French who were now the supermen in Egypt, and the Mamelukes could only fight them out of a sense of blind pride, out of desperation and hatred; they could not hope to win.

After the Jibbrish encounter Murad retreated directly to Cairo, eighty miles away, and probably that was the best thing he could have done, since he thus lengthened Bonaparte's tenuous line of communication with Alexandria, and the country itself was a far more formidable obstacle to the French than anything the Mamelukes could contrive. The heat grew worse as the soldiers moved inland, and although they often camped among wheatfields they had no means of making flour. What they craved for was bread and wine; what they got was water-melons and lentils, and it was a dangerous diet because the soldiers soon began to complain that they were suffering from dysentery, and dysentery on an empty stomach is a debilitating thing, as every foreign army that has invaded Egypt can testify. Even bathing in the Nile was dangerous. It was too early as yet for ophthalmia, an endemic disease in the delta, to take its full effect, but the men were already beginning to feel a painful inflammation of the eyes. Later on this would develop into temporary blindness, and there were other maladies as well – bilharzia and the plague, for example – lying in wait. The French doctors knew very little about these Eastern diseases.

Now, too, the Bedouin began to harass the column in earnest. These tribesmen were a wholly unexpected hazard, since they constituted a kind of third force in Egypt. They had no common cause with the Mamelukes; it was simply in the nature of their grinding life in the desert to fall on any defenceless traveller who came their way, and every invasion or civil war was the signal for them to take to arms. They pillaged and attacked both sides impartially. They did no real damage, but like gnats that set upon an elephant they could make life miserable for the French, and it was impossible to come to terms with them.

'The Bedouin-arab,' Denon wrote, 'who are ill-armed, and can make no resistance, whose ramparts are moving sands, whose lives are space, whose retreat is immensity, by whom can they be vanquished or confined? . . . the Bedouin is the primitive hunter: indolence and independence are the basis of his character . . . he keeps himself in continual motion and endures the siege and tyranny of want. We have nothing, therefore, to offer the Bedouin that is equivalent to the value of robbing us.' And yet, Denon goes on, there were instances of the Bedouin treating captured French soldiers with great kindness once their possessions had been stripped from them. Ferocity and then indolence and generosity – it was hard for the invaders to know where they were in this strange unrelenting world which was so utterly different from everything that they had been told to expect when they left France. There was no wine, no eatable food, no women, no loot, simply this endless march in battle-order under a blazing sun.

ABOVE *French troops parading in the desert. From* Description de l'Égypte

BELOW *A Bedouin camp. From Belzoni's* Researches in Egypt and Nubia

Desaix, moving forward in the van, soon found there was talk of mutiny in his division, and the officers were even louder in complaint than the men. They had not come here, they declared, to die like animals of want, they were hungry, they were tired, they were ill, they could not go on. Some of the discontent was directed against the intellectuals – the famous savants who were forever browsing about like donkeys among ancient stones and ruins;

Bonaparte. After a painting by Pierre Narcisse Guérin

it was they who had persuaded Bonaparte into this mad adventure. This resentment did not run very deep; Monge and Berthollet had both behaved very well on board one of the French gunboats in the Jibbrish engagement, and others like Denon lived almost harder than the soldiers themselves. But by the third week of July, when the march had been going on for ten days or more, everyone, men and officers alike, was looking for scapegoats as an outlet for their grievances. One soldier was bold enough to attempt irony with Bonaparte himself: 'Well, General, are you going to take us on to India too?' Bonaparte is said to have answered coldly: 'No, it's not with men like you that I would undertake that journey.'

It was probably the very fact that they *had* to go on that kept the march intact, for by now they had lost all contact with the coast and the French fleet, their one lifeline to France. It was even a retreat of a kind – less cruel and much smaller in scale than the return from Moscow, which still lay a dozen years in the future – but still a retreat: a retreat to victory.

Had the French known what was happening in Cairo they would have felt a good deal more cheerful. The city was demoralized by the news of Murad's defeat at Jibbrish. He had set out so confidently with his cavalry and his gunboats, and now in a matter of a few days he was back in Cairo, routed and defeated, with this new and terrible French army apparently following on his heels, getting nearer every day.

The first reaction followed the familiar pattern of civilian panic: the run on the food shops, the hiding of valuables and jewels, the preparations for flight. The price of mules and camels rose sharply, weapons of every kind were sold at a premium, and powder and lead became unobtainable in the bazaar. One after another the shops closed their doors and no one stirred in the streets by night. As in every such crisis, when there are signs of fear among those in authority the lowest people in the community came out into the open. Thieves broke into the houses whose owners had already fled, and mobs set upon the homes of the European merchants and the Copt and Greek churches, ransacking them for jewels and arms. It soon became dangerous for a man to appear alone in a deserted street.

The Mamelukes were able to put a check on some of these excesses. Householders were ordered to hang lanterns from their balconies to light the streets at night when thieves were particularly active, and the people who were attempting flight were arrested at the city gates and imprisoned. Ibrahim called a council of war, and couriers were sent off to the Sultan at Constantinople asking for help – a futile gesture since the French were bound to arrive long before the Sultan could move – but no doubt it created a kind of official reassurance. Meanwhile there was a rough and ready attempt to put Cairo into a state of defence: guns were mounted on the walls and a line of boats was sunk across the Nile near Bulaq to prevent the approach of the French flotilla. A tented camp was set up on the west bank of the river around the village of Embaba, and all men of military age were ordered to assemble there.

These preparations did something to calm the population, but the majority of people preferred to put their trust in God. Prayers were said constantly in the mosques, and the great flag of the Prophet was taken down from the citadel and carried in procession with a band of drums and clarinets to the island of Bulaq, where it was thought the French would first appear. But no one knew precisely what the French were going to do. Would they approach on the west or the east bank, or on the river itself? Each day the bazaars filled with fresh rumours, and Murad's return contributed very little to the general knowledge, since after Jibbrish he had broken off contact with Bonaparte entirely. And now it was decided to adopt a plan which was the last extreme of foolishness: Ibrahim was to remain on the east bank with the reserves covering Cairo, while the main bulk of the Mameluke army under Murad was to take up position in the desert at Embaba on the west bank. Thus Bonaparte, who was already on the west side of the Nile, was to be spared the danger and difficulty of crossing the river before the battle was joined.

A general move was now made to Embaba, and traders and food merchants set up their booths there among the troops. Guns taken from the river-boats were placed around the camp, and the digging of a rough system of trenches was begun. By July 20 some sixty thousand men were assembled, but of these only the Mameluke cavalry, numbering about ten thousand, could be described as a coherent force: the remainder were infantry and camp-followers, many of whom were armed only with spears and swords. In Cairo women and children and aged people who had been left behind remained hidden in their houses.

Bonaparte during these eventful days steadily continued his advance up the river. 'Melancholy and sadness,' he records, 'reigned in the army.' But still he pushed his murmuring soldiers on, and ate his own plate of lentils in the midst of their bivouacs at night. The men talked for hours round the camp fires, arguing that they were being got rid of by the Directory in Paris – otherwise what was the reason for this senseless march? But at least they did not have to fight; there had been no sign of the enemy since Jibbrish, and a detachment crossing to the east bank found the country there equally deserted.

On July 19 they reached Umm Dinar, close to the junction with the Damietta branch of the river. Here they were barely twenty miles from Cairo – every man with a spy-glass turned it upon the distant outline of the pyramids – and Bonaparte, hearing at last from spies that the Mameluke army was waiting for him on the west bank outside Cairo, ordered a day's rest. On July 20 a twelve-hour forced march was begun before dawn, and the army bivouacked that night within a mile or two of Embaba. At 1 a.m. on July 21 the camp was already astir, and in the dawn light the soldiers saw the Mamelukes for the first time since Jibbrish: a thousand of them drawn up silently in line across the desert. Bonaparte went forward on horseback and surveyed the position through his glass. He saw beyond the enemy outposts the great camp at Embaba, and judged that there were about twenty thousand enemy infantry there, with perhaps some forty guns in crude entrenchments. The chief interest in these guns for Bonaparte was that they were river-boat guns without wheels or carriages, and therefore immobile. To the west of the camp the bulk of the Mameluke cavalry appeared to be drawn up astride the road to the pyramids at Gizeh, and he judged them to number between 9,000 and 10,000. It was now 10 a.m. and the sun was rising to its full power.

There are many strange aspects about the Battle of the Pyramids; it took place, for example, nowhere near the pyramids – they were eight or nine miles away – and by the same process of romantic association most people remember this day because of Bonaparte's famous exhortation to his troops, 'Soldats! Du haut de ces monuments, quarante siècles vous regardent.' Another version runs, 'Allez, et pensez que du haut de ces monumenst 40 siècles vous observent.' These troops were probably much too busy to pay any attention to it. The battle itself and its drastic aftermath provide many other anomalies. Yet perhaps the really significant factor in the whole affair is that Bonaparte, in these outlandish circumstances, and still a young man of 29, should have divined in one instant, and apparently with absolute conviction, precisely what he had to do. Never was a battle more clearly planned. He sees the fixed guns in the enemy camp and decides at once to keep them *hors de combat* for the time being by remaining outside their range while he tackles the Mameluke cavalry in the open desert. If the enemy infantry choose to come to the aid of the cavalry by sallying out of their camp, then so much the better, they will have to fight without the aid of their artillery. If, however, the infantry decide to remain where they are, it seems not unlikely that he will defeat the Mameluke cavalry with his own mobile guns and the concentrated fire of his squares; and then it will be time enough to turn on the enemy camp. A French detachment placed behind the camp and astride the Gizeh road will prevent the remnants of the Mameluke cavalry from coming to the assistance of their infantry; and indeed the infantry themselves will have no place to which to retreat except into the Nile.

There seems to be no reason to doubt Bonaparte's word that this, in fact, was the way he designed the battle, since these dispositions were those which he actually carried out; at all stages of the action the Mamelukes reacted, not to their own plan (which was presumably to draw the French on to assault the camp while they charged in upon them from the flanks) but to Bonaparte's plan.

So now Desaix was sent off to meet the Mamelukes on the right flank, and it was a long business, a matter of three hours, before all was ready, his infantry marching in squares, with the artillery in between, the baggage to the centre, his scouts at the front. Murad appears to have been confused at first about what was happening; at all events it was not until 2 p.m., when the sun was at its fiercest and a strong wind blowing from the north, that he realized that his cavalry was about to be cut off from his infantry. Then at last he gave the order to charge.

At least six thousand horsemen were involved in this movement, and it is probably true to say that it was the last great cavalry charge of the Middle Ages. The contemporary attempts to describe it both in words and in drawings are not very satisfactory; they leave one with a confused picture of the Moslem pennants flying over the horses' heads, of the Mamelukes in their enormous turbans and fluttering robes, each man leaning forward with a sabre in his right hand, of the foot-attendants running beside them and of scores of camels laden with panniers of ammunition and weapons following on behind. But all this vanishes in a moment of clouds of dust and smoke, and the noise of the charge – the thousands of hoofs beating on the sand, the shouts, the drums and the bugles – becomes lost in the general uproar of cannon. Few eye-witnesses ever really see a battle or comprehend what is happening while it is being fought, every soldier is isolated in the small frantic world of his own experience, and this battle was more tumultuous than most, quicker in action, more savage in character and more concentrated in time; it was, indeed, one long crisis, while it lasted.

Desaix had just reached a sparse grove of palm trees when the charge began, and he had barely time to settle his soldiers into their action stations before the Mamelukes were upon them. They waited until the leading horsemen were within fifty paces. Then they fired. Denon speaks of the enemy riding right up to the mouths of the cannon before they fell or turned aside. Those who wheeled round the squares, seeking to make a breach in the sides and rear, were soon caught in the crossfire of Reynier's division that was coming up behind Desaix; and when they turned to charge again their frightened animals were buffeted back and forth from one square to another. Murad, who had put himself in the van of the first assault, escaped with a slight wound in his cheek, and he appears to have realized that the battle was lost almost before it had begun. He gathered together the remnants of his men and retired towards the pyramids. Desaix's cavalry following up behind

Mameluke cavalry charging the French infantry at the Battle of the Pyramids

soon got themselves behind the enemy camp at Embaba and took up a position close to the river bank.

Meanwhile Dugua's division, with Bonaparte in one of the squares, was advancing on the camp itself. They turned aside a cavalry charge, and seeing the way clear before them rushed straight upon the enemy guns which, up to this point, had taken no part in the battle. Nor were the gunners able to contribute much even at this desperate moment. They fired once, but before they could reload and fire again the French were on top of them, and a hand-to-hand struggle began among the entrenchments and the baggage of the camp. Murad attempted to come to the assistance of his infantry from the rear, but he found himself blocked by Desaix's division; and now in fact the bulk of the Mameluke army and its thousands of camp followers were surrounded. 'From this moment,' Denon says, 'it was no longer a battle: it was a massacre.'

Ibrahim, waiting with his reserves and a huge crowd of townspeople on the east bank, was appalled to see Embaba go up in flames, and presently out of the pall of the sandstorm raised by the north wind thousands of figures, Mamelukes as well as infantry, came running to the river. There were no boats, but apparently these men preferred death by drowning to the bullets of the French, and so they flung themselves into the choppy water, even rode their horses into it, and were soon swept away by the current. This was a great reassurance to the sailors in the French flotilla further down the river. All day they had been struggling against the current, hoping to take part in the action, but at the time of the Mamelukes' first charge they were still miles away. They heard in the distance a tremendous cannonade, and presently this grew fainter – a sign that the enemy were in retreat. But the wind dropped and the noise of the battle grew stronger than before and seemed much closer, almost as if it was Bonaparte who was falling back. In some alarm the sailors listened as the firing continued to increase, but now the bodies of the dead enemy began to float down towards them, at first in twos and threes and then in dozens – the Mamelukes in their gorgeous robes like great tropical flowers on the surface of the water – and they knew that the battle was won. It had been decided in a little more than an hour.

Back on the battlefield and around the camp at Embaba the French soldiers found that they had reached their eldorado at last. The Mamelukes had gone into action carrying their wealth with them. Some had as many as 300 or 400 gold louis in their saddlebags, and their equipment – the inlaid swords and daggers, the silk scarves and the jewelled turbans – were worth a fortune to men who earned only a few sous a day. There was no shortage of this loot; three, perhaps four, thousand Mamelukes and their men had been either killed or drowned, and few of the French failed to get a share; barely two hundred of their own number had fallen. In the camp itself all forty pieces of cannon were recovered intact, together with some eight hundred camels and baggage animals, large stores of food and many cases of silver and other treasure. It was a measure of the ferocity of the fighting and of the bravery of the Mamelukes that only 1,000 prisoners were taken.

It was still daylight. Murad, with about two thousand surviving cavalry, paused only a quarter of an hour at his country house near the pyramids and then continued on into the desert towards Beni Suef. Before he left, however, he found time to make one last gesture. There were about sixty boats anchored in the Nile above Rhoda Island, and before the

LEFT *Dugua and* RIGHT *Reynier. Wash drawings by André Dutertre*

battle they had been loaded with the Mamelukes' personal treasure. Seeing he had no time to man them and sail them away Murad now set fire to these vessels. Bonaparte, coming up to the river in the last light of the evening, saw a marvellous sight: the great grey pyramid of Cheops illumined by the flames, and in the distance, floating in the reflected glow, the domes and minarets of Cairo.

He moved into Murad's house with his staff, and there, in this moment of triumphant relaxation, roamed from room to room marvelling at the cushions and the divans, the damask and the silk hangings fringed with gold. In the garden his officers fell upon the ripe bunches of grapes hanging from the vines.

Towards nine o'clock another, stronger glow lit up the sky, this time over Cairo itself. Ibrahim had not even waited until the French turned their guns upon him across the river; he had retreated directly into the city with his bodyguard, and these, having gathered up their women and portable belongings, had continued directly out of the city towards the east. All night long people streamed through the gates, the men with baggage on their heads, the women with children on their shoulders. A horse, we are told by Abdul-Rahman al-Jabarti, the son of one of the principal imams, fetched a fortune. Only those who could not flee remained behind, for it was believed that the French on entering the city would carry out a general massacre. The refugees, however, fared hardly better than the Mamelukes who had retreated into the Nile: a few miles outside Cairo they were set upon by Bedouin and stripped of their belongings. Only Ibrahim with his column of armed Mamelukes was able to get safely through.

Cairo was now taken over by a mob. They burst into the beys' houses, one after another, Murad's town residence as well as Ibrahim's, looting them of every movable object and in some cases setting fire to the empty shell of the building as well. It was the light of these fires which the French saw from across the river.

Abdul-Rahman al-Jabarti describes this as 'the most horrible night of Cairo's history'. For the French, however, it was the marvellous, almost unbelievable reward for the hardships of the past three weeks, and Bonaparte, his every promise to his men fulfilled, could sit down with some elation in Murad's country house and write his dispatch to the Directory. It was the discipline of his men, he thought, that sang-froid which had enabled them to wait before firing until the Mamelukes had approached to within fifty paces of their ranks, that had won the day. One can imagine him lying down to sleep at last on one of Murad's divans, still dressed in his uniform. He had been awake for some twenty hours. It was a wonderful thing to be young.

7

The Occupation

Bonaparte, after his Italian campaigns, was already an old hand in the business of dealing with captured cities, and the arrangements he now made at Cairo will be familiar to most soldiers who fought in the last world war. The frightened leaders of the community are sent for and are reassured that there will be no reprisals if no further resistance is offered; the shops must be reopened, law and order re-established, and billets made available to the soldiers who are to occupy the city. An officer is appointed as military governor, proclamations are pasted up on the walls, and presently the victorious soldiers come marching in. From the windows of their houses the people watch them silently and intently, fearing the worst, trying desperately to understand what the future is going to bring.

There is a certain arrogance in all soldiers occupying a conquered town. It is muted and disguised for the time being, nevertheless it is there; they despise the helpless, dejected civilians with their meek, averted faces and their shabby houses, and the young officer, ordering his men to ground their rifles in the square, conceals beneath his air of punctiliousness a feeling of secret complacency in his own power. This will change presently as the civilians grow more confident and the soldiers begin to feel the need of more human relationships, especially with women. Food will be bought and paid for, strange faces and manners will grow familiar, and as the soldiers' indolence increases the civilians will learn how to placate their new rulers, how to use them for their own advantage, and perhaps eventually how to cheat them. For the moment, however, all is wariness and suspicious curiosity, with confidence on one side and fear on the other, and when at last the commander-in-chief comes riding into the city he appears to them all, soldiers and civilians alike, to be a very great man indeed, the symbol of absolute power, the final arbiter of all lives.

These effects, which were now about to be produced in Cairo, were of extraordinary interest, not only because it was the French, the most talented people in Europe, who were the victors, and the Egyptians, by nature a devious and long-suffering race, who were the conquered, not only because of the astonishing rapidity of the collapse of the country, but because this was the first real integration of the West and the East in Egypt since the departure of the Roman garrisons well over a thousand years before.

The negotiations were opened at dawn on Sunday, July 22. Having posted a division on Rhoda Island, which was divided only by a narrow channel from Cairo, Bonaparte sent a message to the sheikhs and imams to come to him at Gizeh. The ulema – the religious leaders – had not all fled the city, and they chose two of their number as their representatives. From these men Bonaparte learned that Ibrahim had gone, taking with him Abu Bekir Pasha, the Sultan's Viceroy. So it remained now to find others to take their place. The envoys were sent back to Cairo with assurances of peace, and were instructed that they must return with the leading men who had been left behind in the city. Next day, July 23, a deputation of sheikhs arrived, and after a conference of several hours offered their submission. General Dupuy was now appointed governor, and he followed the sheikhs back to the city. His soldiers occupied the port at Bulaq, the central part of Cairo, and the citadel, while he himself set up his headquarters in Ibrahim's house overlooking the Nile.

Now finally, when all was ready, Bonaparte himself entered Cairo to the sound of drums and trumpets, and the population came out to gaze on him as he rode by. A sumptuous place, the recently built house of Elfy Bey, one of the wealthiest of the departed Mamelukes, had been reserved for him in the centre of the town, in Esbekiah square. It had a garden reaching out to the countryside, and stood on the site where the old Shepheard's Hotel was eventually built. Here the commander-in-chief (or the Grand Sultan, the *Sultan Kebir*, as the Egyptians called him) lived in great style. His coachman Caesar caused much astonishment when he appeared in the narrow streets of Cairo with his coach and six. Other large houses were found for the staff and the savants who were now to set up the new *Institut d'Égypte*.

Awakening from the daze created by the battle, the French and Egyptians now began to observe one another, and the Egyptians at first were immensely relieved. If the French had their mad idiosyncrasies, such as the order obliging the citizens to wear the cockade in their turbans, they were also generous, even to the point of naïveté: they paid for what they bought at very high prices, and the Egyptian bakers, full of wonder at such gullibility, soon began to mix earth with the flour and make smaller loaves. The bazaars and coffeehouses reopened, and many of those who had fled to the desert began to return.

There were excesses of course – despite Bonaparte's orders the French soldiers joined in the looting that was still going on – but the mosques were respected, and householders found that they could get an official paper from General Dupuy's office which, when pasted on the front door, was usually sufficient protection from the mob. During the next few days those Mamelukes who had gone into hiding were informed upon, arrested, and in some cases hanged, but their wives were protected and the French merely demanded of them a ransom – a pretty stiff ransom in the case of Fatima, Murad's wife: she had to pay 720,000 francs.

Bonaparte during these early days tried hard to make himself acceptable to his new subjects. A council of Egyptian elders was set up to replace the Mameluke beys, and a genuine effort was made to encourage them to govern. It was before this council that Bonaparte appeared in Egyptian costume – one marvels at the picture of that pale face beneath the enormous turban – and delivered a harangue on the equality and fraternity of mankind. 'When I am in France,' he is said to have declared, 'I am a Christian, when in Egypt a Mohammedan.' And again: 'The religion of Christ is a threat: the religion of Mohammed is a promise.' At banquets he sat cross-legged among the sheikhs and ate with his fingers. Each guest on one occasion found a copy of the Koran and of Thomas Paine's *The Rights of Man* beside his place.

Egyptians were appointed as governors of the provinces, each with a French commissioner to assist him, and Bonaparte himself designed for these officials a splendid new

Bonaparte, in oriental costume, with the Pasha of Cairo

uniform with a blue-plumed hat. Taxes were imposed on what was believed to be a fair and reasonable basis, and in the law courts and government offices an attempt was made to do away with the Mameluke system of corruption and bribery. Next, an elaborate scheme of public works was set on foot; canals were cleared, rubbish was removed from the streets, a bridge of boats was thrown across the Nile, and engineers repaired the hydraulic machine in the great octagonal tower that supplied the citadel with water. Troops were sent off to rescue a caravan of Mecca pilgims who were being harassed by the Bedouin outside Cairo. In other words, this was the policy of appeasement, and what was to be attempted by the French was nothing less than the regeneration of Egypt.

This was where the intellectuals were to play their part. At the opening meeting of the new *Institut d'Égypte* Bonaparte accepted the vice-presidency under Monge, and he himself elected to direct the work of the department of mathematics, while Berthollet attended to physics, Caffarelli to economics, and Parseval-Grandmaison to literature and the fine arts. The *Institut*'s programme would have done credit to UNESCO and all the combined agencies of the United Nations as well. In the field of arts they were to study the monuments and the antiquities, to write a history of ancient Egypt, to prepare a French-Egyptian dictionary and to publish two journals, *La Décade Égyptienne* and *Le Courrier d'Égypte*. In engineering they were to devise one plan for the cutting of the Suez Canal and another for the preservation of fresh water by the erection of a series of dams on the Nile. The causes of the annual flooding of the river were also to be examined. In agriculture they were to experiment with

Repairing the Nile dam. Bonaparte is watching at the right.

new crops, in medicine they were to investigate the disease of ophthalmia and to reorganize the sanitary and hospital services; in economy a new scheme of weights and measures was to be devised. Monge and others were to busy themselves with such esoteric matters as the desert mirage, the hippopotamus and the crocodile, and the movements of heavenly bodies in the bright Egyptian sky. A census was to be carried out, the country accurately mapped, and a study made of geology and natural history. Egypt, for the first time, was to be revealed to itself and to the world.

It seems clear that the Egyptians themselves, on recovering from the first shock of the conquest, neither liked nor approved of any of these dealings. Bonaparte and his savants were moved by the ardent revolutionary principle that all men wished to be free and to improve themselves, but this, as we have seen, was not necessarily the case in a country that had scarcely ever known either freedom or improvement. The Egyptian sheikhs and imams had no wish to take on the responsibility of government, they were frightened of it. They had had their own devious system for survival under the Mamelukes, and what the French appeared to be offering them was not freedom but a new sort of subservience, worse than the one they had known before because it was alien and strange. The Mamelukes had been lax in gathering taxes, but the French were proving very thorough; they employed Copts and Greeks to ferret out the last piastre, and it was difficult to come to some comfortable arrangement with a bribe. The proposed census was going to make concealment even harder. Everything these new conquerors proposed was a strain; it was a strain *not* to throw rubbish in the streets, *not* to bribe witnesses and officials, and it was upsetting to be obliged to undergo medical treatment where prayers had always served in the past. They had been getting on very well, they felt, as they were before. They had no need for new canals, new weights and measures, and new schools. Above all, they hated the Christian interference in their private lives. They did not believe Bonaparte's protestations of his respect for Mohammed, nor were they much impressed by his dressings-up in turban and caftan or the great celebrations he ordered for the birthday of the Prophet; every move his soldiers made was an affront to the Moslem way of life.

'The drunkenness and frivolity of the French and the liberties they took with women,' Ghorbal says, 'scandalized a society punctilious on these points. The Egyptians suffered all the miseries of a military occupation. When the French took up their quarters in a village the poor peasant would find his utensils, ploughs, doors, roofs, everything, in short, of a combustible nature, burned for cooking, his earthen pots broken, his corn consumed, his fowl and pigeons roasted and devoured, and, worst of all, his daughters ravished.'

Contemporary Egyptian observers make the same point. To quote one of them: 'Cairo has become a second Paris; women go about shamelessly with the French; intoxicating drinks are publicly sold and things are committed of which the Lord of heaven would not approve.'

It was perfectly true that the Mamelukes, in moments of violence, behaved infinitely more cruelly to the Egyptians than the French did. But this was not the point. The Mamelukes were the devil they knew, and Bonaparte was not. His sincerity – and there is no doubt that at first his approach to the problems of governing Egypt was both very sincere and very intelligent – was misunderstood. The Egyptians naturally looked for duplicity beneath the apparent altruism, and at the same time, like spoilt children who are offered undreamed of liberties, they began to expect that more and more would be given them.

The French on their side were no better pleased with the situation than the Egyptians, once the first glow of victory was over. Campaigning with Bonaparte in Italy they had moved among familiar scenes where the inhabitants behaved more or less as they did themselves. But here they were surrounded by dark shuttered houses, by women who in general revealed nothing of themselves but their eyes and the tips of their fingers, by

The sheikhs of Cairo: Sayed Khalil Bahari, Suleiman el Fayumi, Moallem Gerges el Johari

people whose language and religion were a mystery, whose celebrations were gibberish and whose food was uneatable. They had had no mail from home since they had sailed three months before, and now that the first pressure of the campaign was over many of the men fell ill. They were forever hot and uncomfortable, and it was not long before they were beset by that bane of all occupying armies: restlessness and ennui. Bonaparte drew up a list of requirements he wanted urgently from France: a company of comedians, a troupe of ballet dancers, a marionette show, a hundred prostitutes, two hundred thousand pints of brandy and a million of wine. Meanwhile a kind of pleasure-garden was set up in one of the squares of the city.

Bonaparte himself, despite the titanic work that filled his day, appears to have felt a growing home-sickness and a need of relaxation, for he was soon to contract his celebrated liaison with La Bellilote. An order had been given at the outset that no women were to accompany the expedition from France, but this had been evaded by about three hundred officers, who had succeeded in disguising their wives and mistresses in soldiers' uniform. La Bellilote, a young girl named Marguerite Pauline Bellisle, who had married a Lieutenant

Fourès, of the Twenty-Second Mounted Chasseurs, was one of these women. Fourès had found her in a milliner's shop in Carcassonne, and now, having got her to Egypt dressed in a shako and a green uniform, he was unlucky enough to let her be seen by Bonaparte playing *vingt-et-un* in the officers' club. The story that followed (and it can be conveniently anticipated here) has its aspects of farce. Bonaparte packed Fourès off with dispatches for France, and is said to have immediately invited the girl to a dinner party, where he chose a moment to spill a carafe of water over her dress and thus have an excuse for leading her

Abdullah Sharkawi, El Sadat, Mohammed el Mehdi. Paintings by Michel Rigo

to his bedroom. They were absent an hour, and next day Pauline was installed in Elfy Bey's house as his hostess – a role she seems to have performed with a certain gusto, since she dressed often in a general's uniform, was saluted everywhere as the commander-in-chief's mistress, and was a lively figure at the officers' receptions and picnics in the desert. 'She was not serious,' says a French commentator. 'She was not Cleopatra.' Still, she was gay, it was Bonaparte's first affair since his marriage to Josephine, and she wore a miniature of her protector round her neck.

Fourès, meanwhile, had been captured aboard the French ship *Le Chasseur* by the English vessel *Lion*, whose captain, on opening the dispatches, found that they were nothing more than out-of-date proclamations and routine papers of no importance. Suspecting that Fourès was in possession of secret news he was to give the Directory by word of mouth, the English captain put him back on shore near Alexandria. Fourès, who had been shown the papers, at once made his way to Cairo, where, as he half expected, he found his apartment empty. He succeeded, however, in forcing his way into his wife's room in Bonaparte's house. She refused to come away, and Fourès at the height of their argument was about to beat her when some of Bonaparte's staff broke in and dragged him away. A divorce followed, and La Bellilote (a corruption of her name Bellisle), like so many others in this expedition, eventually vanished out of Bonaparte's life and out of history.

Other civilians as well as women had followed the general to Egypt. These for the most part were traders and speculators ('Useless, fickle, wandering and irresolute men,' Denon calls them), who had hoped to mulct the fabulous East in the wake of the army, to buy grain and horses, silk, spices, gold and jewels and sell them at an enormous profit in France, but up to date very little business had come their way. The Mamelukes had departed with their riches, their houses had been pillaged, and trade had been disrupted by the war. Then there were the 'epicures and debauchees who . . . had set out from Paris in search of new pleasures at Cairo', only to find that no recently occupied city ever resembles Sodom or Gomorrah.

These men were now demoralized. Those who had remained in Alexandria found themselves cut off from France, and those who had managed to reach Cairo were unable to get back to the coast because marauding Bedouin blocked the way and no one could stir without an escort. Not even the Nile was safe; the Bedouin waited on the banks until the wind dropped or the boats ran on a sandbank. Then they pounced. In these circumstances even Bonaparte's dispatches were failing to get through, and he had received no word from the Directory since he had sailed. And so each day the malcontents grew in number, and they could talk of nothing except how they could return to France.

But no one could return to France, not for a long time yet. It was soon realized that the campaign which had opened so brilliantly had only just begun, and was about to enter a new phase; in place of pitched battles which were short and victorious they were faced with guerrilla warfare which promised to be long and hard. Bonaparte sent a message to Murad, who had reached the Faiyum oasis, offering him the governorship of Upper Egypt if he would submit, but Murad merely replied with a counter-offer; he said he would pay the French a ransom if they would get out of Egypt. Nor did Bonaparte have any better luck with the Mamelukes who had gone east: when he proposed to Abu Bekir Pasha that he should return to Cairo and resume his role as the Sultan's Viceroy he received no reply at all. The Pasha by now was well on his way to Syria with Ibrahim, each of them with enormous baggage in their train, and they had no intention of returning.

Ibrahim at least, Bonaparte decided to destroy. He himself joined the detachment that set off in pursuit, and although they caught up with Ibrahim's escort – a hand-to-hand skirmish was fought at Salhiya on the eastern edge of the delta – Ibrahim himself and Abu Bekir escaped and continued on their way. Bonaparte spent two days at Salhiya organizing his provincial administration, and it was on his journey back to Cairo that at last he received word from the garrison he had left behind at Alexandria under Kléber. It is said that he read Kléber's message with an air of imperturbability, and if this is true it is remarkable, for it contained terrible news, the worst that could possibly be: the French fleet at Alexandria had been utterly destroyed by the English. The expedition was cut off from France.

'On the morning of July 31, 1798,' Denon wrote, 'the French were masters of Egypt, Corfu and Malta; thirty vessels of the line united these possessions with France.' Now on August 1, the day on which the Battle of the Nile was fought (though Bonaparte did not hear of it until eleven days later), 'the Army of the East was imprisoned in its own conquest.' Overnight the French had become marooned colonists instead of conquerors.

It was many days before the details of the battle reached Cairo, and even at Saint Helena just before his death Bonaparte was still explaining, in his dictated memoirs, his own part in the affair. Brueys had been unwilling to take his ships into Alexandria harbour until its narrow entrance had been charted, and Bonaparte declares that before he began his march to Cairo on July 6 he left definite instructions for the admiral: if he could not get into port he was to discharge his cargoes as best he might and then sail for Corfu. At Corfu he would be safe from the British. Bonaparte in his memoirs goes on to say that he repeated these instructions later, but that instead of obeying them Brueys, still unable or unwilling to go into Alexandria, remained loitering for three weeks in the open sea of Abukir Bay, about fifteen miles to the north-east of the city; and there Nelson caught him.

All this remains true enough, but it is hardly fair to Brueys. Bonaparte's repeated instructions did not get through to him in time; during the whole period that the French army was making its way up to Cairo Brueys had no news at all from Bonaparte. He did not know what had happened to the French army. It was conceivable that it had been defeated and would have to be re-embarked. In those circumstances he could not abandon it and sail for Corfu. And so his ships, anchored by the bow and two hundred and fifty yards apart, remained in a curve about one and three-quarters of a mile long off the coast between Abukir Island and the Rosetta mouth of the Nile. The vessels were at all times ready for action, but their decks were still cluttered with cabins rigged up for the soldiers, a third or more of the crews were on shore, many were ill (Brueys himself was unwell) and morale was low.

Nelson, after leaving Alexandria at the end of June, had doubled back to Sicily in search of the French, and it was only on his arrival at Syracuse on July 19 that he heard that they were in Egypt. Having watered and provisioned his squadron of fourteen vessels, he sailed again for Alexandria and arrived in sight of the French fleet towards dusk on August 1. The sun and the breeze were behind him, the sea was calm. He conceived the dangerous plan of splitting his force into two squadrons, one squadron to run between the French and the shore, the other to go into action from the open sea, and he attacked at once.

The term 'The Battle of the Nile' is another romantic misnomer, since it was not fought on the Nile at all or even at the mouth of the river: it was fought in the Abukir roadstead, where the French had been stationed for weeks. But no one has ever questioned the rightness of Nelson's plan or the brilliance of his victory. As each of his 74s came into range they anchored, and a tremendous broadside swept the French, undermanned as they were, from two directions at once. At 8 p.m. Brueys was wounded on the quarterdeck of his flagship *Tonnant*, and at 9 p.m. he died. The British *Bellerophon* engaged *l'Orient*, the ship of the line in which Bonaparte had sailed from France, and was disabled, but at 10 p.m. *l'Orient* herself blew up with a loud explosion. Thereafter there was a long silence under the full moon and the bright stars, but those watching on shore could see nothing because of the thick clouds of smoke drifting over the water, and presently the cannonading began again.

The dawn revealed a scene of frightful wreckage. Nine British ships were dismasted and

218 of their crews were dead, with 678 more wounded. Nelson himself was hit on the head
by a ball. But the French were annihilated. Of Brueys's thirteen ships of the line and twelve
frigates only four – two 74s and two frigates – were not sunk, captured, or lying unmanage-
able on the water, and these four, cutting their cables, managed to escape. For days afterwards bodies and wreckage of every kind kept drifting on to the shore, there to be seized
upon by the Bedouin. No one ever accurately computed the French losses. It is known,
however, that about 3,500 of the surviving sailors joined Bonaparte's army in Egypt.

Nelson remained for two and a half weeks off Abukir, landing the prisoners taken in the
battle, and refitting six prizes for their voyage to England, and then, leaving Hood to establish a blockade, himself sailed for Naples. He had dealt Bonaparte a blow from which any
other commander would never have recovered.

In one unexpected way the very magnitude of the disaster was of assistance to the
French. It left them without an alternative: being now cut off from all hope of returning
to France, they concentrated their energies upon Egypt and began to accept a life of exile.
This of course did not prevent the soldiers and the camp followers from sending the most
dismal letters home. Egypt, they assured their families, was the vilest and most inhospitable
of countries, its people scurrilous and dirty, its landscape nothing but arid desert, its towns
filled with horrible disease. Even Bonaparte gave way at times to fits of despair. Writing
a little later on to his brother Joseph he spoke of his prospects of escaping:

'In two months it is possible that I shall be back in France, so find me a house where I
may spend the winter alone. I am sick of humanity: I need solitude and isolation. Greatness
wearies me, emotion chills me, my passion for glory has vanished. At twenty-nine years of
age I am worn out. I mean henceforth to live in a country house, but never will I share it
with her [Josephine]. I have no more reason to live.' It seems from this that the news of
Josephine's latest liaison in France had somehow reached him in Cairo.

Such letters as these were dispatched by frigates from Alexandria, and often these
frigates were intercepted by the British blockade, which soon after the Battle of the Nile
had been reinforced by Turkish and Russian ships. Already the British were predisposed
to think it was only a matter of time before the French expedition collapsed of its own
misfortunes, and these letters seemed to confirm that view. There was no need, it was
thought, to land a British force in Egypt; the Turks, who had now declared war on Bonaparte, would be able to deliver the *coup de grâce* without assistance. Nelson gave it as his
opinion that the French could be forced to surrender within three months.

Now in point of fact the French army was very far from being desperate. It suffered
hardly at all from the lack of supplies from France; the soldiers were being amply and well
fed from the rich fields of the delta, perhaps better fed than they would have been at home,
and gradually, with the welcome prospect of the mild Egyptian winter before them, they
were acclimatizing themselves. They had captured a quantity of guns and arms of every
kind, in addition to transport animals and river-boats; a factory for the manufacture of
gunpowder had been set up, and such articles as boots and uniforms could easily be made
in Egypt. The army's losses had been very few; despite sickness the original force of some
36,000 men was still almost intact. To these Bonaparte added local levies of Greeks and
Copts, who could be used for garrison duties and in the transport corps.

Bonaparte presiding over the Cairo Divan. Engraving by A. D. Raffet

Now too Bonaparte began to perceive that his appeasement policy could never convert the Egyptians into active allies or partners. They could be ruled and coerced but never persuaded, or absolutely trusted. He began to take a harsher line with the sheikhs, and to put his government on to a much more realistic basis. The citizens of Cairo now found they had to have a licence for every activity in life, for buying and selling, for the registration of a birth, a marriage or a death, for the transfer of property – and these licences had to be paid for. The discussion of politics was forbidden, and communication with the Mamelukes was made punishable by death. All mules had to be sold as transport animals to the army, and a private citizen found with an animal was fined 1,800 francs. The dead could no longer be buried outside the houses, they had to be taken to the tombs of the Mamelukes outside the city; and amid the fearful screams of the women French soldiers began to tear up the graves in the Esbekiah Square. A quarantine station detained travellers at Bulaq, and as a further precaution against the plague letters had to be dipped in vinegar and every house and its contents were ordered to be cleaned within fifteen days.

One after another the new edicts were shouted through the streets by town criers, and the French soldiers, who imagined that they had come as liberators, now feared to walk about without arms.

The question of the lamps caused as much exasperation as anything; it was the reverse of the black-out regulations in the last world war. Every house was ordered to hang out a lamp at night, and if the light went out a police patrol would at once nail up the door. It remained closed until a fine was paid. Egyptian lamps were primitive affairs, prone to continual failure, and soon the whole town was in a state of resentful agitation – it was even said that the police extinguished the lights themselves in order to raise money.

Bonaparte called a halt in some cases (he settled the lamp affair by putting official lights in the streets and he stopped the desecration of the Esbekiah graves), but now, at last, the Egyptians were beginning to know the true nature of Western occupation, which was bureaucracy enforced by military law. A cannon shot woke the city every morning at daybreak.

The commander-in-chief continued to be very confident. Far from thinking of surrender he set about redesigning Cairo, building new boulevards, no doubt with Paris in mind; he established a mint, and he visited Suez on horseback in order to put his great project for the canal on foot. It was abandoned when Lepère, his engineer, reported (erroneously) that the scheme was impossible because the Red Sea was some thirty feet higher than the Mediterranean.

Conté, the balloonist, managed to get a balloon into the air, and his windmills, the first to be seen in Egypt, were another demonstration of the marvellous inventiveness of the French.

But it was the Nile that preoccupied Bonaparte's mind. He might be able to exist for the time being without contact with France, but it was impossible for him to remain secure in the delta so long as the Mamelukes had control of the river to the south. At any moment they could mount a counterattack from Upper Egypt; and in fact it was known that Murad was already assembling a new army there. Once before he had been driven up the river (by the Turks) and had returned in triumph to Cairo. He might not have stood a chance in a pitched battle against the French, but guerrilla warfare was another matter. He had taken some two thousand Mamelukes with him to the Faiyum oasis together with about five thousand irregular Arab cavalry, and he could count to some extent on the assistance of the Bedouin and of the tribes living along the river bank. This was an ample force for armed raids into the delta, perhaps even for the siege of Cairo itself. He was in contact by courier with the malcontents in Cairo and Alexandria and with Ibrahim in Syria, and every week the ancient cry for a Jehad, a holy war to expel the infidel, was growing stronger. By the middle of August it was apparent that the French would have no peace in the delta until Murad was either destroyed or driven so far off that sheer distance made him harmless. So now, in the midst of his kaleidoscopic activities in Cairo, Bonaparte began to prepare for a campaign on the river.

It has been the fate of this new adventure to be regarded as a sideshow in the French expedition to Egypt, as a sort of appendage to the main operations, and so it was, militarily speaking; not more than five thousand French were involved, and Murad at no time commanded a force of more than about 10,000 to 14,000 men. And yet, like a new branch that becomes more virile than the parent tree, this campaign was to accomplish wonderful things. It was to unlock the forgotten culture and history of the ancient Egyptian past for the first time since the days of the Romans; it was to prepare the way for the penetration of the modern world further and further upstream until the whole mystery of the river system was at last explained, the White Nile as well as the Blue.

Perhaps one of the reasons why the campaign has been so overlooked is that Bonaparte himself did not accompany it; nearly all his senior generals and the historians and memoirists who were later to write about their deeds remained with the commander-in-chief in Cairo, and subsequently went off with him to Syria. The Nile expedition was a campaign within a campaign, and nobody in Europe knew or cared anything about it; England and her allies were concentrated upon Bonaparte and the Mediterranean. And so for fourteen months the two little armies, alien to one another in every aspect of their being, were locked away from the rest of the world on the upper reaches of the river between the pyramids and Philae.

Desaix, who was now recognized as second only to Bonaparte himself as a field commander, was given the French command, and his orders were quite simple: he was to pursue Murad and destroy him on the Upper Nile. To start with he was to have 3,000 infantry, about 100 guns, 1,000 cavalry, and a little fleet of boats and a camel train to convey him up the river. General Belliard, who had accompanied Desaix from Civitavecchia, was to be the second-in-command.

Spies were sent on ahead into the Faiyum oasis, but in general everything on the Nile was unknown to the French. They had studied Norden's and d'Anville's maps, no doubt, they may have read Bruce's account of his journey downstream from Ethiopia, and they acquired interpreters and guides as they went along. But as to the general circumstances of the adventure that lay ahead – the shoals and currents in the river, the rise and fall of the water, the language and the nature of the inhabitants, the heat by day and the cold by night, the sandstorms and the mirages that could always turn out to be the enemy on the horizon, the possibility of finding food and fodder, the existence of forts and of ancient cities that could bar their progress, and the ultimate course of the great river that led them on, seemingly forever, to the south – all this was a mystery that could only be revealed little by little through their own experience, and always in the presence of an enemy who was ready at any moment to strike and then vanish into the desert.

Now, however, the river was high and the wind still conveniently from the north. The boats were loaded, the camel train mustered on the bank, and on August 25 Desaix set out.

One of the last men to join the expedition was Denon, a queer fish in this amphibious operation, since he was a civilian and already aged 51, and therefore something of an oddity among these aggressive young soldiers of the revolutionary army. He was not really interested in war at all, nor even in the present: he was absorbed in the past. Dominique Vivant, Baron de Denon, to give him his full name, had been everything in his time, playwright, artist, diplomat, archaeologist, interior decorator (he had also designed some of the revolutionary uniforms), a favourite of Louis XV (he had arranged a cabinet of medals and gems for La Pompadour), a frequenter of Josephine, a friend of Voltaire, of the painter

David (who had saved him from the guillotine), and now of Bonaparte. Having belatedly followed the army up to Cairo from Alexandria, he went straight on to the pyramids, since an escort of 200 soldiers had been dispatched there at that moment, and it was unsafe to make the excursion alone. Full of excited curiosity, Denon had explored the interior of the Cheops pyramid, had noted of the head of the buried Sphinx that 'its expression is soft, gracious and tranquil', and had gone on to Sakkara, where he had assisted at the de-nesting of 500 mummified ibises from their pots. Now, after a month of investigations in Cairo, terrier-like in its intensity, he hurried on, as the representative of the *Institut d'Égypte*, in the wake of Desaix's men. Through the next ten months he was to prove to be the best of observers, and one of the ablest pioneers in rescuing from oblivion the ancient past of the river.

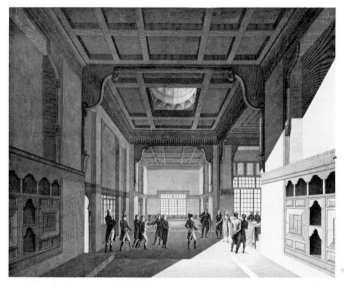

The house of Hassan Kashef intended for use by the Institut d'Égypte
From Description de l'Égypte

Dominique Vivant Denon. From an engraving by Denon after a painting by Jean Baptiste Isabey

8

The Campaign on the River

———

No journey can be quite so soothing as a voyage on the Nile from Cairo to Philae. Day after day as you sail upstream nothing in the general pattern changes. Tonight's incredibly bright stars are the same as last night's and tomorrow's. Each new bend in the river discloses the same buffalo circling his waterwheel, the same pigeon-lofts on the houses, the same dark Egyptian faces swathed in white. The banks are surprisingly green, a patchwork of ricefields and sugar-cane, of palms and eucalyptus, and then beyond them, like a frame set around a picture, one sees the desert and the hills. There is always movement somewhere, but it is of a gentle, ambulatory kind, and one feels oneself going along in a rhythm with the processions of camels and donkeys on the bank, and the feluccas gliding by, and the buffalo, released at last from his wheel, sliding to the blessed coolness of the water in the evening. Occasionally a whiff of humanity comes out from the mud-hut villages on the shore, and it contains traces of the smoke of cooking fires, of dried cow-dung and of Turkish coffee, of some sweet and heavy scent, jasmine perhaps, and of water sprinkled on the dust. It is not unpleasant.

Lying back on deck one idly observes the flight of birds, one dreams, one lets the hours go by, and nothing can be more satisfying than the sight of the brown pillars of a ruined temple that has been standing alone on the edge of the desert for the last two thousand years. This is the past joining the present in a comfortably deceptive glow, and the traveller, like a spectator in a theatre, remains detached from both. He would not for the world live in the dust and squalor of these villages he finds so picturesque, and the ancient ruins he has come to see do not really evoke the early civilization of the Egyptians. The Pharaoh in his tomb, with his stylized head in profile and his retinues of slaves, is an *objet d'art* rather than a symbol of magnificence and immortality, and the images of the gods and goddesses that surround him, Osiris and Isis, Horus, Hathor, Anubis and Thoth, having no longer any power, are not much more than a genial superstition. Even in Pharaonic times they had their legend of a dying god – a god who has no worshippers any more – and now these bird- and animal-headed divinities are very dead. It is the same with the hieroglyphics: after a time one does not look at them for the message they contain, which is usually a bombastic record of wars and massacres, but simply as decorations on the wall, and they are as repetitive as needlework. It is stimulating, of course, to know that Cambyses and so many other conquerors came this way, and that one is following in the path of the Roman legionaries, but they remain securely in their own age; the blood and misery are absent.

It was not quite so, however, with Desaix's little army. The Nile valley was for them a hard and hostile place, and as the soldiers advanced along it they experienced all the brutal realities of life as it was actually lived on the river, whether by invading armies in the past or by the present Egyptians. They ate the native food, drank the Nile water, and camped in the Egyptian houses. Every village had to be reconnoitred, captured or placated, every tomb was the possible hiding place of an enemy. The climate had not altered – the blinding heat of August in Upper Egypt, the sandstorms and the glare – and the march seemed endless; the desert rocks were so hard that each soldier required a new pair of boots every month. At the very outset of the campaign Desaix exclaims: 'Never have I seen the men so tired.'

It was no wonder. They were still dressed in heavy serge, with a collar round the neck – and how spectacular those crimson and yellow facings must have looked in this bright sunlight – and all of them at one time or another appear to have suffered from dysentery and ophthalmia. It was not their sangfroid that took them up the Nile, it was their endurance. Each morning reveille sounded between 2 and 3 a.m., and they were forever on the move, forever fighting, looking for billets, fetching water, cooking, getting up again.

The scenes they saw along the Nile were not quite the same as those we see now. The green belt on either side of the river was narrower then, since there were fewer canals and no locks or dams, and the groves of eucalyptus, a recent importation from Australia, did not exist. So there was less shade. The villages, though smaller, have not altered much in the intervening years, but the ancient temples were then very different. Many were half buried in sand, and successive generations of Arabs had built mud-brick houses among the crumbling walls, throwing out their rubbish everywhere. No one cared for these old columns and statues, no one could read the hieroglyphics on the walls. The mummies hidden in their hundreds in underground caves were of interest solely because the resin with which they were impregnated could be extracted and sold in the Cairo market. The fallen obelisk was simply another rock.

In a way perhaps all this was an advantage. A certain staleness overtakes great monuments that have been too much excavated and restored and then photographed, painted and walked over by millions of tourist feet. But for a man like Denon in 1798 everything was fresh and wonderful. Reading his account of the campaign it is impossible not to feel something of his own excitement as he groped his way down dark passages with a lamp and saw, as few eyes had seen for a thousand years or more, great underground chambers filled with statues and paintings that were still brightly coloured, and mystical inscriptions all around them on the walls. One understands how he marvelled at the sight of huge forgotten temples, like Edfu, rising out of the sand. To have had so much to see, all of it so new, so strange and often so beautiful – this must have filled him with a constricting sense of his own inadequacy, an impatience to see more and more.

Very often his observations on the temples are erroneous, and perhaps a little too mannered, but there is a certain freshness about them, and one has to remember that up to this time Egyptology did not exist; Herodotus, Strabo and Pausanias were almost the only guides to places and monuments which have since become a tourist cliché. Perhaps, too, the very fact that Denon was living in circumstances of some danger and discomfort, and had so little time, sharpened his perception and made him more than usually sensitive.

Denon was lucky to find in both Desaix and Belliard men with educated and inquiring minds, who were ready and even eager to indulge him, but the war had to be fought, and it was hardly ever safe for him to linger. No sooner would he begin a sketch or start to trace an inscription than the trumpet would sound the advance, and he would have to scramble on to his horse and hurry after the others. It was intensely frustrating. He was like the enthusiast who, having come miles to see a painting, is turned out of the museum by the closing bell – except that here he never knew whether he, or any other trained observer, would ever be able to come back again. To have remained alone behind the army meant more or less certain death from the Bedouin, and on several occasions Denon had to gallop off through a fusillade of shots. He pleaded and pleaded for time – just another twenty minutes to examine this mummy, to explore this colonnade, to finish this drawing – and Desaix did what he could, even sometimes allowing a squad of soldiers to remain and guard the artist at his work. But it was never enough, and Denon, who had to live as the soldiers did, sword in hand, sleeping on the ground and often unwell, confessed at times that even his excitement was not enough to drive on his tired mind to further effort.

The army's problems were more exacting. The Mamelukes, after one more futile charge at Faiyum, came to their senses at last and realized that their best means of harassing and even of defeating the French lay in guerrilla tactics. They knew the country and the French did not. The French were impeded by heavy baggage and stores, while the Mamelukes, although accompanied by their wives and followers, travelled light, despoiling the land

Denon preparing to sketch the ruins at Hieraconpolis. Engraving by B. Comte from a drawing by Denon

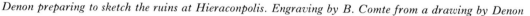

behind them as they fell back. There was every possible advantage to Murad in extending Desaix to the utmost by retreating further and further up the Nile. By doubling back on his tracks through the empty desert, he was then able to cut in on Desaix's line of communication; and this, in a haphazard way, was what Murad now set himself out to do. So what we have to contemplate here is a disjointed running battle on the river. It ranges up and down the Nile as far as Philae, nearly six hundred miles from Cairo, and spreads at times far into the surrounding desert; and it is marvellous that Desaix, far from despairing, never for an instant gave up the chase. 'I think,' said one of his officers, 'that General Desaix is ten degrees colder than ice,' and one remembers Desaix's own admiring comment on Bonaparte: 'He follows his enemy to the end of the world.'

The beginning of the campaign did not altogether go against the Mamelukes. After leaving Cairo Desaix's boats had much trouble with shoals and sandbanks in the falling Nile, and it was not until October 6 that he caught up with Murad at a place called El Lahun, where the Joseph Canal enters the Faiyum oasis. Through his glass he could see Murad himself, sitting outside his tent with his sheikhs on one of the neighbouring heights. They soon retired, however, and Desaix, having spent all the following day getting his boats up, ordered the men to sleep at arms that night and in their squares. On the morning of October 8 he moved forward in battle formation towards Murad's entrenchments, and the leading men had barely got themselves on to a slight rise when a drum was heard in

the enemy camp, and dust, rising from under their horses' hoofs, made it evident that the Mamelukes were coming in for a charge.

The odds against Murad were not so weighted as they had been in the Battle of the Pyramids. Then he had faced some twenty thousand Frenchmen. Now he saw barely three thousand before him, and his own forces at this time outnumbered them nearly two to one. Perhaps, too, he was heartened by the news of the French naval defeat in the Battle of the Nile, and he may even have got wind of the rebellion against Bonaparte that was being planned in Cairo. Desaix had placed his men in a curious arrangement: two small squares of 180 men each were deployed in front, while the rest, with their artillery, remained in one solid mass behind. The commander of the foremost small square, with a matador's bravado, ordered his men to hold their fire until the Mamelukes were only twenty paces away, and this was foolish, because the wounded horsemen in the van were carried by their own impetus into the square, and other Mamelukes, following behind, rushed into the breach. Some twenty of the French infantry were quickly hacked down. The rest, however, had sufficient presence of mind to lie full length on the sand, and this enabled the French artillery to fire over them into the mass of enemy cavalry. A further Mameluke charge on the second small square was held, but by now Murad had one of his own batteries in action, and the French were obliged to rush it with the bayonet before it was silenced. After this the Mamelukes retreated, leaving about four hundred of their men, dead and wounded, on the field.

The chase was now on. Any soldier who campaigned in the desert in the last world war will remember the exhilaration of pursuing a retreating enemy there. A wonderful sense of achievement and spaciousness fills the air, mere distance becomes an object of itself, and the soldiers and the leading columns have an overmastering desire to go on and on, just another mile or two before sunset, just one more view over the next ridge of sand. It is like some mad treasure hunt, except that here the clues are the discarded baggage of the enemy, the broken guns beside the track, a deserted camp where the cooking fires are still warm, a furrow of recent wheel-tracks leading off into the distance.

Something of this sort now happened to the French. They occupied Medinat el Faiyum, and then pushed on to Beni Suef, where there was a short delay while Desaix went back to Cairo for reinforcements. Directly he returned, in Bonaparte's own boat *L'Italie*, they started out for the south again. By mid-December they were in Minia, and at the end of the month in Assiut, one of the principal towns of the Nile, 250 miles upstream from Cairo. Soon after New Year's Day, 1799, they were on the move again, the men marching on the west bank and the flotilla following on the river, and on January 19 they were in Girga.

Murad had kept just ahead of them all the way. Sometimes he waited until the French were only an hour or two behind him before moving on; sometimes his outriders would turn back and cut in upon an isolated French detachment, but then after a quick skirmish they would be gone again. Like Desaix himself, and indeed like every army commander who has fought on the Nile, Murad was having trouble with his transport – at Minia he was obliged to abandon five boats and a dozen cannon – and some of his infantry, mostly Greeks and Copts, deserted to the French. But then he had allies among the local population. The Bedouin and many of the villagers were quite ready to oppose the invaders in the hope of pillage, and there were skirmishes at both Assiut and Girga. Denon speaks of the French being 'exhausted by daily losses and fatigued by victories', in a country where the enemy was 'always conquered but never subjugated', and who 'came on the morrow of a defeat to harass'. Every night thieves 'entered the French camp like rats and left it like bats'. Even Desaix's horse was stolen.

Assiut. Drawing by Gaston Bussière

Yet the French morale was high. For the most part they were moving through cultivated fields and gardens, food was plentiful – Assiut in fact was so rich that not even the presence of three thousand foreign soldiers forced up the price of chickens and fruit – and everything else the men lacked they looted from the villagers. There were also moments of relaxation in the evening, when they sat round their camp-fires under the dom palms on the river bank, and no doubt there were other pleasures as well: rape was not regarded as a great crime in a country that was up in arms, and prostitutes, in any case, were to be found in every town.

Now, in the winter, the heat by day was much more bearable and the nights were pleasantly cool. Once a rare thunderstorm burst upon them with heavy showers of rain, but this was refreshing.

OVERLEAF *The tymphonium of Apollinopolis and the interior of the temple at Edfu Engraving by L. P. Baltard from a drawing by Denon*

On January 22 Murad decided to make a stand at the settlement of Samhud, sixteen miles south of Girga, and close to the temple of Abydos. He had been joined now by some two thousand Turkish janissaries who had been on a pilgrimage to Mecca and who had made their way to the Nile from Kosseir on to the Red Sea. These men, being ignorant of the French, were eager for a battle. Once again it was, in Denon's phrase, a clash of 'northern austerity with eastern pomp: iron seemed to be trying its strength with gold; the plain glittered, the spectacle was admirable'. The janissaries were routed.

The French soldiers were now beginning to know their enemy very well. Hardly a man did not possess loot of some kind – a battle-axe, a quiver lined in red velvet, an amulet or a piece of brocade – and they had long since learned to distinguish the beys from the ordinary Mamelukes, since the beys wore beards. (Many of them, for some reason, also used *noms de guerre*.)

At Girga Desaix had been strengthened by the arrival of additional cavalry with his supply boats, and he now resolved to push on after Murad at greater speed. A series of forced marches was ordered, mostly by night. This was a galling business for Denon; he was rushed in turn through Dendera, Luxor, the Valley of the Kings, Esna, Edfu and Kom Ombo, which were precisely the places he most wished to see.

The temple at Dendera, half covered in sand and disfigured as it was by the tumbledown Arab huts on its roof, moved him to 'a delirium of imagination', but he was barely given time to make a rough sketch of the zodiac there and to snatch up from the debris a few Roman lamps and figurines in glass and porcelain before he was hurried on. Riding regretfully away he noted that the temple was dedicated to Isis (which it is not, Hathor is the presiding goddess), that its bas-reliefs resembled French playing cards since their style never altered, and that the Egyptians, having no rain in their country, had no need of pitched roofs. At Luxor, he declares, 'the army, at the sight of its scattered ruins, halted of itself and, by one spontaneous impulse, grounded its arms'. But when he attempted to enter the galleries with Desaix they were assailed by troglodytes living in the ruins, and the two horsemen, in a shower of javelins and stones, were forced to gallop away: 'this was a war with gnomes'.

Karnak, despite its grandeur, repelled Denon a little: 'Not a circus, not an arena, not a theatre! Temples, mysteries, initiations, priests, victims! For pleasures, ceremonies! For luxury, tombs!' The Colossi of Memnon were also disappointing. Except for their simplicity and gravity and their correct proportions they were 'without charm, without grace, without action: they have nothing to delight'. While the army marched past he sat down to sketch them, and became so immersed that he was horrified to look up and find himself alone.

At Esna, which Murad had left the night before the French arrived, Denon was struck by the reflection that the Egyptian architects had not borrowed from any other country; they owed nothing to the Doric, Ionic or Corinthian styles, they copied from nature; the papyrus stalk inspired the column, the opened bud of the lotus its capital.

At Edfu, Elfy Bey (that same rich Mameluke whose house Bonaparte had requisitioned in Cairo) was sighted with 200 followers, and there was only time to note the temple's resemblance to Dendera and to deplore the Arab village which had been built inside its walls. Kom Ombo Denon scarcely saw at all, since the French were on the opposite bank of the river, but he heard that the crocodile was worshipped there – and indeed he had seen monsters twenty-five feet in length lying on the sandbanks close by.

There now began a final and terrible forced march to Aswan, their last hope of catching Murad before he escaped into the deserts of Nubia beyond the Egyptian border. Already at Edfu the western bank was becoming more and more barren, and the villages more wretched than before. They were entering a region of 'that tranquil monotony which is never disturbed by the shock of a single novelty, of that calm which leaves a length of time between each event in life, of that quiet where everything succeeds peaceably in the soul, where little by little an emotion becomes a sentiment, or a habit a principle, where, in a word, the lightest impression is analysed; and this to a degree, that, in conversing (with the inhabitants) one is altogether astonished to find in them the greatest niceness of distinction and the most delicate sentiment, in company with the most absolute ignorance'. A few earthen pots, a mud-hut, a pigeon-loft, a chicken-run, a field of maize, a few melons and the river – this was life on the Upper Nile. The mind dissolved into an elaborate study of nothingness.

Craving for food and their feet dreadfully blistered, the soldiers crossed the river and entered Aswan on February 1, 1799, to find themselves too late: Murad had gone up the cataracts and had vanished into the unknown wastes that lay beyond. The army was now 587 miles from Cairo, and for the time being strained to the limit of its endurance. Desaix broke off the pursuit and settled into the town.

During the next few weeks Aswan must have borne some resemblance to what it was in Roman times. A fort was built, and a rather grandiose plaque was erected to commemorate the French victories on the river. They found no vines on Elephantine Island as the legionaries did, but they set up cafés and eating houses in Aswan and made the best of the local beer. Having no playing cards they designed their own, and they gambled with their loot. They explored the ruins and carved their names in the stone precisely as the Romans had done a thousand years before. While Desaix went off to organize a chain of posts down the river to Assiut, General Belliard set up a government, and once again the local people saw Western soldiers parading with their bands in the early morning. Spies were sent up above the cataracts and reported that Murad was laying waste the river villages in Nubia, and presently there was news that he was approaching Aswan with a foraging party. At once a French column marched out to meet him, and they surprised the Mamelukes at their evening meal. But it was impossible to come to grips in the darkness, and in the morning the enemy were gone. It seemed for the time being that the war was over.

Since there was then no dam at Aswan, the temples on the island of Philae were not submerged as they are now, and Denon was eager to explore them. His every effort to land by boat, however, was met by the howls, threats and eventually the spears of the natives living in the ruins. The Nubians, it seemed, were people of extreme barbarity: '. . . their costume, as far as regards the males is absolute nakedness, to which they add a morsel of woollen or cotton cloth', while for the women a girdle of little strips of leather 'descending half-way to their knees, suffices, till the time of marriage, to tranquillize all the alarms of modesty'. The Nubian women, Denon remarked, were more beautiful than the women in the Egyptian villages, and were highly valued by slave traders because their skin was cool to touch. (Bruce had noted the same thing: 'The Turks profess to admire the Abyssinians in summer, because, like toads, they have a cold skin.') At all events, the Philae islanders were determined to defend their families against the French, and it was not until the place was taken by assault that they fled. Denon, who had come to admire and sketch the temples, was horrified to see mothers drowning their children in the river rather than allow them to be taken, and his musings on the overlay of Christian and Egyptian paintings in the ruins were interrupted by the cries of a horribly mutilated little girl whom he subsequently adopted.

It was a strange atmosphere, tranquillity blended with the utmost savagery, the silent temples shattered by screams of victims in the villages. Denon's notes take on rather a fated air: 'We sometimes went out at night to breathe for a few instants and our breathing was the only sound that disturbed the frightful sound of nothingness.' 'During the whole expedition we had been followed by a flock of kites and little vultures which . . . instead of being frightened by the cannon, assembled from all parts. . . . On the first discharge of musketry, and especially on the explosion of a mine, they discovered our position and lost no time rejoining.'

And now the heat was beginning again. 'It boiled our blood. . . . Nothing is as frightful as this death: the victim is suddenly surprised with a disorder of his heart and no assistance can save him from the faintings that succeed.'

Moreover the French were much deluded in thinking that Murad had been defeated. At the end of February they had word that, with some hundreds of Mamelukes still in his train, he had made a wide detour through the desert and was descending again from Nubia into Egypt.

The next seven months are a confused story of marches and counter-marches along the Nile valley between Aswan and Faiyum, of ambushes and violent skirmishes on the river. One can hardly fail to sympathize with Murad. He is not Robin Hood, and the Mamelukes were scarcely a merry lot, but they were men fighting for what they believed to be their rights, their pride and indignation were equal to every weariness, and they never gave up. 'Like the Hydra,' Desaix wrote, 'cut off their heads and another grows.' This was the end of a tradition of 500 years of Mameluke rule in Egypt, and it had its moments of nobility. Even the wounded would accept no mercy, and preferred to die fighting so long as there was a hope of killing just one more Frenchman.

Murad was not always unsuccessful. Once he managed to seize a flotilla of French ammunition boats, and even Bonaparte's dahabeeyah, *l'Italie*, was blown up. In one particularly drastic encounter seventy dragoons were killed, and Desaix, desperate for reinforcements, was moved to write bitterly to Bonaparte: 'Eye troubles are frightening. I am deprived of more than 1,400 men, 100 of them blind. . . . We are naked, without shoes, without anything. . . . But I won't bore you with our sufferings.' In May 1799 he was forced to send Belliard off with a column to deal with the Turkish janissaries who kept arriving at Kosseir, and although Belliard left a garrison there no one could be sure that the British might not suddenly land an expedition on the Red Sea coast from India.

By June 1799, however, Desaix could fairly claim that he had the upper hand. For nearly five hundred miles he was keeping the enemy off the river, and many of the local sheikhs had submitted. A headquarters was set up at Assiut to administer the vast territory that had been conquered, and trade was beginning to flow again along the Nile.

Denon went back to Cairo to report to the *Institut* on the scientific and cultural results of the campaign, and he had a wonderful story to tell. He had been defeated in the end in some of his more abstruse inquiries; he had not been able to capture a baby crocodile, and

Slaves resting at Korti. From David Roberts' Egypt and Nubia

many hours spent in putrid tunnels had failed to yield him a mummy intact. But he had brought back with him hundreds of drawings of temples, tombs and inscriptions, and an encyclopedic volume of notes that ranged from a study of the sandstorms and the plagues of locusts to the Nilometer at Aswan and the habits of the troglodytes. He had also secured a number of ancient Egyptian manuscripts which later were to play their part, together with the Rosetta Stone (which had just been unearthed at the mouth of the river and brought to Cairo), in the deciphering of the ancient Egyptian hieroglyphics. The members of the *Institut* listened to these marvels with enthusiasm, and it was resolved that a large party of them must travel to the Upper Nile and continue with the work of research. Modestly Denon could claim that he had 'planted a few stakes along the way'.

It was a moment of stalemate in the campaign. One must envisage a chain of little garrisons dotted up the Nile and divided from one another by about fifty miles or more, the tents pitched on the green bank, the barber and the drinking shops set up in the mud-hut villages, the cow-dung cooking fires under the palms with the French soldiers sitting round them in the evening, the occasional banquets offered to the officers by the local sheikhs – a strange *mélange* of tight uniforms and flowing robes, of French and Arabic – the daily rumours and alarms, the sick lying derelict through endless hot nights, the commotion of the arrival of a boat with supplies from Cairo but never with mail from home, the facetious signposts erected in the camp: 'Route de Paris, No. 1' – the Paris that was impenetrably blocked from them by the desert and the sea beyond, and only to be revived a little in the memory by stories told over and over again until, like repeated proverbs, they had no meaning in them any more. This was exile in its deepest monotony, and no doubt it was only made bearable by the routine of drill and work, by an occasional whiff of danger and by the hope, never quite lost, that some miracle would happen to make it end.

They were establishing a legend, of course, the glory of revolutionary France on the Nile, but one wonders whether this stirred the private soldier very much or even went far to compensate him for those famous promised six acres which, like France itself, were steadily receding into the distance. But human beings it seems will put up with anything, and from one dull day to the next these soldiers went on accepting their isolation, obeying their orders, and making perhaps as great a contribution as any of the learned savants to the awakening of Egypt from its long night.

It was all very well for an artist like Denon to write about the extreme beauty of the river with its feluccas gliding by in the dawn light. He wrote long afterwards, and who remembers or wishes to record the ennuis and pettinesses of an adventure? One makes a virtue of *force majeure*, and the conscripted soldier in recounting his campaigns speaks of them as inevitable and as having an excitement he was often very far from feeling at the time. No one thought this campaign was inevitable or justifiable when they were gasping in the terrible summer heat of the Upper Nile. They hated it and they longed for it to end. And so there must have been a certain stir throughout the column when in July 1799 the calm was broken: Murad suddenly reappeared like some oriental djinn in Faiyum, evidently heading for the delta.

Desaix at once marched north in pursuit, and at the same time another French column came out from Cairo, hoping to intercept Murad before he could reach the delta; now at last they seemed to have him in a trap. July 13 was a dramatic day: Murad was reported to be in the vicinity of the pyramids, and Bonaparte himself hurried to the scene.

During the eleven months that Desaix had been away in Upper Egypt so much had happened to Bonaparte that one can only marvel that he should have kept his sanity, let alone his powers of initiative. Indeed, it was remarkable that he should have survived at all. He had received no help from France of any kind. Russia, Turkey and England had combined against him, and the blockade continued on the coast. Yet he had managed to put down a serious rising in Cairo, he had made his disastrous expedition into Syria, where he had been stopped at Acre by the Turks and Sir Sidney Smith, and now, apparently, unshaken, he was back in Cairo again, his army still more or less intact and Egypt still

The Nilometer at Aswan. From David Robert's Egypt and Nubia

under control. There had been rumours of a Turkish invasion, but he appears to have been confident enough at this moment to turn all his attention to the capture of Murad.

Now in point of fact the rumour of the arrival of the Turks was entirely true. A fleet with sixty transports and an army of 20,000 men was actually about to arrive in Abukir Bay near Alexandria, and Murad had come north with the intention of joining forces with it there. It is not entirely clear how Murad had received word of the approach of the Turks, but it is certain that his wife Fatima had had a hand in the matter. She had manœuvred very adroitly in Cairo. Bonaparte had allowed her to return to her house in the town, and when he sent his stepson, Eugène de Beauharnais, to call on her, she saw to it that she made a good impression. Young de Beauharnais returned with an enthusiastic description of how he had been received by a distinguished and still beautiful woman who retained no less than fifty slaves in her household. He had been taken into the harem, an exceptional honour, and there he had been regaled with coffee and sorbets. At the end of the interview Fatima had taken a ring worth 1,000 louis from her finger and had given it to him.

Bonaparte, if he was not taken in, was at least impressed, and in rather a grand manner he informed Fatima that she was under his protection and would not be molested in any way. 'I am extremely displeased, citizen-general,' Bonaparte wrote to his garrison commander on one occasion, 'to learn that the wife of Murad Bey is complaining of maltreatment . . . her chief eunuch has been beaten. Please find out who did this and put him in prison.' She was not slow in making use of this situation. Messengers were constantly passing to and fro between her house and Constantinople and her husband in Upper Egypt, and she herself may even have been at the centre of a conspiracy to raise a new rebellion against the French, once the Turks were safely ashore at Abukir. On July 13, at all events, she was at her country estate at Gizeh, and Murad by arrangement is said to have climbed to the top of the Great Pyramid and to have signalled to her there.

Now was the moment for the French to pounce, and Bonaparte in fact was deploying his men when couriers arrived from Alexandria with the news of the Turkish landing. Murad had the pleasure of seeing the French army abruptly turn about and march directly for the coast. He himself followed discreetly in the rear.

The Battle of Abukir was not by a long way the most important victory of Bonaparte's career, but certainly he never fought with such devastating effect. On July 20 he was at Rahmaniya, and having paused there for a day or two to await the arrival of his reserves he advanced directly on Abukir with 10,000 men and 1,000 cavalry. The Turks had already killed the French garrison on the shore, and had established a beach-head, but they appear to have been poorly armed; they had no cavalry, no modern artillery, and no bayonets for their rifles. At dawn on July 25 Bonaparte attacked, and in the massacre that followed something like fifteen thousand Turks were killed, captured or drowned in a headlong flight into the sea. Mustapha Pasha, the Turkish commander, was taken prisoner in his tent. Not even the Mamelukes had fared as badly as this, not even Nelson could claim a more decisive victory. When Murad heard the news he turned about and rode back into Upper Egypt, with Desaix at his heels.

But the Mamelukes were now growing very tired. Early in August Desaix surprised their camp far up the river at Samhud, the scene of the skirmish seven months before, and Murad

Bonaparte making a grand gesture in pardoning the rebels. Drawing by A. J. Gros

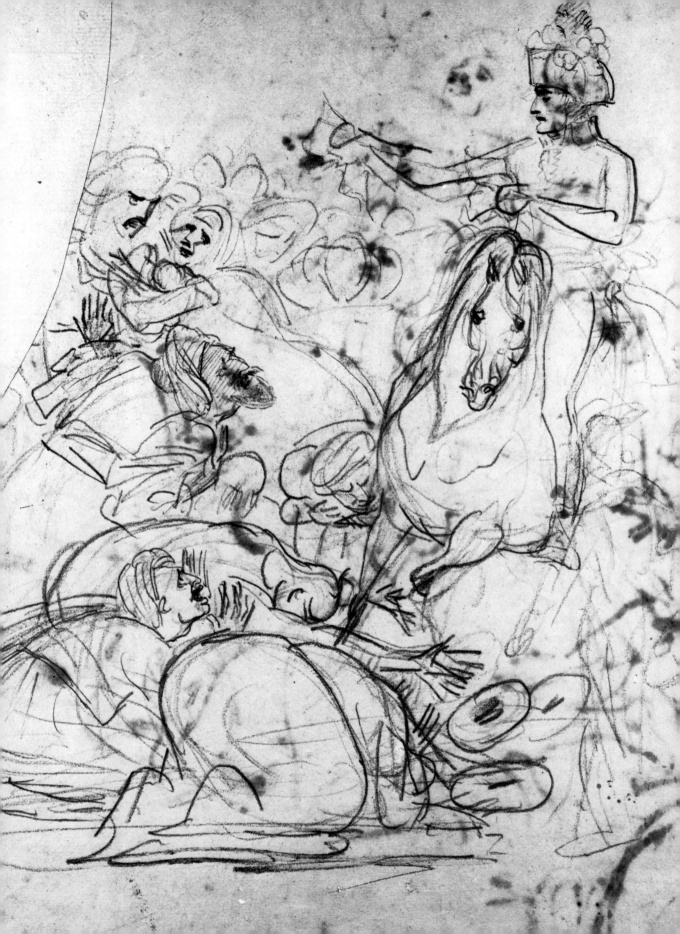

himself was so near being captured that he left behind him in his tent his arms, his clothes, even his slippers. A month later he was still on the run when Desaix's camel corps overtook him near Faiyum. But this was the end. A short sharp skirmish was fought, and soon afterwards a message was received from Fatima saying that her husband was prepared to negotiate. By the terms of his submission he agreed to serve under the French.

It was now mid-October, 1799, and Desaix could look back on his achievements with some pride; those Mamelukes who had not surrendered with Murad were cut off and helpless in the deserts of Nubia, and from Philae to Cairo there was peace on the river at last. In a little more than a year, and with a force of barely five thousand men, he had conquered a territory half as large as France.

PART THREE

———

THE TURKS IN
THE SUDAN

9

The Life of High Crime

———

In this book our course is on the Nile, and so we need do no more here than glance at events in Egypt during the next ten years. Soon after the Battle of Abukir Bonaparte had news at last from France, and it was appalling: the French army in Italy was in retreat, the Ionian Islands had been taken by the Turks, Malta was blockaded and in Paris the political situation was chaotic. He decided to return to France at once, leaving Kléber in command in Egypt.

The arrangements for his flight were made with great secrecy; it was given out that he was to make a tour of inspection on the Lower Nile with a small party of the savants and his generals. There was a last meeting with La Bellilote – she was told that he would be back in a couple of weeks – and soon after midnight on August 18, 1799, three days after his thirtieth birthday, he went on board a boat at Bulaq to sail down the Nile to Alexandria. He had with him Monge, Berthollet, Denon, Marmont, Lannes, Berthier, Bourrienne, Murat, Eugène de Beauharnais and a number of others, including Roustan, a captured Mameluke whom he proposed to exhibit in France. Most of them were not aware of their destination.

At Alexandria the two frigates *Murion* and *Carrière* were waiting. It had been Bonaparte's intention to meet Kléber at Rosetta and inform him that he was to take over the Egyptian command, but on August 21 he was warned that he must sail at once; the wind was favourable and the two British frigates that had been lurking off Alexandria had gone to Cyprus to revictual. There was time only to write to Kléber, 'I will arrive in Paris, I will chase out this gang of lawyers who mock us and who are incapable of governing the Republic and I will consolidate this magnificent colony.' Kléber was to hold on until reinforcements reached him. Only if they failed to arrive by May 1800, or if by then he had lost 1,500 men through plague, was he to negotiate with the Turks.

Early on August 22 Bonaparte boarded the *Murion*, which was waiting two miles out from the same beach at Marabou where he had first come ashore in Egypt fourteen months before. All his fellow passengers agree that the general was in the best of spirits on the hazardous voyage home. As they ran along the North African coast to Cape Bon he played *vingt-et-un*, discussed geometry and physics with Monge, and drew them all into his schemes for the future. They hardly saw another ship until they touched in at Corsica, and then, on October 9, seven weeks after leaving Egypt, ran in through the British blockade to St Raphaël. A month later Bonaparte was dictator of France.

Kléber, abandoned in Egypt and bitterly resentful of Bonaparte's departure, not unreasonably saw very little point in waiting until 1,500 men had died of plague. Soon after

Bonaparte leaving Egypt. A contemporary English caricature

the new year he opened negotiations with the Turks and Sidney Smith at El Arish, and they reached an understanding that the French should leave Egypt, taking their arms with them and with the honours of war. It was the happiest possible end to the affair but it was a little too precipitous to satisfy the hatreds and passions that had been aroused; the British Government wanted harsher terms and repudiated the agreement. This was a decision of the utmost folly, since it condemned Egypt to another eighteen months of war, and in the end, after another few thousand men were dead, the British found themselves obliged to agree to almost the same terms they had rejected at El Arish.

Pitt, it is true, saw his mistake after a few months and might have reopened the negotiations, but by then it was too late: Kléber had demolished another Turkish army coming overland from Syria and had crushed a rising in Cairo. After this it was clear that if the French were to be got out of Egypt at all it was only by sending a European army to fight them. At last, in March 1801, a mixed force of British and Turks landed near Alexandria, and although the French garrison there managed to hold out for a time Cairo collapsed without a struggle.

It was thought surprising at the time that the French should have put up so little resistance – Belliard, who was now in command in Cairo, had 12,000 men and ample provisions – but by then their case was hopeless. The French army was sick of Egypt. All the best generals had gone: Kléber had been assassinated by a fanatic on the terrace of Elfy Bey's house in Cairo on June 14, 1800, that same day on which Desaix, who had managed to rejoin Bonaparte in Europe, was killed at Marengo. Murad had remained faithful to his new alliance with the French, and was actually marching to Belliard's assistance from the Upper Nile, but he died of plague on the way. Soon, too, another British force landed from India on the Red Sea coast, and everywhere the delta was up in arms against the French. Belliard, with his 12,000 half-hearted men, had no real choice but to give in, especially when the British offered to transport the French army back to France.

The last scenes of the campaign were something of an anticlimax. On July 15, 1801, the French marched out of Cairo to the boats that were waiting at Bulaq to take them down

The British troops landing at Abukir. Watercolour by Sir Robert Ker Porter

to Rosetta, a strange procession: the soldiers and the servants, the women and what was left of the crestfallen speculators, the sick on litters, donkeys carrying the baggage and the plunder. Kléber's body, embalmed and coffined, was placed in a leading boat and a black flag flew overhead. By October 1801 the last French soldier had left Egyptian soil, and the British force that had ejected them soon followed them back to Europe.

It was a sad end to a great adventure, and it created the impression that Bonaparte had accomplished nothing very much in Egypt. The Suez Canal was not dug, the new boulevards and waterways in Cairo were abandoned, French military law was forgotten along with their new scheme of weights and measures, their hospitals, their census and their proposed dams along the river. As for Bonaparte's vision of conquering India and the Ottoman Empire, it had vanished as completely as Conté's coloured balloon.

Yet this scarcely states the true case. Almost all Bonaparte's plans for the westernization of Egypt were eventually carried out – it was a Frenchman who built the Suez Canal half a century later – and the work of the savants filled a gap in human knowledge that had persisted since Roman times. There is hardly an aspect of Egyptian life that is not carefully examined in the twenty-four volumes of their monumental *Description de l'Égypte*, and the illustrations, though possibly a little too precise – even the fallen columns and the broken capitals of the temples have been re-erected in the drawings, and in the natural history section the very vultures have every feather in place – give us a picture of the country that has never been surpassed. It was one of the most ambitious publications ever attempted, an enormous guide-book that was used by every successive invader in the nineteenth century. Even its inaccuracies were provocative. This was a true census of Egypt. And when Champollion in the late 1820s began the science of Egyptology by elucidating the hieroglyphics on the Rosetta Stone, a way back into the past was opened up as well. The stone, now in the British Museum, was taken from Cairo to Alexandria and there surrendered to the British in 1801, but Bonaparte, before leaving Egypt, had had impressions of the inscriptions taken, and Champollion worked from one of these copies.

Sir Ralph Abercromby, Sir Sydney Smith commanding the Marines, General Menou mounted on a dromedary, and Lord Keith on board the Foudroyant. *From a watercolour by Sir Robert Ker Porter*

But it was upon the political future of the country that the French invasion had its chief effect. Like land on which oil is found, or like some large neglected property in the path of a new highway, Egypt had suddenly become an immensely valuable territory. It was no

The Rosetta Stone

longer possible for the British to think of India as being tucked away safely at the end of the long route round the Cape: India could now be directly menaced from Egypt, and the Red Sea, instead of a forgotten backwater, had become a vital short-cut to Europe. From now on it was not feasible for the British to allow an enemy to remain in Egypt, and if they were unwilling to occupy the country themselves they were equally bound to keep the French out. Gradually, too, England was forced to enter the Red Sea, to patrol it with her warships, to establish bases on its shores, and to ensure that Ethiopia remained friendly.

Thus all three countries watered by the Nile on its long journey from Lake Tana to the Mediterranean – Ethiopia, the Sudan and Egypt – were drawn into a new scheme of international politics; and in the end, when Britain had failed to guarantee their neutrality by means of diplomacy, she inevitably went to war. Her eventual occupation, at first of Egypt, and then of the Sudan, and her invasion of Ethiopia, were all the indirect result of Bonaparte's invasion.

In 1801 these things may not have been seen at all clearly, indeed, it required nearly a hundred years of complicated political manœuvring before they were all brought about. But the chain-reaction which set events in motion was certainly begun by Bonaparte, he at least had a glimpse of the future, and it was directly due to him that Egypt and the Nile valley became a sort of testing-ground for the rivalries of the West, a process which in one form or another has been going on ever since.

The next figure of importance to appear on the Nile – Mohammed Ali – can be said to have been Bonaparte's logical successor; indeed he himself declared that he was greatly influenced by him, and there were some striking similarities in the lives of the two men. They were of precisely the same age, both (like so many other dictators) came from obscure beginnings in the provinces, both turned rebellions to their own advantage, and both, as though destined for power from the beginning, conquered and handled large empires with apparent ease: some people might say a Machiavellian ease.

Apart from the facts that he was a Turk born in 1769 at the seaport of Kavala, in what is now Greece, that he was a minor government official, and that he married the mayor's daughter and had three sons, Ibrahim, Toussoun and Ismail (from this and other unions Mohammed Ali eventually had ninety-five children), very little is known of Mohammed's early life. He first appears in Egypt as a volunteer in the Turkish army that landed at Abukir in 1799, and like most of the other survivors of that débâcle he rushed for the sea. The story goes that he was pulled out of the water by the crew of a British gig. At all events, he was rescued, and for the next two years, while his hero Bonaparte was conquering Europe, he returned to obscurity. We next hear of him marching with an Albanian detachment to Cairo at the time of the French collapse, and Cairo from now on remained his home, the centre of the new empire to be.

This new empire had begun, as it was inevitably bound to do, with a period of frantic and terrible readjustment. The French, having overturned the Mamelukes, were not long enough in Egypt to set up any other form of government in their place, and the British hardly tackled the problem at all. When the British themselves went away in 1803 Egypt was nominally restored to Turkey, but in reality nothing had been decided; they left a political vacuum behind and the only certainty about the situation was that rival factions of Turks and of Mamelukes (who had by no means been destroyed as yet) would come rushing into this empty space, hating one another to the death. There was no possibility of a peaceful compromise; the Mamelukes were determined to regain what the French had taken away from them. The Turks, who had tried so often in the past to eject the Mamelukes from Egypt, now saw their chance at last.

Few people except passionate amateurs of violent Eastern intrigue can follow the events of the next half-dozen years in Cairo with much interest. It was the worst kind of civil war,

that in which the opponents are more or less equally balanced and equally fanatical, and
the fearful succession of massacres and of bloody *coups d'état* that now took place in the
delta is as meaningless and futile as the battles of the puppet emperors in Bruce's Ethiopia.
The Turks in the main held the towns, and the Mamelukes the Upper Nile and the provinces; and since civil wars end in dictators it was only a question of time before some
leader, more skilful and more ruthless than the others, managed to take control. If Mohammed Ali had not existed he would have had to be invented. However, in a wonderfully
precarious and unpredictable way, he did exist, and when he finally emerged from the
holocaust he restored at least a little clarity to the scene: he set Egypt on the path which, in
general, she has followed ever since.

The departure of the British from Egypt in 1803 found him playing a dangerous game.
By then he had obtained command of a force of Albanians which eventually rose to more
than ten thousand men. With these crude soldiers, who soon became his personal bodyguard, he supported both Turks and Mamelukes in the civil war, while pretending to be
nothing more than a police chief keeping order in the capital, and a good friend of the
Egyptians. No student of the lives of racketeers and party bosses can fail to recognize here
the sly and ruthless manœuvrings of a cunning man. He lurks on the sidelines with the
cold, unblinking eye of the lizard, and then at the right moment strikes. It was a murderous
and reckless world, but Mohammed Ali was murderous without being reckless: he never
tackled a quarry that was too big for him, he never paraded his success, and never forgave
an enemy on any pretext whatever. He was an adept in what Professor Dodwell, in his
study of Mohammed, has called 'that life of high crime which in the east stood for politics'.

By 1805 he felt strong enough to show his hand. With the backing of the Egyptian
sheikhs he besieged the Turkish governor in the citadel, took him prisoner, and set himself
up in his place. A careful message was sent off to Constantinople saying that he was taking
control only as a temporary measure to maintain law and order, and in the following year
the Porte, despairing of finding another man, confirmed him as Pasha of Egypt.

If it was the French who created the conditions for Mohammed Ali to emerge, it was the
British who secured him in his career. By March 1807 Turkey had joined the French
alliance, and as part of a general campaign against Bonaparte the British made a second
landing in Egypt, hoping to support the Mamelukes against Mohammed Ali. It was an
absurd notion. The 5,000 soldiers who were sent on the expedition were largely of non-
British stock and badly led, and the Mamelukes were very far from being the God-fearing
courageous allies the British imagined them to be. The Turks had cut off their supply of
slave-boys from Georgia, and they were a dying race, absorbed in their own desperate
struggle for survival; they detested all foreigners alike, French, British or Turk. 'All the
beys combined,' wrote Drovetti, the French consul, 'have not more than 800 Mamelukes;
the remainder are a mob of Greeks, Osmanlis and Arabs, attracted to their tents by hopes
of pillage. The Mamelukes are no longer the brave soldiers ready to follow their masters to
the death; they have no longer organization or discipline. A bey's court, once a school of
military discipline and morals, has become the source of debauch and disobedience. Their
wandering life of brigandage has degraded them.' Most of them, in any case, were away on
the Upper Nile, with no intention of committing themselves to such a hazardous enterprise.

Thus the weak British force was compelled to fight alone on the beaches of Alexandria, and Mohammed Ali had no difficulty, after two swift and terrible encounters, in pinning them to the coast. A thousand British were killed or captured. Those prisoners who could walk were forced to carry the heads of their dead comrades to Cairo, where some of them were auctioned as slaves, while the heads, about four hundred and fifty of them, were erected on two lines of poles in Esbekiah Square. The British at Alexandria ransomed as many prisoners as they could and then sailed away.

It was a triumph in every way for Mohammed Ali. He had demonstrated his power to the Turks, he had rallied the Egyptians around him, and the Mamelukes on the Upper Nile were now his only opponents in the country. After 1807 he could fairly claim that the delta at least was his, and at once, with the instinct of a born dictator, he set about converting it into his own personal estate. Private property was abolished, taxes were increased, a huge army was conscripted, and the Egyptians after a decade of invasion and civil war could now subside once more into the familiar comforts and miseries of oriental despotism.

Mohammed himself, of course, had no intention of standing still. He had trained his sons for war, and all Arabia, the Sudan, Syria, Greece, even Turkey herself, lay before him. But first he had one last score to settle at home before he could safely set out on his adventures. The Mamelukes were summoned to attend a ceremony in the citadel on March 1, 1811 – one observes how often March is the fateful month in Egypt – and about five hundred of them, lulled by Mohammed's repeated expressions of friendship, got themselves up in their robes and rode in a body to the rendezvous. A narrow road leads down from the citadel to the city, and when the ceremony was over the Mamelukes were invited to ride along it in procession with some of Mohammed's guards going in front and others following behind. Directly the Mamelukes had entered this road the gates at either end were closed upon them, and Mohammed's men, running back to the heights on either side, fired point-blank into the horsemen below. There was a legend afterwards that some of the Mamelukes escaped, but it is more likely that all were killed at once or beheaded afterwards, and the massacre of their followers that continued through Cairo that night brought the total dead to several thousands. As an extra precaution a column under the command of Ibrahim, Mohammed's eldest son, was sent up the Nile to destroy the survivors in Upper Egypt. About three hundred men with their wives, virtually the last of the Mamelukes, managed to escape above the cataracts into Nubia.

'These years,' Ghorbal says, 'present Mohammed Ali at his worst, destructive, avaricious and rigorous.' His power was absolute. 'He may cause any one of his subjects to be put to death,' Lane wrote, 'without the formality of a trial, or without assigning any cause; a single horizontal motion of his hand is sufficient to imply the sentence of decapitation.'

Mohammed was now 42, and contemporaries describe him as a small man, with a dark complexion and a reddish beard, who gave an impression of agility rather than of dignity. There was a defiant air in his manner, and his eyes were restless. He was said to be sober and simple in his private life, and power, not wealth, was his obsession. Yet he was a natural hoarder, and thus he established a tradition among his heirs which continued until the last of them abdicated in this present century; in 1811, as in the 1950s, gold coin, jewels, snuff-boxes and other expensive bric-à-brac were collected in great quantities, and

Mohammed Ali, in addition, was a tax-gatherer of the utmost ruthlessness. When the fellaheen refused to pay they were flogged and dispossessed.

In the museum of the citadel today an effigy of Mohammed Ali has been set up. There he sits cross-legged on the divan in his robes and his turban, the mouthpiece of his water-pipe in his hand and his advisers around him, all equally at ease. They are listening to a petitioner, and a clerk at one side is taking notes. It is a dark, cool, spacious room, with Persian rugs on the floor, and in a waxworks sort of way it is rather impressive. This is the law-giver taking decisions, undisturbed by anything even remotely resembling a telephone or the noise of traffic in the street outside. He has time to think, he cannot be hurried. He is the Caliph dispensing justice.

At what point does the adventurer reform, the murderer become respectable? Is it true that we never feel secure until we have persecuted, and that then our persecution turns to patronage? Mohammed Ali himself, speaking much later on to a European visitor about his rise to power, said, 'I do not love that period of my life, and what would the world profit by the recital of that interminable tissue of combat and misery, cunning and blood-shed, to which circumstances imperatively compelled me? . . . My history shall not commence till the period when, free from all restraint, I could arouse this land . . . from the sleep of ages.'

We know from Mohammed Ali's papers that he was an extremely modern man, a breaker of traditions. Bonaparte had begun the westernization of Egypt, and he was determined to carry it through. His dispatches to his generals and provincial governors are written with a precision and directness which are quite unlike the general idea of oriental correspondence. 'I have given you full powers to govern your territory . . .' he writes to one of these subordinates. 'Do not ask my approval of matters of no importance.' 'You are aware,' he says to his commander in the Sudan on another occasion, 'that the end of all our effort is to procure Negroes. Please show zeal in carrying out our wishes in this capital matter.' He can be very fierce at times when he is disobeyed, but then, having delivered the reprimand, there is a word of encouragement, a paternal pat on the back. He feels at ease with authority, he understands human nature very well, and he is absolutely tireless: even when, later on, he is ruling half the Ottoman Empire he seems to know everything of importance, and no general, however remote, is beyond the range of the courier arriving with commands from Cairo. Almost alone among Eastern rulers he understood the use of sea power.

Visitors from the West – and he welcomed them all, British as well as French – invariably found him courteous and helpful. Lane, the Englishman, by no means an uncritical observer, speaks of how conditions in Egypt have improved under Mohammed Ali; Burckhardt, the Swiss, finds him full of shrewd comment about Napoleon and Wellington; Cailliaud, the Frenchman, greatly admires him for his intelligence. Even the most minor of Western travellers are received and given *firmans* which take them in safety to the Upper Nile. The West, to Mohammed, is the way ahead. He wants European and American engineers to design his bridges and dams, soldiers to lead his troops, and geologists to search for gold. Unlike the Mamelukes, he welcomes foreign traders, and he receives with warmth the French and British consuls. He is even willing to discuss the abolition of the slave trade.

ABOVE *A dredging machine* BELOW *Waterworks at Ismailia*

The evidence is so conclusive that we are bound to agree that it was no accident that he came to power. He towers above his contemporaries, and it is obvious that his best qualities – his grasp of affairs and his understanding of men – were always latent in him when he was young. But one doubts if his character really altered as he grew older; the ambition remained, the passion for power, and if he was a village bully when young he was a tyrant now; if once he killed with his own hand in a street-fight, he now slaughtered thousands without ever leaving his cool divan in the citadel. The manners had changed, of course. In middle age he could speak reassuringly against the slave trade. But that did not prevent him from being the greatest slave-dealer in existence.

Yet, when all this is said, one must in fairness set Mohammed Ali against his time and place. No man could govern for five minutes in the Middle East at the beginning of the nineteenth century unless he was just as violent as the age itself – and government at this juncture was what Egypt needed above all else. The French invasion had uprooted the country's way of life, and turned its economy upside down. Traditions had been thwarted even to the point where the annual pilgrimages to Mecca were abandoned. Mohammed at least restored the country to some sort of stability, and brought it out of the Middle Ages. It might even be argued that, in order to hold his place in world affairs, which had begun to press on Egypt for the first time in centuries, he was bound to raise a large army and to expand. Otherwise he would have gone the way of the Mamelukes.

The first of his foreign conquests began in Arabia in 1811, and concerns us here in only one aspect: it dragged on for seven years, and although it ended in the occupation of Mecca and as complete a victory as any invader is likely to have in those vast deserts, it left Mohammed Ali ruinously short of men and money. There was only one place where he could remedy these deficiencies, and that was on the Nile itself. Both slaves and gold were obtainable in the Sudan, and who knew what other valuable merchandise besides? The French had got as far as Aswan. Mohammed Ali in 1820 decided to push on into the wilderness that lay beyond.

10

Sheikh Ibrahim ibn Abdullah

———

Nothing of much note had happened on the Upper Nile since the French had left. Desaix's carefully organized military government collapsed entirely, and a kind of lethargic anarchy took its place. Wherever the Mamelukes appeared on their restless wanderings they ruled; like a pack of wolves they terrorized the country, stripped it of its food, and then passed on. Wherever the villages were left to themselves they accepted the authority of their local sheikhs, and the Bedouin, another wolf-pack, roamed the desert on either side of the river, making raids on the caravan routes. No traveller went unarmed unless he was poor enough not to be noticed, and everywhere a stranger was at once an enemy. 'The banks of the Nile,' wrote Missett, the British consul, 'formerly so luxuriant, are now condemned to an unnatural bitterness.'

The fierce heat of the sun had taken charge. Nothing was built, every activity was delayed, and the villages turned listlessly in upon themselves, hoping for nothing better than food and peace.

After 1811 Mohammed Ali's Turks gradually set up a chain of administrative posts along the river, and Ibrahim, Mohammed's eldest son, established himself at Assiut as governor of all Egyptian territory south of the delta. He made one final assault on the Mamelukes at Ibrim, in Nubia, but after this no Turk ventured further than Philae, except on raiding parties. The remnants of the Mamelukes were known to be perched at Dongola, above the third cataract, but the rest of the Sudan – that vast arid plain that stretched for a thousand miles to the Ethiopian mountains – was linked to the outside world only by caravans which, at intervals of a year or so, found their way down to Cairo. Beyond Philae all was hearsay, danger and silence; the country was as much cut off from the mainstream of civilization as it had ever been.

But now under Ibrahim's rule the river was fairly quiet as far as Aswan, and European explorers, emerging like inquisitive squirrels after a long winter, were eager to push on above the cataracts. Two of the first to appear were a British Member of Parliament, Thomas Legh, and his companion the Reverend Charles Smelt.

Nothing is more intriguing in African exploration in the nineteenth century than the casualness with which it was often undertaken. A group of friends meet and discuss a trip abroad. Shall it be Vienna, Naples, or the Canary Islands? Or possibly Africa? Yes, of course, Africa. They know nothing about Africa, no shipping lines exist, no one can tell them anything very definite about the climate, the kind of medicines required on the journey, the local languages, the food, the money or the inhabitants; and maps are unobtainable. But presumably, they argue, all these things will be made clear as they proceed along their way. The gunsmith in the Strand supplies them with firearms, the banker gives them a draft on Cairo, the hatter furnishes sun-helmets with flaps at the back, and off they go as light-heartedly as if they were setting off for the south of France to avoid the English winter. Of such were Mr Legh and the Reverend Smelt; and we shall meet others, like the novelist Flaubert, later on.

Legh and Smelt did not even have Africa in mind at all when they first left England. Legh, in his delightful little book, *Narrative of a Journey in Egypt and in the Country beyond the Cataracts*, explains that while Bonaparte was on the rampage in Europe 'a visit to Athens or Constantinople supplied the place of a gay and dissipated winter passed in Paris, Vienna or Petersburg'. And so in the winter of 1812 they travelled at first to Turkey, and it was only when they were driven out of Smyrna by the plague that they directed their attention to Egypt.

As matters turned out, Legh and Smelt did not contribute very much to the exploration of Nubia, but the very insouciance of their journey and the good luck that attended it (there happened to be a pause in the tribal wars on the Upper Nile at the time) were an inducement for more scientific observers to follow them. At Cairo they engaged a guide, who is described simply as a Mr Barthow, an American who had been in Egypt for many years, and armed with *firmans* from Mohammed Ali they proceeded uneventfully up the Nile as far as Aswan. Like Denon, they explored the monuments and admired the women on the islands – 'notwithstanding their colour, the females of Elephantine are conspicious for their elegant shapes, and are, upon the whole, the finest women we saw in Egypt' – and Legh thought it nothing strange to purchase a Negro boy who subsequently became part of the Reverend Smelt's household in England. Far from being put off by the hostility of the Nubians, who regarded them as the forerunners of another invading army, they hired a small one-masted boat at Philae, and in February 1813 sailed up that desolate and forbidding stretch of the river that leads on to the ancient fortress dominating the heights of Ibrim, about one hundred and forty miles from Philae. The village there had been destroyed by the Mamelukes fleeing from Ibrahim two years before, and was deserted; and here they turned back. On their way downstream they were delighted to hear the news of Bonaparte's retreat from Moscow, but they were warned that the plague had broken out again in the delta, and they decided to remain at Minia until it had abated.

They passed the time riding in the desert, visiting the Turkish baths, and at night watching one of the troupes of dancing girls who were attached to every Turkish garrison on the river. But it was a wearisome delay, as Legh with some eloquence explains: 'When the antiquities that may exist in the neighbourhood have been examined, and any local interest ceases to amuse, nothing perhaps can be more melancholy than the prospect of a long residence in a Turkish town, where the absolute want of books, the frivolous conversation and the excessive ignorance of the natives, the daily smoking of tobacco and drinking of coffee, form the chief features of the torpid and listless existence to which a stranger is condemned.'

At Minia they met a Scot named Donald Donald of Inverness, who had been captured during the abortive British landing at Rosetta nearly seven years before. He had been sold as a slave, circumcised, converted to Islam, and was apparently content. At all events he had no wish to accompany the two travellers on their return to civilization, and after an interval of several months they were safely back in Cairo.

There was one other strange man whom Legh and Smelt had met on the river. They had seen him first at Assiut, and then again on their voyage down from Ibrim, and they could not quite make him out. He spoke perfect English and French, and was obviously a cultivated man who knew Europe well. Yet he called himself Sheikh Ibrahim, was 'extremely well-dressed after the Turkish fashion', and was treated everywhere as an Arab. It was not until they returned to England that they learned that this man's real name was

Mohammed Ali's son Ibrahim

John Lewis Burckhardt, and that he had been sent out from England by a group of men who called themselves the Association for Promoting the Discovery of the Interior Parts of Africa. Burckhardt was not at all a casual traveller. He was a scholar and a scientist with definite objects in view, and when Legh and Smelt saw him he was engaged on a journey which was to reveal the Nile in the Sudan as it had never been revealed before.

Burckhardt was a Swiss, born of a well-to-do family in Lausanne, and a more unusual man would be difficult to imagine. His real place, one feels, was in some small but distinguished German university, for he was a scholar of great diligence with a passion for detail. He appears to have excelled in everything he undertook, whether it was the study of

medicine, chemistry or foreign languages, and a sedentary life among his books should have kept him happy for many years. But he would have nothing of all this. A whirlwind of imagination carried him off to Africa and the East, and instead of a schoolmaster in cap and gown we have a nomad dressed in gellabiah and turban and riding on a donkey. He was a man obsessed, but very methodically obsessed. In these wild and dangerous surroundings he was just as painstaking and logical as he would have been in a schoolroom. He is, as it were, a grammarian of exploration, a pedant turned explorer, a classicist in the wilderness, and he is saved from dullness by a very pleasant sense of humour. He is the sort of man who will put up with any hardship to satisfy his curiosity, and as such he belongs to that little group of gifted romantics – Browne and Burton are other members of it – who explore Africa, not for trade, or for Christianity, or reputation, or even for geographical reasons, but simply because they are absorbed by what they see.

No doubt Burckhardt's early life had something to do with his restlessness. His father was ruined by the Bonapartist party in Switzerland – he was even tried for his life for betraying secrets to the Austrians – and Burckhardt grew up loathing the French. As soon as he could he escaped from Switzerland to Germany, and after some years at the universities there emigrated to England. The young man spent a year or two at Cambridge studying Arabic, and then presented himself to the newly formed African Association with an offer to go off and explore on their behalf the sources of the Niger and the centre of the continent. (There was a good deal of confusion about the Niger and the Nile at this time. Many geographers thought that they might turn out to be the same river.) It was agreed that he was to have a small allowance – so small, in fact, that he was never again to know civilized comforts until the day he died – and was to perfect his Arabic by a two years' stay in Syria. After that he was to explore central Africa.

Burckhardt prepared himself for the journey by walking barefoot through the English countryside, sleeping in the open, and living on water and vegetables; and in 1809 he set off. His subsequent adventures are known to us almost solely through the copious notes and letters he sent back to the African Association, for he never returned to Europe, and made very little contact with other Europeans in the East. 'I am proceeding from hence,' he wrote from Malta (where he had grown a heavy beard), 'as an Indian Mohammedan merchant . . . and shall soon be lost in the crowds of Aleppo.' Nearly three years later he turned up in Cairo by way of Petra, which few, if any, other Europeans had visited since the Middle Ages, and by now his mastery of Arabic was such that he had adopted the name of Sheikh Ibrahim ibn Abdullah, and was accepted as an authority on Islamic law. It is some measure of his progress in the language that while in Syria he made a transliteration of Robinson Crusoe into Arabic, and that, there being 150 different words for wine in Arabic poetry, he knew them all.

In May 1813, when he was still only 29, he wrote to the Association from Esna on the Upper Nile saying that he had met Legh and Smelt, and that he had managed to get up the river almost as far as Dongola. He now proposed to make a second journey on the Nile as far as the junction with the Atbara River in the Sudan, and from there make his way across the Red Sea to Mecca. He realizes that this is getting him nowhere near the Niger and central Africa, but he trusts that the Association will approve of his making this small

Sheikh Ibrahim; Burckhardt in Arab clothing
Lithograph by M. Gauci from a sketch by Henry Salt in Cairo 1817

Drawing of Saffa, in Mecca, attributed to Burckhardt

detour; it will fill in the time while he is awaiting the annual caravan which is shortly to set out from Cairo for Fezzan and the interior.

More than a year later he writes again from Jedda saying that he has arrived in Arabia by way of Shendy on the Nile, and is suffering from eye-trouble; and after another twelve months or so he reports from Cairo that he has been to Mecca. He is still awaiting the Fezzan caravan, he says, and he is in rather poor health.

The spring of 1816 brings another letter saying that he has been seriously ill, and that in order to escape the plague in the delta he has been to the monastery at Sinai. Still another eighteen months later, in October 1817, the Association is shocked to hear that their traveller has died of dysentery in Egypt, aged only 33. He has left his eight hundred volumes of oriental manuscripts to Cambridge University, and for some time after his death the Association continues to receive delayed letters in the handwriting it knows so well.

Poor Burckhardt. He dies protesting that he really does mean to go to central Africa, he is most anxious that the Association will understand the reasons for the delay and give him just a little more time; perhaps next month at last the caravan will set out. Knowing this warm-hearted and devoted man as well as we do, we cannot doubt that he would have gone, caravan or no caravan, had he lived. But it is clear that he was captivated by the Near East; he could not bring himself to go just yet. The fact that he was buried as a Moslem may not prove very much, since in 1817 it may have been difficult to obtain a Christian burial in Egypt, but it is certain that his eight years of wandering in the East can hardly be explained away entirely as a preparation for a journey to central Africa: his heart, his head, the whole of his generous nature was involved in Islam and the desert. One cannot even really claim for him a great place in geographical discovery; his journeys to Mecca (nearly fifty years before Burton arrived there) and to the Upper Nile were remarkable achievements, made in conditions of poverty and hardship which would have destroyed a less determined man, but they did not add much to what was already fixed on the map.

It is only when we come to the letters and the notes, and the splendid volumes that were subsequently developed from them, that we realize that Burckhardt was one of the most observant travellers who ever lived. A good deal of his writing – his meteorological observations, his analyses of local dialects, his lists of place-names – make rather dull reading, but when he is on the move one travels with him. Never for an instant does one doubt the truth of what he says. He is a superlative non-exaggerator, and he makes the smallest objects sing. He is the miniaturist who reveals the age.

Thus on his first journey up the Nile beyond Philae he speaks of the gazelles that then roamed the desert in large herds and at night came down to feed on the maize crops on the river bank. The Nubians, Burckhardt says, kept them off by erecting scarecrows of hyenas made of straw with wooden legs. On the whole he liked the Nubians very much; one might describe them as naked savages who put butter on their heads 'to refresh the skin and keep the vermin at bay', but they were a brave and independent people, and thieving as well as disease and prostitution were almost unknown among them – a very welcome change from Egypt. Highway robbery was not regarded as theft among the Nubians. If they chanced upon an unprotected traveller they demanded ransom, and it was unwise, says Burckhardt, to refuse – at once the Nubians would start digging your grave. Burckhardt, riding on an ass with a single servant, and so poor that he lived on dates and maize bread, protested in vain to a man who waylaid him that he had nothing to give, '. . . and as soon as he began to construct my tomb I alighted, and making another, told him that it was intended for his own sepulchre. . . . At this he began to laugh; we then mutually destroyed each other's labours.'

Then there was the pleasant interlude with a guide whom he had hired, a man who would never reveal in advance how far they had to travel to get from one place to the next. 'May God smooth our path . . . God is great, he can prolong distances or shorten them,' was all that could be got out of him. The man was not a good guide, and when they came to part Burckhardt felt himself obliged to do no more than say, 'May God smooth your path.' 'No,' the guide answered, 'for once I ask *you* to smooth it.' He then demanded Burckhardt's shawl and Burckhardt let him have it.

During this earlier part of his journey Burckhardt was in the vicinity of the Nubian temples which now have either been removed or flooded by the waters of the new dam. No one who has seen the temples can fail to regret their disappearance from their present setting, for it is an exhilarating experience to come up in the evening, or better still in the moonlight, to some such place as Wadi es Sebur, and see, close to the shore, the great propylon of Rameses' temple with its avenue of sphinxes half buried in the sand. But to have been there in 1813, as Burckhardt was, and to have known that nothing but an utter barbarity lay around, that there was no easy way back to civilization, and that this sight, unrecorded, unexplored and unknown, was standing there for your eyes alone: this must have provided sensations which were the justification for all the dangers and miseries of the journey. Denon in Egypt at least had the French army to protect him and transport him. Burckhardt in Nubia was alone. He was less ebullient than Denon, and less of an artist. But he had a trained eye, and his descriptions of the Nubian temples are not only the first to be made since ancient times; they are still among the best that have been written.

On March 22, 1813, he reached Abu Simbel, which had escaped the attention of all other travellers, and thus he was the first educated man in modern times to look upon a scene which perhaps might be described as the finest spectacle on the Nile.

He thought nothing much of it at first. Abu Simbel lies in an angle of the cliffs on the western bank of the Nile, and Burckhardt approached it from above. Looking downward he could make out only the façade of one small temple cut into the face of the rock. This was the temple of Rameses II's wife Nefertari, and no doubt when Burckhardt descended the cliff he had much the same view of it as we have now. He was able to enter by the main door, but the interior must have been much cluttered up by grime and rubbish, for he makes no special mention of the brilliant frescoes and carvings within; and in fact he says that Abu Simbel at that time was used by the inhabitants of the surrounding country-side as a place of refuge when warlike tribes were on the move; people camped in the temple for weeks or months at a time until the trouble blew over.

Burckhardt was a little disappointed at what he saw, for he had been given 'many magnificent descriptions' of the place by neighbouring villagers. However, by chance he turned upstream a little way, and caught sight of the head of one of the four colossi which have been carved out of the cliff-face and form the main decoration of the façade of the second, much larger temple which was excavated in honour of Rameses himself. Here his view was absolutely different from what we see now. Nine-tenths of the colossi he could not see at all: '. . . they are now almost entirely buried beneath the sands which are blown down here in torrents, only the left-hand figure showing as much as the head and part of the breast and arms.' The head of the next figure had broken off, and of the remaining two 'the bonnets only' appeared. In other words, what he saw was a long slope of yellow sand, and he had to guess what lay beneath. 'I expect,' he wrote, 'could the sand be cleared away, a vast temple would be discovered,' and he speculated intelligently that if it proved that the colossi were not standing but sitting they would be very large indeed.

Of the single exposed head he wrote: '. . . a most expressive, youthful countenance, approaching nearer to the Grecian model of beauty than that of any ancient Egyptian figure I have seen . . . it might pass for the head of a Pallas'; and he goes on to speak of its 'incomparable serenity and god-like mildness'. Clambering up the sand he measured the shoulders (seven yards across) and one ear (three feet four inches long), and correctly guessed from these dimensions that the whole statue, if sitting, was from sixty-five to seventy feet high.

With this discovery alone he had justified his first excursion on the Nile. But it was his other experiences that were to be of more interest to Mohammed Ali, for he had also visited on this first journey the territory of the Mamelukes and the Shaiqiya tribes. The Mamelukes retreating up the Nile from Ibrahim had done fearful damage, and Burckhardt, following in their wake, found many ruined villages. These 'tyrannical and unprincipled slaves', he says, still managed to travel in luxury with their wives and retainers. In the ferocious Nubian heat they continued to wear thick woollen robes, but they lived on rafts in the river, and day and night slaves were engaged to throw water over the awnings. They had laid waste the country around Derr, the principal settlement in Nubia, and had gone on through the trading post of Wadi Halfa to pillage Dongola above the third cataract.

The Nile here described a tremendous S in the desert, and this was the country of the Shaiqiya tribes. It was in many ways one of the most beautiful parts of the river. Hundreds of waterwheels pumped life into the sand, and on either bank fertile crops and forests of

A waterwheel. From David Roberts' Egypt and Nubia

mimosas and acacias spread away. Wild thyme grew on the many green islands in the river, and water birds in thousands were constantly lighting down to feed or passing overhead. Every few miles there were villages with boats tied up on the bank, and on the cliffs behind quite large crenellated sandstone castles, with walls thirty feet thick, the relics of the great days of the Fung empire. It was true that flies and midges infested the river at certain seasons, that the heat was overpowering and that rain hardly ever fell, but it was a calm and refreshing prospect for the traveller to come upon, and the only vile, or at any rate violent, thing about it was man. The Shaiqiya, like the Fungs, were a mysterious people, neither Nubian nor Arab, and no one seems to know where they came from. There was some strain in their blood, however, that made them rise above all the surrounding tribes, and in their prowess and appearance they were every bit as formidable as the Mamelukes. They lived by pillaging the settled communities along the river bank, and they were said to be able to muster some ten thousand warriors, of whom at least two thousand were mounted. All through this part of the Sudan their name was a byword for piracy and destruction.

'They all fight on horseback,' Burckhardt wrote, 'in coats of mail which are sold to them by the merchants of Suakin and Sennar. Firearms are not common among them, their only weapons being a lance, target and sabre; they throw the lance to a great distance with much dexterity, and always carry four or five lances in the left hand, when charging an enemy. They are all mounted on Dongola stallions, and are as famous for their horsemanship as the Mamelukes were in Egypt; they train their horses to make violent springs with their hind legs when galloping; their saddles resemble the drawings I have seen of those of Abyssinia, and, like Abyssinian horsemen, they place the great toe only in the stirrup. The Shaiqiya are a perfectly independent people, and possess great wealth in corn and cattle. . . . They are renowned for their hospitality; and the person of their guest or companion is sacred. If the traveller possess a friend among them and has been plundered on the road, his property will be recovered, even if it has been taken by the king. They all speak Arabic exclusively and many of them read and write it. Their learned men are held in great respect by them; they have schools, wherein all the sciences are taught which form the course of Mohammedan study, mathematics and astronomy excepted. I have seen books copied at Merawe [Merowe], written in as fine a hand as that of the scribes of Cairo. Whenever young men are sent to them from the adjacent countries for instruction, the chief of the Ulema distributes them amongst his acquaintances, in whose houses they are lodged and fed for as many years as they choose to remain. Such of the Shaiqiya as are soldiers, and not learned men, indulge in the frequent use of wine and spirits made from dates. The manners of their women are said to be very depraved.'

These impressions were confirmed by Waddington, the English explorer who followed Burckhardt up the Nile. He found these warriors a proud and beautiful people. 'The Shaiqiya,' he wrote, 'are black – a clear, glossy, jet-black, which appeared to my then unprejudiced eyes to be the finest colour that could be selected for a human being. They are distinguished in every respect from Negroes, by the *brightness* of their colour, by their hair, and the regularity of their features; by the mild and dewy lustre of their eyes, and by the softness of their touch, in which last respect they yield not to Europeans.'

These men, like the Mamelukes, despised agriculture or work of any kind – that was for the servile Nubians – and their term for a Turk or an Egyptian was dog. They feared nothing, Waddington says, and went very gaily into battle: 'The signal for attack among the Shaiqiya, as I believe among other Arabs, is given by a virgin, richly dressed and seated on a dromedary, who is held sacred, even by the enemy. The signal is *lilli-lilli-loo* frequently repeated.' As they rode up to the enemy they shouted *Salaam aleikum* – peace be with you: by which they meant the peace of death. Among these people 'arms were playthings and war a sport'. They sought from their enemies 'nothing but amusement and in death feared nothing but repose'.

It was the old story of a fierce and predatory conservatism, of a military caste that had not grown decadent, and although they bore obvious resemblances to the Mamelukes one tends rather to compare them with the Central Asian warrior tribes. The Shaiqiya might easily have gone raiding through the steppes, and with them too the horse was a symbol of power and life, and their women were said to be quite as brave as the men. They were parasites, of course, and very destructive ones at that, since they regarded every travelling caravan as fair game, and every field and village on the river as an invitation to help themselves. They could change sides in a campaign when it suited them, and in a civilized world most of their pretensions would have been absurd. Yet there was a kind of primitive chivalry in their traditions – firearms, for instance, they regarded as cowardly – and they contributed an element of freedom and vigorousness to the slow lethargic life along the Nile.

At the time of Burckhardt's arrival in the Sudan the Shaiqiya occupied a stretch of about eighty miles along the river below the fourth cataract, and they were divided into three tribes each under a chieftain called a *mek*, who lived in his castle on the Nile. The tribes operated separately on pillaging raids, but they tended to combine when faced by an invader. In combination they were by some way the most powerful force on the Nile in the Sudan, and any enemy advancing up the river from Egypt was bound to come into conflict with them. Even Burckhardt, a persistent man, hesitated to venture alone far into their territory, and at Dongola he decided that if he was going to get any further up the river he would have to by-pass the Shaiqiya by making the desert crossing from Aswan to Berber. And so he turned back to Esna in Egypt.

Here in the security of a Turkish garrison town he was able to assemble his notes and write a description of a part of the river – the 500-mile stretch from Aswan to Dongola – that was very little known. Nothing was omitted: the overlay of Moslem mosques upon the more ancient Christian and Pharaonic temples, the languages and habits of the tribes, the annual rise and fall of the river and the cultivation of its banks, 'the deep hoarse murmur of the cataracts', the hippopotamuses, the crocodiles and the white ants, the caravan routes and the great pointed rocks that rose in natural pyramids from the desert, an exact calculation of distances. It was the first clear spotlight that had fallen on Nubia since ancient times, and the gentlemen of the African Association in London, on opening Burckhardt's letters, were in the position of knowing more about the Upper Nile and its past than anyone in Egypt.

Burckhardt's health had been undermined by the journey – he had marched ten hours a day and had covered 900 miles in a little more than a month – and he was laid up for a long time with eye-trouble. But in March 1814, before he was fully recovered, he was ready to set out again.

CAPTIONS TO COLOUR PLATES

1   *The Tisisat Falls.*

2   *Two aquatints of Ethiopian landscapes, after Henry Salt:* ABOVE *Macalle;* BELOW *Abha Moneim.*

3   *Desaix. Painting by Andrea Appiani.*

4   *The mosque of Sultan Hassan and the entrance to the citadel, Cairo. From David Roberts'* Egypt and Nubia.

5   *Bonaparte toured Alexandria shortly after the landings. He visited Pompey's Pillar (he is on the right) when it was being measured by means of a kite attached to two strings. Watercolour by Dominique Vivant Denon, who is holding the horses.*

6   *Detail from the slave market at Cairo. Painting by William James Muller*

7   *Detail from the Battle of the Pyramids. Painting by Louis Francois Lejeune.*

8   *Detail from Bonaparte giving a sabre to the military commander of Alexandria. Painting by François Henri Mulard.*

9   ABOVE *Kom Ombo, by Edward Lear.* BELOW *Philae. Watercolour by Owen Jones.*

10 *Detail from the massacre of the rebellious Mamelukes. Lithograph from a painting by Joseph Vernet after a sketch by Forbin.*

11 ABOVE *Outside and* BELOW *inside Abu Simbel. From drawings by G. Belzoni.*

12 *Detail of the Storming of Magdala by the British troops under General Sir Robert Napier, Monday, 13 April 1868, by Alfred Concanen from a sketch by a staff officer.*

13 ABOVE *The countryside in western Ethiopia.* BELOW *The royal palace at Gondar. From Heuglin's* Reisen in Nord-Ost Afrika.

14 *Robert Napier. Painting by Lowes Dickinson.*

Kôm Ombos.
A.M. & P.M. 10. Feby. 1856.   & loose sand   & pots & brix & broken pans —

all sand &
pots —
(& some pans)   oh! pots!

11

Shendy Market

———

The desert crossing from Aswan to Berber had become by now a regular caravan route, since it avoided both the Shaiqiya and the great loop in the Nile, but it was a dangerous journey involving an almost waterless march of 400 miles across the sand. Since Bruce had made this journey in the opposite direction forty years earlier no other European had attempted it, and in the intervening years a fierce xenophobia had sprung up among the Arabs. Foreigners were not liked in the caravans, and Burckhardt, being alone, gave it out that he was a poor trader who was travelling on the Upper Nile in search of a cousin who had vanished on a journey to Sennar some years before. On these terms he was accepted as a travelling companion by the leader of a group of about one hundred traders and their families who were setting off on March 1, 1814, but even so he was despised as an intruder and a Turk. The women especially, he says, were filled with horror and disgust at his beard and white skin, and as a poor man he was reiegated to the worst part of the caravan. His constant note-taking, he knew, would have aroused the deepest suspicion, and so he used to ride a little way ahead each day and hide behind a rock, writing rapidly, until the caravan caught up with him.

Compared with the equipment carried by later scientific expeditions his baggage seems recklessly pathetic. He gives an inventory of it: a watch (broken), a pocket-compass, writing materials, penknife, tobacco-purse and steel for striking a light, a light axe, needles and thread, one spare shirt, a comb, a small medicine-box, a sleeping carpet, a few cooking pots and water-skins, and a store of the usual native food – flour, dates, biscuits, salt, rice, lentils and coffee. So as not to cause suspicion he also took with him a small quantity of merchandise and the obligatory firearms, a gun and a pistol. At this juncture he had no slave or servant, which meant that he had to gather his own food and firewood and cook at the end of every march, and his sole transport was an ass and a share of a camel. The only money he possessed was fifty Spanish dollars and a couple of sequins – and this was to carry him through a ten months' journey that was not only to take him up the Nile as far as the Fung kingdom but across to Mecca as well.

His companions were small traders for the most part, carrying up from Egypt to the markets of the Sudan such things as sugar, soap, beads, cloth, mirrors and ancient firearms, and hoping to bring back with them the well-known products of the Sudan: gum arabic, ostrich feathers, ivory, and the black slaves and gold upon which Mohammed Ali had set his heart. It was a dreadful life, and Burckhardt's account of the behaviour of the traders who made up his caravan reads like nothing so much as a description of Captain Kidd and the pirates of the Spanish Main. The conditions of the journey itself, one would have thought, were hard enough – they had scarcely started before they were attacked by Bedouin and once they nearly all died of thirst – but these men by their inhumanity to one another contrived to make it harder still. They quarrelled, they stole from one another, they abandoned the weak and dying along the way.

The actual start was made from Kom Ombo, a little to the north of Aswan, and before they left the green banks of the Nile the camels were stuffed with three times the usual amount of maize, which it was intended they should slowly masticate in the empty desert that lay ahead. When an animal died – and many did die of exhaustion from the very outset of the journey – its head was turned towards Mecca and its owner at once set about selling the meat. The bones of camels were scattered everywhere along the route. At every halt the traders dug holes in the sand for water, sometimes finding it and sometimes not; they marched from the freezing cold of dawn to the ferocious heat of midday, when they camped and slept (each man perched on his baggage lest it be stolen by his companions), and then moved on again in the cool of the evening. And so it went on from day to day and it was not unlike a voyage at sea. One looked ahead to one's arrival at Berber as the sailor looks forward to a landfall, and like the sailor these traders promised themselves a glorious debauch once they were delivered from the hazards of the journey. This happened on March 23, 1814, when they had been over three weeks on the way. All at once they were aware of a breath of freshness in the air, and Burckhardt heard one of the Arabs exclaim, 'God be praised, we smell again the Nile'. Two hours later they struck the stream just below its junction with the Atbara, and the bedraggled travellers, now reduced to about eighty men, entered the settlement of Berber.

Berber, with its four squalid villages of tumbledown huts, would appear to have been somewhat less than the Islamic prospect of paradise, but it was all this and more to these worn-out men. Burckhardt, a serious man on a scientific expedition, describes the place with a good, Swiss, Protestant abhorrence. Of the Berberines he exclaims, 'Never have I seen so bad a people'. Drunkenness and debauchery governed their lives. They were liars and hypocrites to a man. He concedes that the Abyssinian slave-girls who infested the town were good-looking and astonishingly merry, and that the dry desert air kept them healthy, but for the rest they were animals. A great shout of delight from these girls greeted the caravan's arrival, and within a few minutes the traders were dispersed among the huts. Each man took a girl for the duration of his stay in the town. She prepared his grog and his meals, massaged his body with grease, and joined him in his drunken orgies through the night.

Berber was the first entrepôt of importance on the great trade route up the river to Sennar, but Shendy, another one hundred miles upstream, was a larger centre, and Burckhardt pushed on there as soon as he could. He stayed a month in Shendy before setting off for Mecca, and his study of the town is a fascinating piece of anthropological research. It is the most complete picture we have of life in the central Sudan as it was on the eve of Mohammed Ali's invasion.

There are some curious aspects about this part of the Nile. It is the beginning of the rain belt on the river, but the heat is very great throughout the entire year. It is the sort of climate that drives people to extremes: either the lassitude and debauchery which Burckhardt had already seen at Berber, or a fanatical asceticism. On his way to Shendy Burckhardt passed through the holy town of Damer, close to the junction with the Atbara River, and here he found a large mosque and a settlement of fakirs who denied themselves every comfort and observed the Islamic law to the letter. In Shendy he was back in a more venal atmosphere again. The green strip on either side of the river here, moreover, is not very wide in the dry season; beyond a few hundred yards there is nothing to be seen but stark outcrops of blackish rock in a vast plain of sand and gravel, mirages quiver in the midday heat, and often great clouds of locusts and suffocating storms sweep across the country. One would have thought, therefore, that there would never have been much inducement for human beings to settle here. Yet Burckhardt found the region was fairly populous, and Shendy itself, with about six thousand inhabitants, was the largest town in the central Sudan.

Clearly there was some special reason why so many people should have chosen to live in this unattractive place, and the answer, as Burckhardt soon discovered, lay in Shendy market. It was a fabulous market for so small a place. In an open space in the centre of the town three rows of huts had been set up, and here every Friday and Saturday, a thousand miles away from any part of the world that one could call civilized, you could buy such things as spices and sandalwood from India, antimony to blacken the eyelids, medicines, German swords and razors, saddles and leather goods from Kordofan, writing paper and beads from Genoa and Venice, cloth, pottery and basketware of every kind, soap from Egypt, cotton, salt and Ethiopian gold. There was a lively sale in monkeys that were trained to do tricks, and Shendy's wooden dishes, battered and blackened by being held over a fire, were famous. The market was also renowned for its sale of Dongola horses, and for camels and other beasts to carry these goods across the desert.

The stalls where most of the merchandise was displayed were miserable affairs, little cells measuring six feet long by four feet deep with grass matting for a roof. There were no means of locking up these stalls – in the absence of nails the doors were tied together with rope – and so each night the merchants bundled up their goods and took them to their homes in the town. Their money (mainly Spanish dollars, but any currency served) they buried in the ground, and even the richest men affected to be very poor by living in one room, sleeping on the ground and wearing little more than a loincloth. There were no fixed prices in the market (Burckhardt thought the bargaining more like downright cheating), barter often took the place of money, and quarrelling was continuous. There was little agriculture at Shendy, and the local crafts were nothing very wonderful. 'Commerce,' Burckhardt says, 'was the very life of society', and the people never looked much further than the bouza shop or the swarms of prostitutes for their distractions. Yet it was an animated existence, and the traders, ranging from the fairest Arabs to the blackest Negroes, from Moslems in turbans and robes to naked pagans, were a wonderful hotch-potch of the tribes and races of north-eastern Africa. In the heat and the dust they squatted in front of their stalls, bargaining from early morning until late at night, and there was always some new caravan arriving, another taking off again into the desert. Looking up into the sky Burckhardt saw great flocks of storks migrating northwards to Europe.

What he had discovered here, in fact, was the great cross-roads of the Nile. The river at this point made its closest approach to the southern end of the Red Sea, and thus the way was opened up to Arabia, India and the Far East. To the west the caravan routes, keeping as far as possible within the cover of the rain belt and south of the Sahara, led on from oasis to oasis, to Lake Chad and Timbuktu. The Nile valley itself provided a highway to Egypt in the north, and Ethiopia could be reached by the track that led up through Metemma to Gondar. In a curious but inevitable way all the themes of the river were gathered here. The pilgrims from central Africa came through Shendy on their way to Mecca. The slaves captured on the Upper Nile were inevitably bound for Shendy market. Here, for the first time, the traveller ascending the Nile came into touch with Ethiopia, and here on his return journey downstream he was once more drawn into the influence of Egypt and the north. Shendy was also known as 'The Gates', and it lay in the heart of the ancient 'Island of Meroë' – the area bounded by the Atbara and the Nile. From Meroë the Ethiopian Pharaohs and their queens had ruled the river almost as far north as the delta, and it was on this part of the Nile that Cambyses had been finally driven back. On his way into Shendy Burckhardt had passed through the ruins of the ancient capital of Meroë, and although he failed to investigate the place ('I was in the company of a caravan, and had the wonders of Thebes been placed on the road, I should not have been able to examine them'), he had correctly divined that important discoveries would be made on the site.

In Herodotus' day all this country had been known as Ethiopia, and at the time of Burckhardt's arrival the Ethiopians were still laying claim to it. They threatened to come down the Blue Nile once again and seize it, just as Mohammed Ali was now threatening to lead an invasion up from Egypt. Mohammed in fact had already sent agents to Shendy and Sennar to spy out the land. Invasions, slave-raiders, traders' caravans and the Mecca pilgrimage – Shendy had known them all for a thousand years, and its market place was still a genuine capsule of the past. There were other markets upstream and down on this part of the Nile, but none was so important as this, none stretched out its contacts so far, none had such a continuous tradition or was able to reveal so much. It was, in a way, a microcosm of the river, and what happened at Shendy was, very largely, the fate of all the other inhabitants on the Nile from Lake Tana to the sea.

It was extraordinary, of course, that Shendy, being so much in touch with the outside world, should still have been in 1814 so much cut off from it. Bonaparte's invasion as yet had scarcely sent a ripple up the river, and Mohammed Ali was simply a menacing name in the distance. Protected by the surrounding deserts and the cataracts on the Nile the little town continued with its own affairs, and if its inhabitants, like the Berberines, were a depraved and lazy lot, they also had the power of survival. They had worked out a valid way of life depending upon the waterwheel on the river and the caravan in the desert, and the crudities and wastage of this existence were perhaps not quite so drastic as missionaries and explorers were later to make out. The touchstone of all this was the slave trade, and Burckhardt went very thoroughly into the matter, since Shendy was also a great slave centre, probably the greatest in central Sudan.

About five thousand slaves passed through Shendy market every year, and they were drawn from every tribe along the Nile, but the Ethiopians were regarded as superior to all the rest, the females, says Burckhardt, 'being remarked above all other black women for

An Ethiopian slave-girl. From a drawing by Henry Salt

their beauty, and for the warmth and constancy of their affection to the master who has once taught them to love him'. Ethiopian men made the best house servants and clerks. The chief buyers were traders who came up from the Red Sea coast with Indian goods which they exchanged at Shendy for slaves, gold and horses. The slaves were then taken back to the coast at Suakin, some to be shipped north to Egypt, the rest east to Arabia. The other slave route was the one Burckhardt had followed along the river from Egypt, and at Alexandria many of the slaves were passed on by sea to Turkey. Slaves might be bought and resold several times on their journey down to the coast, their value going up steadily as they got nearer the sea.

Most of the natives offered for sale at Shendy, Burckhardt says, were under 15 years of age, about fifteen dollars being paid for a male provided he bore the marks of smallpox (the price dropped two-thirds if he did not), and twenty-five dollars for females. One could buy a slave upon a three days' trial, and many of the traders hired out girls as prostitutes – indeed, it was customary for all traders to sleep with the women they had bought, and very few of them reached the coast as virgins. The traders liked to get the young girls drunk at their parties in the bouza shops at night.

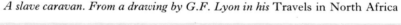

A slave caravan. From a drawing by G.F. Lyon in his Travels in North Africa

As soon as a boy was purchased by a Moslem trader he was circumcised and given an Arab name; and it was an odd fact that many of them, though never taught to read or write, often became religious fanatics, more Moslem than the Mohammedans themselves. The trade in eunuchs was very small – about one hundred and fifty of them reached Cairo every year – but they were regarded as immensely valuable. 'Two years ago,' Burckhardt wrote, 'Mohammed Ali caused 200 young Darfur slaves to be mutilated, whom he sent as a present to the Grand Signor.' Even the Moslems flinched from carrying out the horrible operation on their victims; for the most part, Burckhardt says, the work was left to two Christian Coptic priests at Assiut, and he gives an appalling description of it. Two in every hundred of the boys died, and the survivors could always be detected by 'a skeleton-like appearance'. But already, he goes on, the demand for eunuchs was dropping under Mohammed Ali's régime; a eunuch was a status-symbol, and if a man possessed one it was a sure sign that there were many women in his household, and that therefore he must be wealthy – and wealth attracted Mohammed's tax-gatherers.

At Shendy slaves were regarded as neither more nor less than livestock; when a trader bought a slave he would say to the owner, as at a cattle sale, 'Drive him out'. And yet, Burckhardt wrote, 'the treatment which the slaves experience from the traders is rather kind than otherwise'. In the main they were treated as children; they called their masters 'father', were seldom beaten, were well fed and not overworked. It was regarded as wrong to separate a mother from a young child. He admits that this clemency was not so much due to compassion as to a desire to stop the slaves running away when they were in settlements like Shendy, and that in the desert, where they could not escape, the traders became much more brutal. Even so the slaves were not shut up in houses – the Negroes especially hated being inside and rapidly deteriorated under a roof – and on the march the young girls rode on camels. Only the men were chained.

There was a great fear of Egyptians among the slaves; they believed that they would be murdered if they were sent to the delta, or at any rate mutilated. Yet the truth was, Burckhardt thought, that in both Egypt and Arabia 'slavery had little dreadful in it but the name'. In both countries there was a very good chance of a slave obtaining his freedom, and in Egypt if he was maltreated he could insist on being sold to another master. Inside a household a slave often got more consideration than a servant; after all, he was a valuable property, and it was thought disgraceful for a master to sell a slave whom he had possessed for a long time. Female slaves, however, suffered from the jealousy of their mistresses.

In general Burckhardt was inclined to think that the worst part of the traffic was the effect it had upon the nature of the victims themselves; it made them, he said, lazy, hostile, gluttonous and apathetic. He was convinced that there was not the smallest hope of abolishing slavery in Africa.

One notes in all this a lack of moral indignation which is a little surprising, since Burckhardt was a kindly and warm-hearted man. And yet he is convincing. He drives one to the conclusion that slavery in Africa was not something you could regard as an implacable and unchanging evil, something like malaria or dysentery. It differed very widely in different times and places. In these early years of the nineteenth century it was enmeshed in ordinary life in Egypt and the Sudan, and the average slave accepted his status just as the factory worker or the bank clerk accepts his status today. It is certainly true that the kind of slavery Burckhardt saw in the Sudan was nothing like as cruel and inhuman as it became after Mohammed Ali's invasion in 1820. Mohammed Ali imported something new and dreadfully barbaric into the scene: the wholesale deportation of people for political purposes, a shocking device which was hardly to be seen again in the world in its full brutality until Hitler's and Stalin's day. But in Burckhardt's time slavery was no more than an established domestic custom, and its evils were probably not much worse than many other aspects of life along the Nile at the beginning of the nineteenth century.

Shendy Castle. From a drawing by Linant de Bellefonds

Shendy, like all these small principalities on the river, had its *mek* or king, and the line dated back to the end of the sixteenth century. The incumbent in 1814 was a man called Nimr, and although Burckhardt does not say much about him (possibly because Nimr filched his precious gun), it is apparent from other accounts that he was a very considerable figure. Nimr was six foot tall, a man with a proud and reserved manner, who proceeded on state occasions wearing a leopard-skin (usually a sign of royalty on the Nile) and with a servant carrying a sunshade above his head. His castle on the banks of the Nile, a structure of whitewashed mud-brick, was the only two-storeyed building in the town, and it was furnished with bedsteads inlaid with mother-of-pearl. In addition, he had three other houses, each containing a separate harem, and these he visited in turn for periods of a fortnight. His army or bodyguard consisted of only three hundred horsemen and about twenty obsolete firelocks, but with these he was able to rule with absolute authority and even carry on war with the neighbouring Shaiqiya tribes. His wealth was very great, and was derived chiefly from slaves, many of whom he hired out for immoral purposes in the market and the surrounding villages. He was a literate man, a reader of the Koran, but he had a reputation for ruthlessness; Burckhardt translates Nimr as meaning 'the Tiger', which can hardly be correct since there were no tigers in Africa – 'the Leopard' was a better term – but at all events this last of the Shendy kings was very greatly feared.

Burckhardt seems to have enjoyed his stay in Shendy. 'Nothing unpleasant occurred to me during my stay,' he says. 'Our house and courtyard were soon filled with slaves and camels; we separated into different messes, and everyone delivered a daily ration of dhourra (or maize) to the female slaves, who cooked for the mess; we defrayed all our common expenses with dhourra. Every evening some of my companions had a bouza party; the day was spent in commercial pursuits. Soon after our arrival in order to conciliate the Ababdes (the guides of his caravan) I bought a young sheep, and I always kept my tobacco pouch well supplied for their use. I attended the market regularly, and courted the acquaintance of some Fakyrs. . . .'

It was true that the noise, the heat and the confusion of the market made his head ache, and he used to go home to his hut in the middle of the day to sleep. Nevertheless, he continued to attend the little stall he had set up, and by questioning the fakirs and the traders who were constantly arriving he was able to press his inquiries far and wide.

Everywhere it was a story of decline and disintegration. Abd-el-Rahman, the ruler of Darfur, had died, and the tribes who inhabited that vast province were now largely a law unto themselves. On the Nile itself above Shendy there were several other semi-independent little kingdoms, but they were moribund. At Halfaya the White Nile flowed down from a wilderness where no traveller ever seemed to go, and the Negro tribes who inhabited that unknown region were said to be barbaric in the extreme. The caravan route up the Blue Nile was fairly well developed, but Sennar itself, Burckhardt learned, had collapsed into a welter of futile rebellions against a monarchy that had ceased to stand for anything any more. A regent or vizier named Mohammed wad 'Adlan, a descendant of the regent who had held the real power in Bruce's time, had seized control, but it was apparent that the little empire was at its last gasp and could offer no strong resistance to an invader.

The route down to Suakin on the Red Sea coast Burckhardt was able to investigate for himself. In May 1814 he purchased a 16-year-old slave-boy and a camel with the last of his money, and set off with a party of 150 traders and 300 slaves. They struck off from the Nile by way of the Atbara River, on the pilgrim route to Mecca, and reached Suakin at the end of June. Burckhardt was the first European in modern times to set eyes on this famous seaport, and he was not impressed. It was the same story – 'ill-faith, avarice, drunkenness and debauchery'. About eight thousand people were living in the town, but nearly all their houses were falling down, and the real activity of the place was gathered round the island off the shore where the traders' boats were moored. They were taking away between 2,000 and 3,000 slaves every year.

By now Burckhardt had built up a fairly complete picture of the Nile valley in the Sudan, or at any rate the northern part of it, and his meticulous notes covered every aspect of life along the river. Despite its incredible anachronisms and disparities it was, in a way, a familiar picture: the little feudal kingdoms emerging from barbarism under the cover of Islam and then declining again, black Africa penetrated by the Semitic east, the Koran and the leopard-skin. For the rest – nothing but the vast untenantable desert with its lonely and dangerous caravan routes winding back and forth to the river.

So long as the outside world was kept at bay chieftains like Nimr at Shendy could continue to lord it over their subjects, but it was obvious to Burckhardt that they would collapse at the first approach of an invader equipped with modern arms. Firearms were unknown to the majority of the Sudanese and they were terrified of them. The Shaiqiya might well be another matter, but for all the other little principalities on the river it was the same. Time here had been standing still, and the astonishing thing was that places like Shendy had been preserved for so long from outside interference. Burckhardt thought that the whole of this part of the river from Berber up to the Blue Nile could be conquered by 300 Europeans. The Sudan, in short, lay open to an intruder like some vast tumbledown house whose original owners have died or gone away, leaving a rabble of itinerants and beggars to settle in the ruins.

It was a situation that in many ways reminds one of Egypt on the eve of Bonaparte's invasion, and we are to meet a very similar scene later on in Ethiopia. It contained every element of tragedy: the unarmed, defenceless people quarrelling among themselves, the lure of loot in the form of slaves and gold, the indifference of the outside world. No one cared what happened to Shendy. Few people had even heard of the place until Burckhardt wrote about it. And now the town and its ancient market were ready to be swept away. Like some proliferating plague the politics of the West were working up the Nile, and Shendy's fate was to be the fate of Nilotic peoples everywhere.

Burckhardt sold his slave-boy and his camel in Suakin and departed from the scene in the direction of Arabia, where he met Mohammed Ali, and no doubt informed him of all he had seen in the Sudan, and thus, unwittingly, he hastened the tragedy on its way.

Suakin. Engraving from Heuglin's Reise in das Gebiet des Weissen Nil

12

Salaam Aleikum

Despite the helplessness of the Sudan there were good reasons for Mohammed Ali to hesitate before he committed himself to an invasion. It was a problem of geography rather than of warfare. To surmount the cataracts, to get a force 2,000 miles up the Nile, to venture into a country that had scarcely been explored and never invaded for the past 300 years – this was an enterprise that required a Bonaparte's imagination and the tenacity of the conquistadors.

There was no question of the army making the desert crossing from Aswan to Berber since it would certainly have died of thirst on the way. It was bound to stick to the river, and this meant surmounting no less than six cataracts before it arrived at the confluence of the Blue and the White Niles – and still Sennar, the main object of the expedition, lay another two hundred miles to the south.

Nor could the opposition of the Sudanese be absolutely disregarded. The Nubians above Aswan might be too docile to fight, and the Mamelukes at Dongola too few (they numbered only 300 fighting men), but the Shaiqiya would certainly resist. Presuming that they could be defeated, the way up to Berber and Shendy would be clear, but who was to say that all these old dependencies of the Fung empire might not reunite in the face of an invasion? If that happened the expedition was doomed from the start.

There was still another obstacle, and it was of a more complicated kind. England since the fall of Bonaparte at Waterloo in 1815 was emerging as a great sea power in African waters, especially in the Indian Ocean. Although the Suez Canal was not yet built, the trade route up the Red Sea was steadily increasing in importance, and in order to guard it England had already sent a mission to the emperor of Ethiopia to conclude an alliance and obtain concessions in the Red Sea ports. It was clear that she would not see Ethiopia invaded without making a protest of some kind. In London Mohammed Ali was regarded as an ally of the French, and the English did not trust him. By now (1820) Bonaparte was safely marooned on Saint Helena (where he now had but one year more to live), but there was always a possibility that the French might return in force to the Near East and make some deal with the Turks.

Mohammed Ali was perfectly aware of all this, but to Sennar at least he was determined to go. He already knew some facts about the place from the accounts of earlier explorers. Poncet, the French doctor who had visited it in 1699, had been able to give a description of the mysterious empire of the Fungs, whose kings could once have travelled for a thousand miles on the Nile without going beyond the bounds of their authority. Their rule extended to the Red Sea in the east, to the White Nile in the west, to the Ethiopian mountains in the south, and almost as far as the Egyptian border in the north. The Fungs had appeared suddenly out of nowhere at the beginning of the sixteenth century, and seem to have been neither Arabs nor Moslems at first; they may have been descended from the black Negro tribes on the White Nile, for their rulers were originally known as the Black Sultanate. Later on they had intermarried with Arabs and had embraced Islam, and in Poncet's day they were still very powerful indeed. Their capital, Sennar, lay on the west bank of the Blue Nile, a little below the present town and about 150 miles from Khartoum (which was not then in existence). Poncet speaks of a population of 100,000, which was probably an exaggeration, and he says they were a crafty, suspicious and deceitful people. Most of the houses were of one storey with a flat roof, but there was a large mosque, and the king's palace was a solid bastion with a five-storey tower and elaborate doorways of carved wood.

In 1699 Sennar had an extensive trade with India through the Red Sea port of Suakin, and many rich women about the court were to be seen wearing silk, with silver rings on their arms and ankles, and their faces made up with kohl. They were attended by servants naked from the waist up. In the market, where prices were very cheap, one could buy in addition to slaves, camels and horses, such things as ivory, tamarind fruit, civet for fixing scent, gold-dust and tobacco. There were large forests outside the town with wild animals roaming about in them. A good deal of the Fungs' wealth was said to come from the fabulous gold mines at Fazughli, on the Ethiopian border, and the king, according to Poncet, kept up considerable state. Once every week he would ride out to one of his country houses, accompanied by three or four hundred horsemen and footmen, who sang his praises and played the tabor while they marched. They were followed by hundreds of women who carried on their heads baskets of fruit for the royal *fête champêtre*. Medieval tournaments with jousts and mock battles were often held, and the king, who never appeared in public without a piece of coloured gauze over his face, presided at his court of law with the authority of a Roman governor. Criminals, on being convicted, were thrown to the ground and beaten to death with clubs.

Theodore Krump, the Bavarian missionary who followed Poncet to Sennar in 1701, confirmed Poncet's account, and he added that the central square of the town was 'as big as that of Munich'. It was here that the satellite kings from Berber, Shendy, Damer and other regions came to pay homage to the Fung monarch, kissing his foot and offering tributes of slaves, horses, camels and money. On one of these occasions Krump said he witnessed a procession of 300 slave-girls wearing silk loincloths and many bangles and beads, and carrying baskets of incense on their heads. They came shouting and singing into the square and were formally delivered to the king.

Bruce, as we have seen, found things much declined when he reached Sennar seventy years later. Most of the forests had been cut down, the palace was crumbling, and the weak and nervous little king was entirely in the hands of his Grand Vizier. By then too the Shaiqiya tribes in the Dongola region had revolted, and one after another Shendy and the other riverine states had thrown off their allegiance. After what Crawford has described as 'three centuries of barbaric squalor' the Fung dynasty was worn out and ready for collapse.

As for the western regions of the Sudan, Mohammed Ali also possessed some desultory facts about them. Browne had been to Darfur in 1793, and his book about this journey had

Sennar in the early eighteenth century. From Krump's Hoher und Feuchtbahrer Palm-Baum desz Heiligen Evangelik

come out in 1806. He related that he had sailed up the Nile as far as Assiut, and from there had ridden on camels to the Nuba mountains, where he had been detained, robbed and maltreated by the Arab king, Abd-el-Rahman. Nearly two years had passed before he had been allowed to return to Cairo. Thus he had had ample time to observe the country (he grew so bored with his detention that he devoted himself to bringing up two lions), and was able to produce many fascinating details about the caravan routes, the Darfur markets, and the habits of the local people.

Since that time the French invasion and the civil wars in Egypt had interrupted exploration on the Upper Nile, and only a few adventurers like the invaluable Burckhardt had been able to describe conditions on the river. Yet there were pressing reasons for Mohammed Ali to venture on his expedition; it was not only a question of the gold he hoped to discover, nor of seizing the slaves who were, in Richard Hill's phrase, 'to swell the black army of his dreams'; something had to be done about his huge Albanian bodyguard which had hoisted him into power. By 1820 it was becoming a menace in Egypt, and the Sudanese invasion was an obvious means of diverting its energies.

It remained, however, a very dangerous enterprise, and perhaps the most astonishing part about it was that Mohammed thought that he could carry it through with so small and irregular a force, and without himself ever stirring from Cairo. The command was to be given to his third son Ismail, a young man barely 25 years of age.

Ismail is something of a conundrum in this semi-barbaric world, and we have the most disparate descriptions of him by his contemporaries. None go so far as to compare him with his elder brother Ibrahim, who was a military commander of genius, but Ismail, we are told by more than one observer, was a most intelligent young man, in manners extremely courteous, and by nature generous and kindly. This description hardly squares with his behaviour on the campaign, when he conducted himself more like Genghis Khan than a civilized human being. Nor does it quite fit in with the fact that his father in Cairo more than once sent him messages telling him to act more leniently towards the Sudanese. He was very young, of course, and for that reason all the more prone to violence, and his cleft palate, his high, rapid, almost unintelligible voice, may have been disadvantages that he tried to overcome by an outward show of grandeur. Yet he had a certain adroitness in taking political decisions, and he easily out-manœuvred Waddington and his companion when they wanted something he was not prepared to give. He was reckless, he was high-handed and quick-tempered, and the whole army went in fear of him; yet he never seems to have lost his nerve during the dreadful two years that were all that remained to him of his life, and he was not without a sort of humour. He liked to play chess with his buffoon during the campaign, paying a gold piece for every game he lost, and inflicting twenty blows on the buffoon for every game he won.

Like his elder brother, Ismail had a tremendous respect for his father, and perhaps it was respect that went as far as fear. Never for a moment, even when he is a thousand miles and many months away from Cairo, does he forget that cold, crafty, watching eye in the citadel; never does he neglect to send dispatches or strive, a little pathetically, to win a word of approval. Mohammed Ali was a man who ruled not only empires but his own house as well.

The force that Ismail was to command, and which was to get him twice as far up the Nile as the French had ever been, consisted of no more than four thousand soldiers. One even hesitates to describe them as soldiers at all, for they were as strange a band of desperadoes as ever travelled on the Nile either before or since; indeed, they can have resembled nothing so much as the crowds of extras in some lurid historical spectacle on the films. The Turks and Albanians who comprised more than half the expedition were got up in limp red or green tarbushes, short blue jackets encrusted with gold braid, a cummerbund, billowing pantaloons and red slippers, and each man was followed by a slave and a donkey. Others wore the Evzone uniform – white pleated kilts and long stockings – and the Kurdish cavalrymen, who were mounted on horses padded with arrow-proof mattresses, sported steel breastplates and tall conical hats as well. About a thousand Bedouin were supplied with helmets and chain-mail, and a swarm of hangers-on, who probably brought the total numbers of the force up to ten thousand, dressed as they pleased, though mostly in the loose white robes of the East. Nearly all the men in the expedition were mercenaries hired by the month, but it was probably not their miserable pay that made them enlist: it was the hope of loot and the promise Mohammed gave them that he would pay fifty piastres for every human ear obtained in battle.

The young commander-in-chief of the expedition kept up a state which was quite equal to the flamboyance of his little army. His tent was a magnificent affair made of canvas dyed green, one hundred feet long and surmounted by a large gilt globe, with smaller balls stuck on the top of every tent pole. The interior was lined with tapestries and silk hangings, carpets and cushions were spread upon the floor, and a chandelier of glass oil-lamps was suspended from the roof. All this paraphernalia was transported up the Nile, and as the march went on Ismail was to be found each day in his great tent, seated cross-legged on a divan, and attended by his bodyguard, his senior captains, his Greek and Italian secretaries and surgeons and his buffoon.

The general plan of the campaign was quite simple: the force was to move upstream in two echelons, Ismail to lead the way and to advance directly to Sennar and the Ethiopian border, while his brother-in-law, Mohammed Bey, who was known as the Defterdar, was to follow on and strike further west into Kordofan. The general objectives were precise: Mohammed Ali wanted slaves – at least forty thousand of them – and as much gold and other precious metals as the force could lay hands on.

A good deal of our knowledge of the campaign comes from three Western witnesses who described their experiences, and it is worth pausing here for a moment to identify them, for they were an odd group, almost as odd as the little army itself. George Waddington, a fellow of Trinity College, Cambridge, was aged 27 at this time, and he came to Egypt just as haphazardly as Legh and Smelt had come eight years before. While on a tour of Europe he happened to meet the Reverend Barnard Hanbury, of Jesus College, in Venice in 1820, and was persuaded by him to go on 'an antiquarian visit' to the Upper Nile. They arrived in Cairo in August of that year, and were received by Mohammed Ali, who gave them permission to follow the army into Upper Egypt. Dressed as Turks, and accompanied by a young Irishman named James Curtin, two Maltese and a setter dog which they christened Anubis (after the dog- or jackal-headed Egyptian god), they ascended the river as far

as Merowe, where Ismail, who had no use for foreign observers, politely sent them back.

Waddington was destined to end a long life as a church historian, and as dean and then warden of Durham University, and was perhaps not ideally suited to describe a brutal filibustering expedition on the Nile. He was scholarly, dilettante, elegant, a mighty indulger in his own prejudices, and often inaccurate. He greatly admired Burckhardt, but himself lived in a donnish cocoon which enabled him to observe the world comfortably at second-hand. Nevertheless, he gave a polished and amusing account of his experiences, and he could write poetically about such things as the mirages which the Arabs called 'the lakes of gazelles' because of the large herds then grazing in the desert. These mirages, Waddington says, really did seem to be 'haunted by the antelope, as if she loved the banks of that fairy sea, and delighted to chase or graze upon its fugitive waters'.

At Merowe Waddington met a very strange character indeed, and, as a devout and uncompromising churchman, detested him on sight. This was George Bethune English, an American who had been born thirty-three years before in Cambridge, Massachusetts, and who had been educated at Harvard. English had begun his career as a minister of religion, had switched to the editorship of a newspaper, and a year or two before this had obtained, through the influence of John Quincy Adams, a commission in the United States marines. He was a man of distinguished and grave appearance and a good linguist, but he was given to sudden and dramatic decisions. Early in 1820 his ship had put into Alexandria while on a Mediterranean cruise, and at once the East had swallowed him up. He resigned from the United States navy, became a convert to Islam, and entered Mohammed Ali's service under the name of Mohammed Effendi. This move was not wise, and was to end in recriminations and his departure for Constantinople, where he subsequently became an agent of the United States government.

For the moment, however, English was a man with a mission: Ismail put him in charge of the expedition's artillery – ten light field guns, a mortar and two howitzers, and a loose assortment of 300 native gunners – and with these he eventually got as far as Sennar. He had as his second-in-command of artillery another American, a man named Bradish, whose name can be seen now cut into the altar in the inner sanctuary at Abu Simbel. Little else is known of him. Waddington in his description of their meeting at Merowe calls English 'a renegade', and was forced to apologize later on; and indeed it was unfair, because English really did believe in his apostasy and served Ismail well. He, too, in the book he wrote had his poetic moments; he speaks of Arab stallions that 'tossed their flowing manes aloft higher than the heads of their turbaned riders, and a man might have placed his two fists in their expanded nostrils', and on the whole he is a closer though duller observer than Waddington.

Then there was a third traveller, French by birth, whom one can only describe as a one-man *Institut de France*. Frédéric Cailliaud has resemblances to Denon. He is the intellectual fox-terrier, tireless, excited, expostulatory, brave, endlessly interested in everything. No hardship and no rebuff can damp his overwhelming curiosity. Temples, battles, Shendy market and the slave trade, languages and religions, wild life and gold mines, the Nile itself – with a meticulous zest he absorbs them all, and of the three Western accounts of the campaign his is incomparably the best.

George Waddington. Painting by Frederick Richard Say

Cailliaud was born in Nantes in 1787, the son of a jeweller and watchmaker, and already at the time of the campaign had been in Egypt for some time. Five years before Mohammed Ali had sent him off as a geologist to look for emeralds on the Red Sea coast, and in a series of other adventurous journeys he had visited nearly all the great Egyptian oases and had actually succeeded in forcing his way into the temple of Abu Simbel shortly after Burck-hardt (whom he also greatly respected) had been there. Like Waddington he was not welcomed by Ismail when he first presented himself at Aswan, and was bundled off down the river again. Back in Cairo he knew how to soften Mohammed Ali's heart – he offered to prospect for gold mines in the Sudan – and with two European companions he managed to catch up with the expedition again not far from Berber. This time Ismail let him continue to the Ethiopian border. On the way up the river near Wadi Halfa Cailliaud had fallen in with Waddington, who had not failed to be almost as offensive to him as he had been to English. Waddington says airily in his book that Cailliaud and his companions 'were both in the Turkish dress, and most cautiously defended from sand and sun by long Muslim shades projecting before their eyes. We merely exchanged a few words of civility in passing, and proceeded on our respective destinations with as much indifference as if we had met in the park or on the boulevards.' Cailliaud, who was burning for information about the antiquities in the Sudan, especially at Meroë, gives a different account. He says he questioned Waddington on the matter but Waddington would tell him nothing.

Here then we have our three Western eye-witnesses, British, American and French, all

The cataract at Absyr. From Cailliaud's Voyage à Méroé

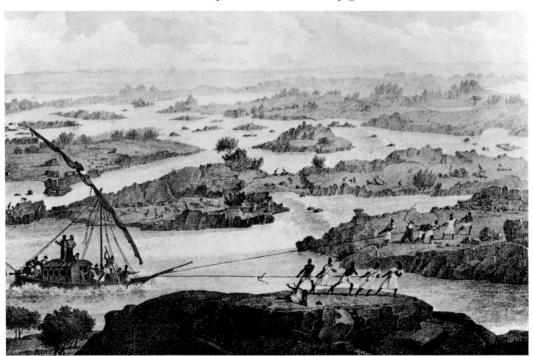

heartily disliking one another (Cailliaud never even mentions English), all rather under suspicion from the Turks, all suffering varying degrees of ill-health and hardship, and all – as it so happened – absent from the only battle that counted in the campaign. Fortunately, however, there are Turkish sources as well, and by putting all together one can arrive at a fairly coherent understanding of a campaign that lacked all coherence and was colonial warfare at its worst.

By the summer of 1820 all was ready. Some hundreds of boats were assembled at Bulaq, and all through July and August a long disorderly procession of men, animals and arms made its way up the river to Aswan. At every stage of the advance the heat was appalling.

Above Aswan the boats were dragged with immense labour up the first cataract into Nubia, and by September most of the force was assembled at Wadi Halfa. Here there was a further delay while they tackled the second cataract, but by the end of October they were through it. Up to this point there had been no opposition. The Nubians had collapsed, and the Mamelukes had fled from Dongola and had taken refuge at Shendy. But now, as they rounded the bend of the Nile near Korti, they were in the Shaiqiya country and the tribesmen came out to do battle.

Ismail attempted to negotiate. He induced a deputation of Shaiqiya sheikhs and imams to come to his camp, and he told them that it was his father's desire that henceforth they should become cultivators; if they would surrender their arms and horses he would impose only a light tribute. According to English the dialogue ran as follows:

Ismail Pasha's camp at Singa. From Cailliaud's Voyage à Méroé

The Shaiqiya: Why are we being invaded?
Ismail: Because you are robbers.
Shaiqiya: We have no other means of livelihood.
Ismail: You should cultivate the land.
Shaiqiya: We have been born and bred to what you call robbery, and we will not work.
Ismail: Then I'll make you.
Upon this the negotiations broke up, and Ismail sent off a party of 100 Bedouin horsemen

A Shoa warrior. From a drawing by P. Blanchard

to reconnoitre the enemy territory. They were at once engaged, and only twenty-five of them were able to fight their way back to the Turkish lines. On the night of November 3 both armies were encamped on a wide plain on the west bank of the river a little above Korti, and the Shaiqiya made the fatal mistake of not attacking in the darkness when their spears and swords would have been just as effective as firearms. The encounter that ensued on November 4 was a pathetic affair and might be dismissed, like the rest of this monstrous raid, as merely another massacre of defenceless tribesmen, were it not for the fact that this action, like the Battle of the Pyramids, was followed by immense consequences. It was the end of an era on the Upper Nile; it decided, as Professor Dodwell says, the fate of the Sudan for the next hundred years.

A young girl, Miheira bint Abud, mounted on a gorgeously caparisoned camel, gave the Shaiqiya the signal to attack – that warbling cry, *lilli-lilli-loo* – and then a horde of unarmed peasants came running down on the Turks in a cloud of dust. They had been assured by a religious fanatic that bullets could not kill true believers, and they carried ropes with which they hoped to bind the Turks they captured. Behind came the Shaiqiya cavalry, about a thousand of them in all, accompanied by a roll of drums and uttering their sardonic war-cry *Salaam aleikum* as they charged. Incredibly they did make a little headway at first, since they were better swordsmen than the Turks, but then the Turks took to their guns and pistols and before nightfall it was all over. About eight hundred men, mostly peasants,

The mountains and ruins of Jebel Barkal. In the foreground to the left can be seen a young woman, reputed to be Safia, being brought before Ismail Pasha, who is on the right. From Cailliaud's Voyage à Méroé

were left lying on the field, with the Turks running among them cutting off their ears. Waddington, arriving after the battle was over, says that the expression on the faces of the dead warriors was one of anger rather than terror, and some were smiling. That night the inhabitants of Korti were massacred by the Turks, and the town was destroyed by fire. Some three thousand human ears were sent to Cairo and they were taken from the living as well as from the dead.

The Battle of Korti was followed a month later by a second encounter on the other side of the river at Jebel Dager, where once again the Shaiqiya were annihilated by guns. This time they were led by Safia, the daughter of one of the leading Shaiqiya chiefs, and she was taken prisoner. Ismail behaved very shrewdly. He had her washed, perfumed and splendidly dressed, and then sent her back to her father. Waddington, describing the incident, says,

'As soon as the chief recognized his daughter and saw how she had been honoured, "All this is well," he said with impatience, "but are you still a virgin?" She assured him she was, and when he had ascertained the truth of this, he withdrew his troops, and swore that he would not fight against the man who had spared the virginity of his daughter . . . this little anecdote was generally spoken of and made a great noise in both armies.'

Whether or not the actual event was as dramatic as Waddington says, it is certainly a fact that this was the end of all organized resistance in the Sudan for the time being. If there had ever been a hope of the different tribes and river settlements combining against Ismail, it was gone now. One after another the Shaiqiya chiefs came in to surrender and to enlist in Ismail's ranks, and in February 1821 the advance was resumed, one half of the column continuing along the river and the other making directly across the desert towards Berber. English tells us that for the most part the marches were made at night to the beat of kettledrums, the soldiers following a route that had been laid out for them by an advance guard who lit fires and sent up rockets along the way. But it was a straggling and disorderly advance. Sentries were not posted at night, little pockets of men turned aside to loot villages or simply scattered themselves over the open desert; and the boats were abandoned at the fourth cataract to await the next annual flood. 'Ismail,' Crawford says, 'had "divided and conquered" in a new way. Every one of these detachments could have been cold meat for an enterprising and mobile force, which could have annihilated each in turn with the utmost ease, operating from Shendy or Berber; but the Shaiqiya had emasculated and estranged those once warlike states, to which the Turks came in the role of deliverers from Shaiqiya oppression, and nothing was attempted . . . and now they could gloat on the prospect of an orgy of killing, ear-cutting, looting, burning and rape as good as, or perhaps even better than that they had indulged in at the expense of the Shaiqiya.'

Early in March 1821 they reached Berber. The little town, once so confident with its beer shops and its debauchery, collapsed at once, and on March 12 Ismail had word that Mek Nimr of Shendy, 'the Leopard' himself, was coming in to surrender. Nimr arrived a few days later, seated on a palanquin between two camels, and bringing with him a gift of two fine horses. In the great green tent he prostrated himself before Ismail, kissing his foot and placing it on his head. Ismail, foolishly and arrogantly, was a little distant with him, since he thought that Shendy should have been surrendered much sooner. The interview lasted only ten minutes and Nimr was not offered the customary coffee and pipe until he was outside the tent. Soon after this about a hundred of the Mamelukes came in to offer their submission, and were added to Ismail's bodyguard.

Cailliaud now seized his chance of indulging in his passion for antiquities, for they had reached a region which had been a matter of archaeological speculation since Herodotus' day, and neglected ruins were to be found at every vantage point on the river. When Cailliaud writes about these places he is fascinating. In his account of his journey through this part of the Sudan he gives a shape and a perspective to the history of the Nile that not even Burckhardt was able to surpass. One begins to see through his eyes the great down-slide of civilization on the Upper Nile. Everywhere from Aswan upstream he discovers, in the sand-filled temples, arts that had long since been forgotten, traces of civilizations that had become utterly submerged by the general decline into barbarity. By 1821 the population had dwindled almost to nothing, and where once there had been great cities and palaces with fleets of 200-foot galleys on the river, there now existed precious little but mud-huts and crude rafts, and the use of the sail had been forgotten.

Sic transit gloria mundi – it was a wonderful text, and Cailliaud, in the prevailing mood of the early nineteenth century, exploits it with romantic ardour. One night, he relates, when he was far down the river at a place called Gournah, he had set up his camp in a painted tomb. But it was too hot to sleep, and in the middle of the night he lit a lamp and began to study the paintings on the walls. There were scenes of a Pharaoh and his wife and daughter fishing in the Nile; the sky was brilliant blue, the banks of the river were covered with flowers. Then on another wall he found a funeral procession: the despairing wife and daughter were shown following the body of the Pharaoh on his sacred boat to the door of the very chamber where Cailliaud himself had been sleeping. All had been order, dignity and civilization in that other age. To leave the tomb was like coming out of a theatre into the harsh light of day, out of a glorious past into a squalid present. Cailliaud was overcome with a philosophic melancholy.

Now at Berber he was within sight of the greatest goal of all, the ruins of Meroë, which in ancient times had been the capital of the Sudan and of most of Egypt as well. With the exception of Bruce and Burckhardt who had made only passing references to the place, no one had described the ruins for a thousand years at least, and there was even some doubt at this time as to whether or not they really existed. Cailliaud had read everything he could about Meroë, dreamed of it, schemed to get there (he had to pretend to Ismail that he was searching for diamonds), and finally in a transport of excitement he reached it. Using Bruce's map, he and his companion Leztorec went on ahead of the army, and they arrived at Meroë at dawn on April 25, just in time to see the first rays of the sun gilding the tops of scores of stepped pyramids. Most of them were in a state of crumbling ruin, and in size they were nothing to be compared to those at Gizeh or even at Sakkara. But it was the same effect of grandeur, the same attempt to create, in Professor Stevenson Smith's words, 'a gigantic staircase to the heavens', and Cailliaud, beside himself with a discoverer's joy, climbed the highest he could see and there carved the name of the French geographer d'Anville who had mapped the Nile – a tribute that can still be seen on the pyramid today. He and Leztorec spent a fortnight in fearful heat, drawing the inscriptions on the tombs and the plump, lordly figures of the kings and queens, who were so different in their *embonpoint* from the thin and graceful Pharaohs of Egypt. The maps and drawings Cailliaud prepared (and he was a careful man) became the basis for all subsequent archaeology at Meroë.

The campaign now resolved itself into what it was originally intended to be, a slave-raiding expedition. Those prisoners Ismail could not enslave he butchered, and his soldiers, throwing off all control, looted and destroyed every village in their line of march. On May 24, 1821, the army reached Halfaya, at the junction of the Blue and White Niles, and Ismail gave orders for the soldiers to cross the White Nile roughly at the point where the modern bridge has since been constructed. It took them three days to get across, either by hanging on to their horses' tails or using improvised rafts, and 30 men and 150 camels were drowned.

OVERLEAF *Cailliaud's drawing of himself in Turkish dress, sketching a fallen colossus on Tombos Island. From his* Voyage à Méroé

Now at last Ismail heard the truth about Sennar. Nothing had happened to rejuvenate the place since Bruce's day. Its great empire had become a myth, and in fact at the news of the approach of the Egyptian army civil war had broken out. He gave orders for an immediate advance on the town.

At Halfaya Cailliaud obtained a boat, and in it he sailed up the Blue Nile to Sennar, reflecting pleasantly that this was probably the first time that a sail had been seen on the river since Pharaonic times. His notes on the country will be recognized at once as authentic by anyone who makes this journey today. Then, as now, groves of acacias and reeds lined the banks, and as the traveller penetrated upstream into the rain forest he found himself in a pristine world of brilliant birds and flowers. There were more wild animals to be seen then; Cailliaud speaks of many hippopotamuses, of monkeys, hyenas and giraffes, and of the

Sennar in 1821. From a drawing by Linant de Bellefonds

fresh tracks of elephants. Ostriches were fairly plentiful, and the natives hunted them down with dogs. The sacred black and white ibis, long since driven out of Egypt, reappeared, and gay green parrots followed him all the way among a galaxy of other birds. He took a clutch of crocodile eggs and made precise notes on the foot-long hissing little monsters which emerged from the shell and headed by instinct for the river.

When he reached Sennar in the middle of June Ismail had already arrived. Not a shot had been fired. Badi, the last of the Fung kings, had himself come out of the town to surrender and offer gifts of horses and their trappings to the conquerors. Ismail had served coffee, had presented Badi with a somewhat unsuitable fur-lined cloak, and on June 14 had led his rabble into the town, where they began their usual lootings and reprisals, including one particularly horrible impalement.

A victory parade in honour of Ismail was held a few days later, but it was a pathetic affair compared with the great festivals which Poncet had seen in 1699. Badi, who had been reinstated by Ismail as the nominal ruler, seemed to Cailliaud to be an extremely limited little man who was stunned by what had happened: he was intrigued by Cailliaud's gift of a box of matches. His palace and the mosque, the only two buildings of any consequence in Sennar, were tumbling down, and the remains of the forests outside the town had been demolished by goats. As for the inhabitants, Cailliaud found them a dowdy lot, especially the women, who were much given to smoking and beer-drinking. Their hair was still piled up on their heads in an infinity of little plaits, but the silver and the splendid robes were lacking, and the young girls wore nothing at all but a fringe of leather trimmed with cowrie shells, a sign of virginity. Of the famous 'Black Horse' of Bruce's day there was no sign at all, and Sennar's last armament, four rusty antique cannon, had been flung into the Blue Nile in order to appease the Turks. As Crawford says, 'the long-drawn-out death agony of the Kingdom of Sennar was finished'.

Up to this point – and he was now 2,000 miles from the sea – Ismail's passage had been fantastically easy, so easy indeed that there is an air of unreality about it. His little band of marauding soldiers do not really have the appearance of conquerors. They crawl across an immense landscape that is much too big for them, and the Nile, one feels, was not to be so effortlessly won as this; one expects Ismail to be swallowed up in these wastes in the manner of Cambyses and his army over two thousand years before. And in fact it was the Nile, or at any rate the climate of the Nile, that was Ismail's real enemy now. In June, soon after he had settled into Sennar, he said to Cailliaud that Bruce (whose account of the town he had read) was a liar: the climate of Sennar was very bearable. In July, when the rain arrived, he changed his tune. Malaria and dysentery swept through the little army. There were no medicines and no qualified doctors. By the end of September 600 of his men were dead; by mid-October, when he was still unable to move because of mud, only 500 were fit for active service and these, being half-starved, were threatening mutiny. As for gold, none had been found, and only a trickle of slaves had been sent down to Cairo.

The arrival of Ismail's elder brother Ibrahim was just in time to prevent disaster. Ibrahim himself was ill with dysentery, but he managed to reorganize the expedition, and by the beginning of December, in cooler drier weather, the army was ready to go on again. They headed south on the Blue Nile, Ismail taking the right bank and Ibrahim the left, and the objects were the same as before: gold and slaves.

All such raids on the Nile have a brutal similarity, and the events of the next three months are interesting only so far as they reveal this then unknown part of the river. They entered now for the first time the territory of the Negroes, of the Dinkas, Shilluks and Nuers, who with their immensely long legs stood like storks in the swamps, and of other tribes so primitive that they smeared their bodies with red ochre and displayed, as their only adornment, great self-inflicted weals on their faces, breasts, backs and arms.

Frazer was to write later on in *The Golden Bough* of the legend of the prehistoric priest-kings of Nemi, in Italy, who prowled about by night with a drawn sword, knowing that sooner or later they were destined to be destroyed in single combat by an enemy who in his turn would rule and be murdered in the same way. Such kings actually existed here on the White Nile, close to the junction with the Blue. And there were other pagan tribes who, like the ancient Egyptians before them, worshipped the sun and the moon and who even made sacrifices to the baobab tree.

On the raid south of Sennar to the Ethiopian border, Cailliaud was the only European

Ismail's army encamped on the shores of the Blue Nile at Agady. From Cailliaud's Voyage à Méroé

left with the expedition, and he dined with Ismail every night, listening to his endless speculations about the gold they were to discover in the fabulous mines at Fazughli. '*Cette soif de l'or,*' Cailliaud writes, '*était le principal mobile qui poussait ce prince en avant.*' They followed the line of the Blue Nile past Roseires, rounding up without pity every Negro they could lay hands on, and when the villagers tried to fight back – shooting off their arrows and rolling boulders down from the heights – they were obliterated. Cailliaud grew sickened with the massacre, but he stayed on hoping that in the end he would be given a chance of exploring the White Nile, which he believed, quite rightly, would lead on to the true source of the river.

On the first day of the new year, 1822, the army beheld a marvellous sight: foothills and rocky outcrops appeared on the flat plain, and beyond them the beginnings of the great mountains of Ethiopia rose up. Ismail called a halt. Even if he had wanted to go on – and there was a sinister quality in the mountains for men who had lived all their lives in the desert – it was soon discovered that the Blue Nile here vanished into an enormous gorge which was impassable even to men on foot. At Fazughli, where the local king hurried to prostrate himself before Ismail and the power of his frightful guns, Cailliaud threw himself into the business of acquiring gold. The famous mines, however, proved to be another disappointment, and several weeks of hard prospecting in the hills yielded nothing more than a few yellow grains washed down from the mountains. The villagers were well aware of the value of gold; they stored it in the quills of vultures' feathers and used it for money, but the quantity was pitifully small.

Nor was the slave hunt much more successful. Of the total of some thirty thousand sent down the river it was estimated that only fifteen thousand got through to Cairo, and many of these were women and children. Death by sickness, ill-treatment and fatigue claimed the others on the road.

Crossing over to the camp of the other branch of the expedition, Cailliaud found Ibrahim broken in health and on the point of returning to Egypt with his Italian doctor, a certain Ricci, who was promised 10,000 dollars if he got Ibrahim to Cairo alive. He did this in the remarkable time of thirty-six days, and was paid. In mid-February, 1822, Ismail also turned back and settled again at Sennar.

The hatred of the Turks along the river was now intense. Everywhere their name was a byword for brutality and heartlessness, and Ismail, enduring another wet season at Sennar, surrounded once again by sickness, sent messages to Mohammed Ali asking for permission to return. Apart from terrorizing the Sudan he had really accomplished very little, and Mohammed Ali's repeated requests for more and more slaves must have added to the young man's frustration and restless irritation. Two years of campaigning had exhausted his mind as well as his body. It is also not inconceivable that Ismail, having killed and uprooted so many helpless people, may have had a premonition that retribution might overtake him if he remained too long in the Sudan. At last in October 1822 Mohammed Ali sent him a message telling him to come back, and Ismail set off at once. Late that same month he reached Shendy on his way down the river.

Here he sent for Mek Nimr, that same proud, reserved chieftain whom he had humiliated eighteen months before, and he made impossible demands: 30,000 dollars in cash, 6,000 slaves, and a mass of general stores were to be delivered within forty-eight hours.

There are several versions of the drama that followed, but the general theme seems clear enough. When Nimr declared that the demands were impossible – already the country was facing the prospect of famine – Ismail struck him across the face with his long wooden pipe. Nimr drew his sword but was at once overwhelmed by Ismail's Mameluke bodyguard and was forced to apologize and withdraw.

That night a banquet with a native dance was arranged, and while it was in progress Nimr and his men set fire to Ismail's house. Those Turks who rushed out were instantly cut down. Ismail remained trapped indoors, and died either by suffocation or by burning. It was said that he had been warned of this attempt, and had refused to believe that Nimr would act. But it was not only Nimr who had been provoked to a passion for revenge; 'the killing', as Richard Hill says, 'set the Nile valley afire'. In every village where Turks were quartered the Sudanese rose up against them, a futile protest, for they could never hope to win against firearms or escape Mohammed Ali's fury at the death of his son. It was the end of all freedom in the Sudan, the final breaking of its fragile isolation, and even now one can hardly tolerate the story of the Turks' savage reprisals.

The work of massacre was entrusted to the Defterdar, Mohammed Bey, who had been out raiding in Kordofan as far as El Obeid. The town of Metemma was first sacked and burnt, and then it was the turn of Damer and all the other settlements along the Nile from Berber to Sennar. The people in Shendy erected mud walls around the town and managed to hold out for a little, but finally their houses took fire and the Turks rushed in with the sword. Nimr at the last moment managed to get away with his family, and Mohammed Bey pursued him up the Blue Nile, leaving an appalling trail of atrocities in his wake. All male prisoners he took were emasculated and the breasts of their women were cut off; the wounds being filled with boiling pitch to prevent the victims dying at once. Nimr at last took refuge with the Ethiopians, and the Defterdar, unable to follow him into the unexplored mountains, turned back through Kassala to Omdurman. By the end of 1823 he could fairly say that the Sudan was subdued, and that all the valley of the Nile from the Ethiopian mountains to the sea was in Mohammed Ali's hands. Some fifty thousand Sudanese had been killed in the process. It was the peace of death along the river.

A Shoa warrior

13

A Thought Threading a Dream

The Nile was now revealed as far as the Ethiopian border, but vast areas of the Sudan remained ungoverned and unknown, Ethiopia was still intact and the ultimate source of the river was still a mystery. From the 1820s onward there was a slow but persistent penetration into these empty spaces. After Ismail's death a succession of Turkish governor-generals came up from Cairo, and although they were the worst of colonizers and explorers they extended their grip on the Sudan with a predatory tenacity. They educated nobody except as a convenience, they thought nothing of the ancient monuments except as a useful store of building materials, they explored merely to destroy, and their government was directed towards one single end: to mulct the country of all the money, cattle and human beings they could lay hands on. Flogging, blowing from guns, impalement – these were the normal punishments for anyone who opposed them, and every governor-general was judged by the success of his slave-raids and military expeditions.

One marvels how any human beings could have survived such harsh treatment, but the Sudan was vast, the pressure was not continuous, and if the Turks were destructive they also had a talent for administration. Then too, the Moslem religion was a steady and coherent influence, and through the early years of their rule at least the Turks were not demoralized by the enervating climate of the Upper Nile. They were very active.

In 1824 they moved their headquarters from Omdurman across the river to a fishing village on the promontory of land formed by the confluence of the two Niles – an area known to the local Arabs as El Khartoum from its supposed resemblance to an elephant's trunk. It was a wise decision, for Khartoum lay fairly centrally in the Sudan astride the main caravan route to Cairo, and from this point they could take their boats on both Niles to the south. The young city, with its mud-hut buildings and narrow dirty streets, was hardly a very impressive capital – vile, squalid, filthy, are the usual epithets bestowed upon it by early travellers – but it was at least an outpost of civilization where both European and Eastern wares could be bought, and its population soon rose to thirty thousand. Other garrisons were established at Kassala on the Ethiopian border, Wad Medani on the Blue Nile, El Obeid in Kordofan and on the Red Sea, and by the 1830s the Turks had a chain of forts reaching all the way down the main Nile to Cairo.

'The White Nile,' Crawford says, 'was virtually a cul-de-sac ending at El Ais (about one hundred and eighty miles south of Khartoum) beyond which lay the savage realm of the Nilotic tribes. It led nowhere, was of relatively little importance, and therefore was little spoken of or known; whereas the Blue Nile was a thoroughfare throughout history.' In 1839, however, the Turks decided to investigate the White Nile. An expedition (to which the

Royal Geographical Society in London contributed fifty pounds) was dispatched by boat from Khartoum, and got as far as Bor, on the sixth parallel, where it was blocked by the vegetation in the swamps of the Sudd. In 1840 and 1841 two further expeditions were sent and got a little further to Gondokoro, in the vicinity of the modern town of Juba, but here they were baulked by cataracts. Another twenty years were to elapse before explorers were able to penetrate into the unknown country that lay beyond. Meanwhile the main Turkish effort was concentrated upon the Blue Nile and the great stretch of savanna between the river, the Ethiopian mountains and the Red Sea. Mek Nimr was still holding out in the Ethiopian foothills, and as late as 1846 Mansfield Parkyns, the English traveller, met him there. Nimr, Parkyns says, had a great reputation as a brigand and a cut-throat, but the old man was now blind and feeble. He welcomed Parkyns very hospitably to his camp, and he seemed to be, Parkyns says, 'a good-natured old grand-dad with a bald pate and a comfortable rotundity'. He was rather anxious to re-establish his good name, and he felt homesick for Shendy, but the Turks, he knew, would never allow him back. And so he fought feebly on. It was a sad end to the Leopard King, but still he had about him something of black Africa's instinctive defiance of the West.

A dinner party at Aduwa. From Parkyns' Life in Abyssinia

In 1838 Mohammed Ali, aged 69, visited the Sudan for the first time, bringing with him a large party which included a number of European engineers. The old tyrant, now the ruler of an empire which his son Ibrahim had pushed to the Euphrates, was full of projects: he wanted to clear the Nile cataracts, build a railway and a telegraph to Khartoum, and establish cotton and indigo growing in the land between the two Niles. Like Bonaparte in Egypt he had to leave it to his successors to carry through these excellent plans. From Khartoum Mohammed travelled up the Blue Nile to Fazughli, still dreaming of the conquest of Ethiopia perhaps, and certainly still dreaming of gold, but after four months in the country he departed for Cairo, never to return. Ten years of increasing weakness and, eventually, imbecility, were all that were left to Mohammed of his life, but he survived by nearly three decades his great mentor, Bonaparte, and a part at least of his empire was to prove more durable than all the conquests of the French.

In 1826 Cailliaud, who had returned to his native Nantes to become Keeper of the Natural History Museum there, published his *Voyage à Méroé*, with a folio of drawings. It was the first serious study of Sudanese antiquities to be made, and it stimulated a new band of European adventurers to follow him up the Nile. It is from these people that we

Linesmen of the Oriental Telegraph Company on the road to Suez

get the best picture of the river through these years, for they were an unusual group of men, ivory traders, scientists, sportsmen out for big game, soldiers and casual tourists, and they surveyed the scene from very different points of view.

There were the Mellys, for instance. George Melly went even a step further than his predecessors in the casual approach by taking with him his father and mother, and his brother and sister. He claims, probably quite rightly, that the ladies in his party were the first ever to visit Khartoum (this was in 1850), and he writes in a pleasant, intimate, privileged way as though they were all on a jaunt to Brighton. From him we learn what Philae looked like in those days when there was no dam to cover it (a scene which, incidentally, was beautifully and brilliantly drawn by Edward Lear a few years later), and of how then one crawled through a four-foot hole in the sand to reach the interior of the great temple at Abu Simbel. Climbing like Burckhardt to the head of one of the colossi, Melly stood on the lip and found he could not reach the eyebrows. He speaks with some annoyance of the way travellers on the Nile carved their names on these ancient monuments – and lost no time in adding his own. Khartoum, he says, had about three thousand houses in 1850, and most European luxuries could be purchased in the bazaar. There was a Roman Catholic Mission in the town, and the governor-general, Latif Pasha, kept a most elaborate household among gardens on the river bank.

The slave trade was now starting to reach its peak in the Sudan, and Melly gives a decidedly complacent account of it. 'Just before reaching the boats [near Aswan],' he says, 'we came upon a large party of female slaves on their way down to Cairo, where, in the lottery of the slave market, they were to pass to new masters. . . . They were nearly all young girls, varying in age from twelve to sixteen, and a merrier set could not be met with. The woods rang with their pleasant laughter; and one might have thought – what perhaps was not very far from the truth – that in place of now entering a house of bondage, they had left it behind in their own country. Their masters, from all we could learn, were universally kind to them; and wherever we encountered a party, we found that the girls were much attached to the head of their caravan. The bevy we now saw was from Abyssinia – whence, indeed, most of the female slaves are drawn – and was destined, as the Abyssinian girls usually are, for the Turkish harems, or as wives of shop-keepers and affluent Arabs.

'Their colour was a glossy black; they were exceedingly well made, and had bright cheerful faces, lit up by sparkling black eyes. They all seemed very shy, and could not be induced to come out of their huts, or even to let us approach them. There was but one who showed more confidence, a very fine young woman, apparently about twenty-five years of age, who brought out her baby, a most beautiful child, almost a Murillo in colour, and exquisitely formed. We offered to purchase it, but, though she seemed flattered, the mother's heart clung to her child, and she would not be tempted to part with it. We gave her some money for grease, which had an immediate effect on her spirits, making her as blithe as a bird, and then left her, the envy of the whole sisterhood.'

Having described this idyllic scene, Melly goes so far as to admit that the male slaves he saw being marched down from the Sudan showed signs of great exhaustion, and that the Nubians, rather than be conscripted in the Turkish army, often mutilated themselves by putting out an eye or cutting off a hand. It was a hard world, and it could be hard on the visiting tourist too. Melly's father died during the awful desert crossing from Berber to Aswan.

Flaubert's appearance on the Upper Nile in 1850 was an even more unlikely event. Drawn apparently by a romantic vision of the East, he ascended the river as far as Wadi Halfa with Maxime du Camp, the French journalist and photographer. In his letters Flaubert, then aged 29, reveals very little interest in the antiquities ('I generally think of nothing at all, despite the elevated thoughts one is supposed to have in the presence of ruins'), but the people captivated him, and Egypt fulfilled all his expectations 'so excel-

Drawing of Gustave Flaubert when young by Delaunay. Maxime du Camp, a photograph by Nadar

lently', he says, 'that it is often as though I were suddenly coming upon old and forgotten dreams'. There had been other European artists and writers on the Nile before this, but none so responsive, none so well able to communicate his feelings. It is a curious mixture of voluptuousness and fastidiousness that Flaubert describes. In Cairo he debates religion with the Coptic bishop and visits the Turkish bath where he watches 'the daylight fade through the great glass bulls-eyes in the dome'; and where he finds it 'sweetly melancholy to take a bath like that quite alone, lost in those dark rooms where the slightest noise resounds like a cannon shot, while the naked Kellaks call out to one another while they massage you, turning you over like embalmers preparing you for the tomb.'

In Nubia he reads the *Odyssey* in Greek while the boatmen chant on deck, and he watches 'everything that goes by: camels, herds of oxen from Sennar, boats floating down to Cairo laden with Negresses and elephants' tusks'. Writing of the performances of the male dancers he says, 'It is too beautiful to be exciting. I doubt whether we shall find the women as beautiful as the men; the ugliness of the latter adds greatly to the thing as Art. I had a headache for the rest of the day.'

At Esna he visited a celebrated courtesan named Kuchiouk Hanem, and the letter he wrote about it to Louis Bouilhet is a remarkable evocation of the gaudy squalor and the sensual excitement that reconciled the Turks to life on the Upper Nile. The woman, he says, 'was just leaving her bath. She wore a large tarboosh topped with gold and green and with a tassel falling to her shoulders; her front hair was braided in thin braids that were drawn back and tied together; the lower part of her body was hidden in immense pink trousers; her torso was entirely naked under purple gauze. She was standing at the top of her staircase silhouetted against the blue background of the surrounding sky. She is a regal-looking creature, large-breasted, fleshy, with slit nostrils, enormous eyes, and magnificent

Dancing girls. From David Roberts' Egypt and Nubia

knees; when she danced there were formidable folds of flesh on her stomach. She began by perfuming our hands with rose water. Her bosom gave off a smell of sweetened turpentine, and on it she wore a three-strand golden necklace. Musicians were summoned and she danced. . . .

'When it was time to leave I did not go. Kuchiouk was not eager to have us spend the night with her, out of fear of thieves who are apt to come when they know strangers are there. Maxime stayed alone on the divan, and I went downstairs with Kuchiouk to her room. A wick was burning in an antique-style lamp hanging on the wall. In the adjoining room guards were talking in a low voice with a serving woman, an Abyssinian Negress whose arms were scarred by plague-sores. Kuchiouk's little dog was sleeping on my silk jacket. Her body was very sweaty; she was tired from dancing, and cold. I covered her with my fur coat and she fell asleep. As for myself, I didn't close an eye. Throughout the night I had experiences of a dream-like intensity. . . .'

Some echo from these letters no doubt reached the dreaming mind of Pierre Loti when he too was on the Nile half a century later, and protesting against the submerging of Philae under a new dam.

A myth was growing up about the Nile, a fantasy embellished with ancient temples and ferocious animals, with harems and savage tribes, with jewels and manuscripts lost in the arid sand. This was a new kind of decline and fall, where the sophisticated past was overwhelmed by the primitive present, and the great river, flowing out of nowhere, upon which one now so pleasantly sailed in a dahabeeyah, carried one back and back towards the mysterious origin of things. These were the years when Shelley could write of the truncated

Nubian women. From David Roberts' Egypt and Nubia

statue of Ozymandias, king of kings:

> *Nothing beside remains. Round the decay*
> *Of that colossal wreck, boundless and bare*
> *The lone and level sands stretch far away;*

when Keats could apostrophize the Nile:

> *Son of the old moon-mountains African!*
> *Chief of the Pyramid and Crocodile!*

and Leigh Hunt could write:

> *It flows through old hushed Egypt and its sands,*
> *Like some grave mighty thought threading a dream.*

In the early 1860s Lady Duff Gordon came to live on the Upper Nile in the vain hope of curing her consumption, and she more than any other European since Lane grew into the

OVERLEAF *The entrance to the temple at Luxor. From David Roberts'* Egypt and Nubia

lives of the ordinary people on the river; loving them she understood them. Already by then Luxor had become an English watering place, with as many as eight or nine houseboats tied up on the bank, and a steamer from Cairo called every fortnight during the winter months. A trade in bogus antiques was flourishing, and white-robed guides hovered like ghouls round the ruins. Lady Duff Gordon, observing this scene with the detachment and sympathy of someone approaching her own death, learned things the tourist never knew. She studied Arabic, she sat with the sheikhs and the imams at their ceremonies, and acted as physician to the fellaheen; and never for a moment was she anything but English. When

Luxor from the Nile. From David Roberts' Egypt and Nubia

she speaks in her letters of 'smelling the smell of a slave ship', of the kindness of the village people and of the Biblical cycle of their lives – the annual rising and falling of the Nile, the harvests, the plagues, the tax-gatherers and other calamities – it is the reality behind the fantasy. She saw by night 'the moon rise over the mountains and light up everything like a softer sun'. 'The night here,' she goes on, 'is a tender, subdued, dreamy sort of enchanted-looking day'; but the days with their overpowering sunshine were hard to bear: 'The silence of noon, with the *white heat* glowing on the river which flowed like liquid tin, and the silent Nubian rough boats floating down without a ripple, was magnificent and really

awful.' Every modern tourist will recognize her description of the Valley of the Kings at
Luxor: 'The road is a long and most wild one, truly through the valley of the shadow of
death; not an insect nor a bird'; and she has a splendid outburst against the desecrators of
Abu Simbel: 'The scribbling of names is quite infamous . . . Prince Pückler Muskau has
engraved his and his *Ordenskreuz* in huge letters and size, on the naked breast of that
august and pathetic giant who sits at Abu Simbel.'

Then there were others who came to Egypt and went up the river, rather less emotionally,
though still responding to the attraction of a country that seemed so familiar and yet was
so entirely new. Bayard Taylor, the American poet-diplomat who translated *Faust*, got a
fair distance up the White Nile beyond Khartoum in 1851, and wrote a book about his
journey; in 1852 the German doctor Theodor Bilharz arrived in Egypt and discovered a
parasite which causes the disease now known as bilharzia, and which is the curse of the
river; in 1845 a German peasant named Bauer set up a soap and brandy works on the
Blue Nile; and in 1846 John Petherick, the Welsh mining engineer turned elephant hunter,
naturalist and consul, reached Khartoum and began a series of explorations to the south.

Year by year these people penetrated into the unknown corners, gradually filling out the
picture of the Sudan and revealing it as something more than an aberration in history and
a blank space on the map. But still by the middle of the century the river system of the
Blue Nile and the other great tributaries that poured down once a year in flood from the
Ethiopian highlands remained more or less unexplored. For the earliest and best account of
this region we are indebted to the formidable, fifteen-stone figure of the Englishman,
Samuel Baker. (For a description of Baker's character and his subsequent journeys on the
White Nile, see the author's *The White Nile*, 1960, 1971.)

Baker, at this stage of his career (1861), was not an explorer at all: he was a wealthy big-
game hunter, and he came up to the Sudan from Cairo with his young wife in search of
large wild animals. His book *The Nile Tributaries of Abyssinia* is dedicated to King Edward
VII (then the Prince of Wales), who visited Egypt in 1867 and went up the river as far as
Luxor. Baker describes him as 'the first of England's Royal Race who has sailed upon the
waters of the Nile'. It is, in the main, a sportsman's record of a year's wandering in the
Eastern Sudan. But before he reached the end of the book it was the inhabitants who
really interested him, and the great mystery of the river itself. No one understood the Nile
better than Baker, no one could write about it so clearly.

'The two grand affluents of Abyssinia,' he wrote, 'are the Blue Nile and the Atbara,
which join the main stream respectively in N. lat. 15 deg. 30 and 17 deg. 37. These rivers,
although streams of extreme grandeur during the period of Abyssinian rains, from the
middle of June until September, are reduced during the dry months to utter insignificance:
the Blue Nile becoming so shallow as to be unnavigable, and the Atbara perfectly dry. At
that time, the water supply of Abyssinia having ceased, Egypt depends solely upon the
equatorial lakes, and the affluents of the White Nile, until the rainy season shall again have
flooded the two great Abyssinian arteries. That flood occurs suddenly about the 20 June,
and the grand rush of water pouring down the Blue Nile and the Atbara into the parent
channel, inundates Lower Egypt, and is the cause of its extreme fertility.'

The Bakers reached the junction with the Atbara just before this annual flood arrived, and found that there were pools up to a mile long in the dry river bed, with wild life teeming in them and around them; huge fish and crocodiles, turtles, hippopotamuses, gazelles and hyenas, and the migrating sand grouse flew in thousands. The nights were cool and free of mosquitoes, but by day the temperature went up to 137 degrees in the sun. It was so hot that Baker's writing paper broke into fragments when he crunched it in his hand. On the night of June 23 the flood came roaring down, and the travellers, waking in the morning, beheld a stream 500 yards wide and fifteen to twenty feet deep. Floating islands of broken bamboos and other debris were being carried along in the muddy current. There was no rain, but with miraculous speed every dead-looking tree along the banks sprouted into leaf directly the water penetrated through the sand to its roots.

The rhinoceros at bay. From Baker's The Nile Tributaries of Abyssinia

The Bakers journeyed for 220 miles up the Atbara and then struck off across the desert to Kassala, where the famous mountain, a smooth block of granite, rose up for 3,500 feet. Here the River Gash was in spate, and it rushed past the walled town to lose itself at last in the dry sand of the desert. Kassala stood at the limit of Egyptian territory, and a desultory border warfare was going on between the Egyptian garrison and the Ethiopian tribes. It was ideal country for guerrilla fighting: plantations of cotton and tobacco ran up to the foothills of the Ethiopian plateau, and here the jungle took over, forming a sort of no-man's-land between the Ethiopians and the Turks. Now that the rain had arrived, all the nomadic cattle-grazing tribes were on the move northwards into the desert to escape the mud and the tsetse fly, and the Bakers turned back to the Atbara again. They travelled in some style. Rising at 5.30 a.m. they rode on ahead of their party on fast camels, and at 10.30 a.m. stopped for the day, having by then covered some twenty-four miles. A Persian carpet was

OVERLEAF *Samuel Baker and his wife on a journey through the desert*
From Baker's The Nile Tributaries of Abyssinia

spread out under a shady tree, and while breakfast was being prepared (a cold roast fowl, biscuits and a pot of coffee), Baker smoked his pipe and wrote up his journal. After breakfast he went out with his gun and shot game or fished for the afternoon meal. About 4 p.m. the baggage train caught up with them, and there then occurred the pleasant activity of the tents being erected, the campfires lit, the antelopes skinned and the guinea fowls prepared for the cooking pot. Mrs Baker made shoes and clothes from the wild animal skins.

One feels comfortable with the Bakers. Theirs was a Robinson Crusoe existence in the wilderness, and to read about it is a delightful change from the slave-raids and the massacres along the Nile. Baker recommends the following for African travellers: a large umbrella with a double lining, a quart syringe for injecting brine into meat, sticks of Indian ink that can be 'rubbed up in a few moments to write up the notebook during the march', tinted writing paper (the glare of the sun is too strong for white), burning glasses and flint and steel, quicksilver and lead for making bullets.

They were in no hurry – they camped for three months at one spot waiting for the rain to stop – and consequently Baker's notes on the country have the impress of a quiet and observant mind. As his knowledge of their language increased, he grew to like and under-stand the desert Arabs. They were conservative people, nomads with few possessions and a hatred of towns. They spoke, he says, the language of the Old Testament, and 'the name of God was coupled with every trifling incident in life'. The women after marriage wore clothes but went unveiled, revealing three tribal knife gashes on their cheeks, and he describes how they contrived for themselves an exotic sort of Turkish bath: a hole was made in the ground inside a tent and filled with burning embers upon which were thrown a variety of perfumes – ginger, cloves, cinnamon, frankincense, sandalwood and myrrh. The woman then crouched naked over the embers, her robe arranged like a tent round her so that none of the fumes could escape.

'She now begins,' Baker goes on, 'to perspire freely in the hot-air bath, and the pores of the skin being thus opened and moist, the volatile oil from the smoke of the burning perfumes is immediately absorbed.' Afterwards generous quantities of fat were rubbed into the skin and hair. Baker claimed that he could smell an Arab woman from a hundred yards away. Slaves were attached to all the tribes, but they were hard to obtain, and Baker, in need of a cook, was obliged to pay the equivalent of seven pounds for a not very competent woman. He paid in Austrian Maria Theresa dollars, which had by now become general currency in the Sudan – 'The effigy of the Empress, with a very low dress and a profusion of bust, is, I believe, the charm that suits the Arab taste.'

By the end of the first week in September the rains were slackening, and the Atbara, running through a gorge a mile wide near the Bakers' camp, had fallen eighteen feet. Immense crocodiles began to bask along the sandbanks. By the end of October the rains had entirely gone, the green was withering from the trees and the tsetse fly had vanished. In the pools of the river, now sparkling and clear, Baker found eatable oysters, and hordes of bee-eaters and other brilliant small birds were flying about. Ducks and storks, the first of the migrating birds, arrived.

It was now possible for the Bakers to get on the move again, and with three newly purchased Abyssinian horses they crossed eastwards to the Setit River and followed it far upstream through regions never visited by white men before. Here on the Ethiopian border he saw to the south and east 'a confused mass of peaks of great altitude', and like Cailliaud on the Blue Nile at Fazughli he found that he could get no further; the river vanished into an impenetrable gorge. Even today this country is only passable on a few tracks and by mule or on foot.

It was now March 1862 and the Bakers turned back into the Sudan. They were forced to proceed very cautiously, keeping well away from villages, since the dry season, as Baker says, had 'introduced a season of anarchy along the whole frontier'. Presently they arrived in the territory where Nimr had set up his headquarters when he fled from Shendy in 1822, and now in the 1860s Nimr's son still carried on the war with the Turks. He had formed an alliance against them with the Emperor Theodore of Ethiopia, and every dry season he raided down into the Sudan. 'The society in this district,' Baker says, 'was not *crème de la crème*, as Mek Nimr's territory was an asylum for all the blackguards of the adjoining countries, who were attracted by the excitement and lawlessness of continual border warfare.' The Mek himself was 'a man of about fifty and exceedingly dirty in appearance', but he received Baker well and even agreed that he would accept a truce with the Turks if Baker cared to arrange it with the Turkish governor-general in Khartoum.

In mid-April the Bakers crossed the Atbara again and arrived at Gallabat, their camels laden with the skins and heads of the rhinoceroses and other wild animals they had shot and here they fell in with two German missionaries on their way into Ethiopia. Baker did not think much of missionaries, and these two in particular aroused his irony. It was their intention to convert the Jews of Ethiopia, and for this enterprise they had equipped themselves with a number of Bibles printed in an Ethiopian dialect, and a medicine chest filled with bottles from which the labels had become unstuck. Baker helped them sort out the medicine chest, and warned them that Theodore 'regarded missionaries as an unsavoury odour', but they insisted on going on. And thus, Baker comments, 'provided with a medicine chest they did not comprehend, and a number of Bibles printed in the Tigré language they did not understand, they were prepared to convert the Jews who could not read.'

Gallabat at this time lay in Ethiopia, and everywhere the Bakers found fierce resentment against the Turks. The local sheikh was even reluctant to allow them to return to the Sudan, fearing that they were spies. At the end of April, however, they got away, and striking north-west along the Rahad and Dinder Rivers reached the Blue Nile above Khartoum at Wad Medani. On June 11, 1862, just a year after the outset of their lonely journey, they reached Khartoum. Baker was not impressed with the place: 'The difference between the view of Khartoum at the distance of a mile, with the sun shining upon the bright River Nile in the foreground, to the appearance of the town upon close inspection was about equal to the scenery of a theatre as regarded from the boxes or from the stage . . . a filthy and miserable town.'

They found their way through the decrepit streets to an open square where they 'perceived a large archway with closed doors; above this entrance was a shield, with a device that gladdened my English eyes: there was the British lion and the unicorn! . . . This was the British Consulate.' John Petherick, the consul, was away, but the Bakers were invited to stay in one of the cool and airy upper rooms. In the walled garden below, Petherick kept a menagerie of ostriches, wild boars, hyenas, dog-faced baboons and leopards, and no doubt the Bakers felt at home.

Baker lost no time in presenting himself to Musa Pasha, the governor-general, and in raising the question of Nimr's offer of a truce. There was a violent reaction. Musa Pasha declared that Nimr was a criminal, his ally the Emperor Theodore was mad, and that both would have been destroyed long ago had they not been under the protection of the British. Quite recently, Musa Pasha added, Theodore had written him an insolent letter laying claim to all the territory over which the Bakers had travelled between the Atbara and the Blue Nile, and even demanding the surrender of Khartoum and Shendy as well. The Egyptians were now determined to launch a campaign against him.

Seeing that argument was useless, Baker returned to the consulate. He now had time to survey the results of his journey, and they were considerable. He had traversed, as he had intended to do, nearly all the tributaries that descended from Ethiopia to the Nile, and was able to produce for the first time a very plausible map of the river system in the Sudan. He had explained the action of the annual floods, and had seen with his own eyes gorges on the Atbara and elsewhere which were miles in width – the displaced soil, presumably, having been carried down to the delta. In a huge area which until now had been a closed book he had compiled a mass of original information upon the tribes, the wild life, the meteorology, the vegetation and the minerals. And he had discovered one broad simple fact that was so apparent that it had been generally overlooked: a new frontier had been created in Africa. Islam had pushed up the Nile as far as the Ethiopian mountains, and now in the very nature of things it was likely to go on and attempt the conquest of Ethiopia itself. Thus Egypt's domination of the Blue Nile upon which she so vitally depended would be complete.

The idea that the Blue Nile might be blocked or poisoned at its source in Ethiopia as a means of destroying Egypt had been canvassed in every age: in 1093, for example, the Nile flood was very low, and the Egyptians sent an embassy to Ethiopia to persuade the emperor to release more water – a thing he could not possibly do. It was nonsense of course. Even now, all the genius of modern engineering could not divert the Nile from its course or prevent its annual flood, and the poisoning of such a vast amount of water is a childish dream of evil. But in the early 1860s nobody was at all sure of this. Nobody had followed the Blue Nile from Lake Tana to the Sudanese border; nobody even knew where the White Nile came from. And so the politics of Ethiopia were bound up in the politics of the river, and the struggle for the control of that country that now began was largely a struggle for the control of the Blue Nile. The importance of Baker's journey was that he had under-lined these things. Like Bruce before him, he and his fellow explorers once again called attention to the strange Christian country locked away from the rest of the world in her mountains and surrounding deserts like an island rising from the sea. In particular they aroused the attention of England. The work on the Suez Canal was now far advanced, and it was apparent to any sensible observer that the Red Sea route would soon abolish the need for the long voyage round the Cape. Now, less than ever, could England afford to have an enemy in control of Ethiopia and the Red Sea ports, and whether that enemy were Christian or Moslem made no difference; she would be bound to intervene. In the 1860s such an enemy appeared, and the last phase of the conquest of the Blue Nile began.

PART FOUR

——

THE BRITISH IN ETHIOPIA

14

The Power of Theodore

It has always been accepted that the Emperor Theodore was a mad dog let loose, a sort of black reincarnation of Ivan the Terrible and the Russian tyrants, and so he was in many ways, even by the savage standards of Ethiopia itself. Yet Theodore's appalling reputation does not fit him absolutely. A touch of nobility intervenes and although just possibly, in better circumstances, he could have become Othello he could never have been Iago. He was far too emotional to be a calculating villain, and there was no real method in his madness. Plowden, who knew him well as far back as the 1850s, says that as a young man Theodore displayed 'great tact and delicacy'.

'His wrath,' indeed, 'was terrible, and all trembled.' But then he was energetic and decisive, and he was also very religious, and very generous. He was a courteous man, even at the height of his frenzies, and nobody ever contested the fact that he had that sort of unthinking courage that comes to some people as naturally as the air they breathe. The rest of the pattern is the familiar one of the dreaming megalomaniac, of the raging reformer who finds his reforms rejected and wants to pull the whole world down in ruins to appease himself for his failure. Plowden thought he was entirely sincere in the beginning; he really did attempt to abolish slavery, to reform taxation, to pay his soldiers instead of allowing them to plunder, and he even introduced into the country those extraordinary white jodhpurs in which Ethiopians still get about at the present time. He believed right up to the moment of his death that he was destined to restore the glories of the ancient Ethiopian empire, and in that cause, Plowden says, 'his personal and moral daring were boundless'.

That was the trouble. He had no judgment and he never knew where to stop. When he was finally defeated in the long chaotic struggle to coerce, bludgeon and bully his people out of the Middle Ages he turned, like an animal at bay, to senseless butchery. He was like a child who knows that he is doing wrong, yearns for forgiveness, for a way out, and finding none gives way entirely to his anger, hoping that it will create its own justification. Had he had anyone to help him in the terribly difficult business of adjusting himself without loss of dignity to the modern world it might have been a different story. But he was surrounded by ignorance and superstition, and a wilder, more barbaric place than Ethiopia in the nineteenth century cannot be imagined.

Since Bruce's departure in 1771 nothing had happened there but anarchy, and it was anarchy so deep that even the records are silent. We do not know in any precise detail what the politics were, what chieftains marched against each other, or by what laws and forces the people managed to survive. Their battles were fought in a black night of isolation, and were forgotten as soon as they were lost and won. It is only with the emergence of Theodore that

Theodore. From Le Jean's Théodore II [*sic*]

light begins to fall on the scene, and with Theodore the history of modern Ethiopia begins.

Theodore claimed that he was of royal blood and in the direct line of kings descending from Solomon and Alexander the Great. He was nothing of the sort. He was the son of a small local chieftain, and he had no connection with the royal line. He was a self-made king if there ever was one, and his dynasty begins and ends with himself. He was born in 1818 in the border district of Kwara, close to the source of the Blue Nile in the Christian province of Amhara. Amhara was closely invested by Moslems – by the Turks, Egyptians and Arabs in the deserts of the Sudan, and by the Galla tribes of central Ethiopia itself – and Theodore grew up knowing hardly anything but war against Islam. It is true that he had other quarrels as well, and could kill his brother Christians with a clear and determined conscience, but in the main he considered himself a crusader against the Moslems, and if we are to understand him this is an aspect of his character that one ought never to forget. From the earliest beginnings he seems to have been singled out as an exceptional man. He looked like a leader. He was black and very beautiful, a man with a high forehead, a lithe, athletic body, and there was a certain air of grandeur in his bearing. He was educated in a monastery, but very soon abandoned the priesthood to become a soldier: and in the ruthless arts of Ethiopian tribal warfare he was a master.

By 1853, when he was 35, he had defeated all the rival chiefs on Lake Tana and had overrun Amhara. Next he turned with his little army to the neighbouring provinces of Tigré, Gojjam and Shoa, and by 1855 most of the ruling families in those areas were either killed or in his hands. The Turks were still threatening him from the Red Sea coast and the Sudan, but in Ethiopia itself this new St George was triumphant. Both Gondar and the great mountain fortress of Magdala had fallen to him, but he still preferred to move about the countryside in a vast tented camp with his court and his army around him. He now declared himself Theodore III, Emperor of Ethiopia, and it was a title which, for the moment, nobody could dispute. It was even thought worth while in England to appoint a consul, Walter G. Plowden, to conclude a treaty with him.

Plowden, at the time of his appointment, had already been in Ethiopia for a number of years, and had become an intimate of Theodore's, while his companion, an engineer named Bell, had even been appointed to act as a kind of grand chamberlain and secretary at the court. A number of missionaries of German extraction, but sponsored by British religious organizations, were also on the scene. By the late 1850s, therefore, things were going very well with England's policy of building up friends along the Red Sea route. But in 1860 disaster suddenly intervened: Plowden on one of his journeys through the country was killed by tribesmen near Gondar. Theodore at once marched with Bell against the culprits, and as a gesture of condolence to his dead English friend slaughtered and mutilated about two thousand of them – a holocaust exceptional even for Ethiopia. During the fighting Bell rushed to the assistance of Theodore and was killed.

It now became necessary for the British Government to find a new representative at the emperor's court, and their choice fell on a Captain Charles Duncan Cameron of the Indian Service. One does not know quite what to think about Cameron. Although he was to become the *casus belli* of the British expedition, and although his subsequent sufferings aroused the sympathy of all the civilized world, he does not really emerge as a well-defined individual outside of his consular office, and if he was competent he was not very far-seeing. Most of the contemporary accounts of these years merely refer to him as 'Consul Cameron', and leave him at that, a somewhat faceless image. Plowden, one feels, would have acted very differently had he lived; certainly he would have handled Theodore more adroitly.

Charles Duncan Cameron

But then Theodore himself was changing about this time. His first wife, a chieftain's daughter named Tavavich, had recently died, and she appears to have been a steadying influence upon him. Theodore married again but his new queen, Teru-Wark, was a twelve-year-old girl who soon bored him, and he fell into the habit of taking up with any woman, married or unmarried, who happened to please him for a night or two. Up to this point, too, he had been a sober man, but he now gave way to bouts of heavy drinking. These were hardly the ideal circumstances for a new consul to make his appearance.

At first, however, all was warmth and friendship. Cameron arrived at Gondar in 1862, and there presented Theodore with a brace of pistols, each with a silver plate on its stock inscribed with the words, 'Presented to Theodore, Emperor of Abyssinia, by Victoria, Queen of Great Britain and Ireland, for his kindness to her servant Plowden, 1861.' Whether or not Theodore took this to be a gracious acknowledgment of the massacre he had just carried out is not known, but it is certain that he was delighted by the gift, and Cameron, encouraged by his reception, suggested to Theodore that he should send envoys to England to conclude a new treaty of friendship with the Queen. Probably what Cameron intended was nothing more than a formal exchange of civilities, but Theodore took up the idea with all the seriousness of a petty African chieftain wishing to establish his importance in the great outer world. He drafted a letter to the Queen and directed Cameron to deliver it, probably thinking that Cameron would do so in person. Since this fatal letter was the source of all the misunderstandings and tragedies that were to follow it is worth quoting a full translation from the Amharic:

In the name of the Father, of the Son, and of the Holy Ghost, one God in Trinity, chosen by God, King of Kings, Theodore of Ethiopia, to her Majesty Victoria, Queen of England.

I hope your Majesty is in good health. By the power of God I am well. My fathers, the Emperors, having forgotten the Creator, He handed over their kingdom to the Gallas and the Turks. But God created me, lifted me out of the dust, and restored this Empire to my rule. He endowed me with power and enabled me to stand in the place of my fathers. By this power I drove away the Gallas. As for the Turks I have told them to leave the land of my ancestors. They refuse. I am now going to wrestle with them.

Mr Plowden and my late Grand Chamberlain, the Englishman Bell, used to tell me that there is a great Christian Queen, who loves all Christians. When they said to me this: 'We are able to make you known to her and to establish friendship between you,' then in those times I was very glad. I gave them my love, thinking that I had found your Majesty's goodwill.

All men are subject to death, and my enemies, thinking to injure me, killed these my friends. But by the power of God I have exterminated those enemies, not leaving one alive, though they were of my own family, that I may get, by the power of God, your friendship. I was prevented by the Turks occupying the sea-coast from sending you an Embassy when I was in difficulty. Consul Cameron arrived with a letter and presents of friendship. By the power of God I was very glad hearing of your welfare and being assured of your amity. I have received your presents and thank you much.

I fear that if I send ambassadors with presents of amity by Consul Cameron, they may be arrested by the Turks. And now I wish that you may arrange for the safe passage of my ambassadors everywhere on the road. I wish to have an answer to this letter by Consul Cameron, and that he may conduct my Embassy to England. See how Islam oppresses the Christian.

This letter eventually found its way to London, and in the normal course of events a polite, though possibly non-committal answer would have been returned. But on this occasion someone in the Foreign Office slipped up: the letter was read, perhaps smiled at a little, and forgotten. To a man of Theodore's prickly *amour propre* this was already an insult, and now the Foreign Office proceeded to injury: they sent Cameron an instruction to make his way down to Kassala in the Sudan, where, among other matters, he was to inquire into the prospects of growing cotton (cotton prices had quadrupled since the Civil War had cut off supplies from the United States) and investigate the slave trade.

Now the Moslem Sudan was Theodore's bitter enemy, and, as we have seen from Baker's experiences in Khartoum, the Turks were at that moment actively preparing to invade Ethiopia. No Ethiopian could visit the Sudan without being branded as a traitor. Undeterred by this Cameron set off, and it was only some months later that Theodore, who imagined he had gone down to the coast on his way to England, heard of his real destination. He flew into a rage that presently suppurated into a sullen resentment. One cannot but sympathize with him a little; what was this Englishman doing, coming to him with professions of friendship, and then surreptitiously going off into the camp of his enemies? The absence of any answer to the letter was now explained: England was plotting a campaign against Ethiopia from the Sudan. Theodore had been brought up in a world of treachery and of quick revenge, and so now he naturally fell upon the European missionaries at Gondar – those same missionaries, incidentally, whom Baker had encountered in Metemma in 1862. They were put into irons and held as hostages, and when Cameron returned in January 1864, all unsuspecting, from his mission, he too was thrown into prison. Explanations were useless. A savage hatred and a savage pride had been aroused, and in the extremity of one of his rages Theodore ordered Cameron to be tortured. Things were made even worse when a young Irishman named Kerans arrived from England as an assistant to Cameron; although he carried other messages from the Foreign Office there was still no answer to Theodore's letter. Kerans was put into chains with the others.

The news of these dealings reached Aden in April 1864, and in Aden the British Political Agent was a shrewd and energetic man named Colonel William Merewether. He at once got through to London with an urgent request that Theodore's letter, now two years old, should be answered at once. The government was further prodded into action by *The Times* newspaper which published a communication that Cameron had smuggled out of his prison in Gondar. 'There is no hope of my release,' he wrote, 'unless a letter is sent as an answer to His Majesty.'

It was not an easy situation. The prisoners were held by a half-civilized chieftain well out of the range of British power or influence in the heart of Ethiopia, and a threatening reply might well mean their further torture or even death. Eventually a careful and mollifying document was drawn up addressed to 'Our Good Friend Theodore, King of Abyssinia' and signed at Balmoral on May 26, 1864, 'Victoria R.' with the royal signet attached. It thanked Theodore for his good wishes, congratulated him on having established his authority in Ethiopia, and promised to receive an Ethiopian embassy in England. The pith of the letter, dealing with the release of Cameron, was as follows:

> Accounts have indeed reached Us of late that your Majesty had withdrawn your favour from Our servant. We trust, however, that these accounts have originated in false representations on the part of persons ill-disposed to your Majesty, and who may desire to produce an alteration in Our feelings towards you. But your Majesty can give no better proof of the sincerity of the sentiments which you profess towards Us, nor ensure more effectually a continuance of Our friendship and goodwill, than by dismissing Our servant Cameron, and any other Europeans who may desire it, from your Court, and by affording them every assistance and protection on their journey to the destination to which they desire to proceed.

A strange choice was made of an envoy to deliver this message. Hormuzd Rassam was not an Englishman by birth: he was an Iraki born in Mosul of Christian parents. As a young man he had been attached to Layard, the archaeologist in Mesopotamia, had studied at Oxford, and had eventually adopted British nationality. Some time before this he had found his way on to Merewether's staff in Aden. Perhaps it was thought in England that a wily oriental would be the best man to handle Theodore, perhaps it was simply because Rassam was on the spot and Merewether supported him, but at all events this unusual

LEFT '*This photo of Rassam was taken about the time of these stirring incidents*' and RIGHT
Colonel Merewether

agent was instructed to negotiate with Theodore on behalf of the British Government, and he was soon to prove himself very able indeed. He was a supple and persistent man, not at all lacking in bravery. Two assistants were given him for his long and dangerous journey into the interior: a doctor named Henry Blanc, and later, a Lieutenant Prideaux of the Bombay army.

In July 1864 Rassam and his party were taken in a British gunboat from Aden to Massawa, which was then in Egyptian territory, and the customary gateway into Ethiopia. Even here the fear of Theodore was so great that many of the natives believed that he heard everything that was said about him even though he was hundreds of miles away, and Rassam was warned that he should on no account enter Ethiopia without the emperor's permission. He wrote a letter to Theodore saying that he was the bearer of a letter from Queen Victoria and asking, very politely, for this permission. With some difficulty he then obtained messengers who were willing to convey it to Gondar. Other letters and a sum of money were dispatched to Cameron, and Rassam sat down to wait.

It was a long wait indeed. All the rest of that year went by in the fetid and plague-ridden port of Massawa with no word from the interior, and it was not until early in 1865 that Rassam began to get messages from the captives. Cameron wrote that some twenty or thirty Europeans and their families had been rounded up, some like the missionaries Mr and Mrs Flad being with Theodore in the field near Lake Tana, and in relative freedom, while others like himself and the missionaries Rosenthal and Stern were now in Magdala

The house at Magdala where Cameron and Stern were first imprisoned. From Stanley's Coomassie and Magdala

and chained in such a way that it was difficult to stand upright. Rassam had written a second letter to Theodore in October 1864, but to this there was still no reply. A third letter, even politer in tone, was now sent off and remained unanswered. Cameron, who now began corresponding fairly freely from Magdala, suggested that Rassam might perhaps try a stronger tone. He added, 'But, for God's sake, do not come up here; he will cage you as sure as a gun, as he thinks that while he has us in his hands he is safe from attack, and, of course, with a swell like you in addition, matters would only be better for him . . .'

At last in August 1865, more than a year after Rassam's arrival at Massawa, word was received that Cameron had been released from his chains, and this news was followed by a letter from Theodore himself. Most of it was a self-righteous and petulant outburst against the British Consul, but there was a gleam of hope in the last paragraph: 'Be it known to Hormuzd Rassam that there exists just now a rebellion in Tigré. By the power of God, come round by way of Metemma. When you reach Metemma, send me a messenger, and, by the power of God, I will send people to receive you.'

There were difficulties here. Metemma lay hundreds of miles away in the Sudan, south of Kassala, where the wet season had begun, spreading disease and making all travel impossible. Rassam, who preferred on this and on all other occasions the soft tone, replied: 'Most Gracious Sovereign. I . . . beg to inform your Majesty that, in consequence of the prevailing sickness at Kassala and the neighbourhood, I dare not for the present come up to you via Metemma, as you have directed'; instead he would go up to Cairo and there await the ending of the wet season in October.

Rassam had a twofold motive in going first to Cairo: he wanted to get fresh instructions from London by telegraph, and he wanted to buy suitable presents to carry in to Theodore. The presents at least were easy enough to obtain in the Cairo bazaars, and an exotic lot they were: several chandeliers, mirrors and glassware, two cases of Curaçao and a mass of general stores. His instructions, however, came rather as a shock; he was told that he had been replaced as envoy by a diplomat, William Gifford Palgrave, who had already arrived in Cairo. A little deft string-pulling was required (probably by Merewether in Aden) before this matter was straightened out, and Palgrave, no doubt with some relief, went back to London, while Rassam returned with his packages to Massawa.

The first news he received when he disembarked there was that Cameron and his fellow-captives, far from being released from their chains, were more heavily bound than ever. Rassam and his party now lost no further time, and on October 16, 1865, they set off from Massawa in the midst of a cholera epidemic, the chandeliers and other baggage securely lashed to a string of camels. They had 620 miles to go, much of it over country that had barely been explored or mapped. Skirting the edge of the Ethiopian plateau in the Sudanese desert, they reached Kassala in the not bad time of three weeks, and on November 21 they arrived at Metemma. Here they were inside Ethiopian territory for the first time, and on the track that led up to Lake Tana, only 100 miles away. Rassam hastened to send off messengers to Theodore announcing his arrival. After a week's delay a note came in from Cameron, urging haste. 'The King,' he wrote, 'sent us a cow a-piece sometime back – the first notice he has taken of us since the torturing. He has spoken rather kindly about us lately in public. But we are still chained hand and foot.'

This was followed by an effusive letter from Theodore himself, calling Rassam his 'beloved' and saying that an escort was on its way to him. On December 28 the British party set off into the cold of the mountains and was duly met by the escort – a horde of 1,400 men – close to the western shores of Lake Tana. They were nearing their goal at last.

Years afterwards Rassam wrote an account of this journey, and in a remarkable way it reads like an exact repetition of Bruce. Here it all is once more, the unchanging black Biblical world of Ethiopia: the raw beef banquets, the swarms of tribesmen in their white robes trailing across the landscape, the villages ruined by war, the gaunt prophet-like figures of the Coptic priests emerging from their round hut-churches, the childish posturing of the officials, the abject fear of the king, the tej drinking, the flowers and the honey, the lions roaring at night, the vast horizons of mountains, the bigotry and violence of the Middle Ages in surroundings of fantastic natural beauty; nothing had altered.

For some days they marched on, rounding Lake Tana on the west, and finally on January

Ethiopian tribesmen on the Wadela plateau. From Holland and Hozier's
Record of the Expedition to Abyssinia

26, 1866, they reached the source of the Little Abbai – the Little Blue Nile – where Bruce
had had his great moment of discovery a hundred years before. Perching on a green hilltop
close by was Theodore's camp, his own great white tent in the centre and surrounding it
on every side thousands of other smaller tents and makeshift huts.

Theodore sent a warm message to his guests to advance, and Rassam was presented with
a mule upon which he was to make his ceremonial entry into the camp. Hastily he got
into his 'blue political suit', while Blanc and Prideaux changed into scarlet jackets, and as
they went forward they were met by Aito Samuel, the emperor's chamberlain, and officials
of the court. The escort, now swollen to 10,000 men, fired off a ragged salute as they passed
the first tents. Rassam was much moved. 'After dragging out a miserable existence for
eighteen weary months,' he writes, 'in an unhealthy climate and among semi-barbarous
races . . . in vain efforts to reach the most impracticable man that ever swayed a sceptre . . .
here we were at last, about to obtain the long desired audience.'

A red tent had been erected for the occasion, and here Theodore received them, sitting
on a sofa, his long robe muffling up his face and his courtiers in a circle round him. Rassam
opened the proceedings by producing his famous letter from Victoria, now eighteen months
old, but Theodore did not read it at once. Instead he launched into a long and involved
harangue about his grievances. Speaking in Amharic through an interpreter, he declared
that Cameron had behaved very badly, that the missionaries had slandered him, that he

was surrounded by treachery even among his own followers. The Ethiopians, he went on, were 'a wicked people', always ready to reject good government, always in revolt; 'If I go to the south my people rebel in the north; and when I go to the west they rebel in the east.' And so instead of good government he now gave them war. Then there were the Turks: they had seized Sennar and the Sudan which rightly belonged to Ethiopia. For them too he was preparing war.

Rassam listened to this diatribe without comment, and Theodore brought the interview to an end by appointing his chamberlain, Samuel, to be the cicerone of his guests, and by declaring that he would see to their every want. The British party then retired to the tents which had been prepared for them a short distance away inside the royal enclosure.

Next morning there was a second interview. Rassam was informed that orders had gone to Magdala for the release of the captives, and Theodore handed him a reply to Victoria's letter. It was a strange document. In it Theodore described himself as 'an ignorant Ethiopian', and he asked the Queen's pardon: 'Counsel me but do not blame me, O Queen. . . .' But once again he could not prevent himself from reverting to his grievances, and Rassam was forced to listen to another long outburst of complaint.

Choosing his moment, Rassam presented his chandeliers. They were well received and the second interview closed.

So far so good. But the British were soon to discover that things do not move quickly in Ethiopia. It was announced that the capital was to be transported into the Damot province, where Theodore intended to demolish some tribes he suspected of rebellion. Rassam and his party were to accompany the march as far as Lake Tana, and were then to go off to the village of Korata on the south-eastern shore. Here they were to await the arrival of the prisoners from Magdala.

The march was an astonishing affair. Each day some ninety thousand people, men, women, children, and their herds of sheep and cattle, got on the move, straggling over the hills and valleys like some enormous crawling dragon. Theodore led the way, and he showed great skill in keeping order among his rabble. Starting each morning at seven they sometimes covered as much as thirty miles in a day, and they kept this up for a week on end. At every ravine and difficult river crossing Theodore turned back to see his followers across, often himself lending a hand with the older women and children. Each night a city of 20,000 tents and huts sprang up in an instant. Each day skirmishing parties of warriors replenished supplies by pillaging and despoiling the wayside villages.

The British party was given a place of honour in the van of the march, and Theodore was almost embarrassingly attentive to Rassam. At their first camp on the Little Abbai Rassam slipped and nearly fell into the stream. Theodore rushed forward and grasped his arm. 'Cheer up,' he said, helping Rassam up the bank, 'don't be afraid.' Each day there was a gift: an antelope which Theodore had shot, a brace of partridges, a battery of firearms, a message saying that all the expenses of the British party while they were in Ethiopia would be met by the royal treasury.

Close to the lake, on February 6, they parted, Theodore going south to continue his marauding, while the British, attended by Samuel and a strong escort, crossed in boats to the opposite shore. They embarked with their baggage on a fleet of rush-bottomed rafts at the little port of Adina, and after spending the night on the island of Dek paddled across the outlet of the Blue Nile from Lake Tana and reached Korata a few miles to the north on February 14. By Theodore's orders the local elders had prepared a ceremonial welcome for them, and they moved into a collection of ramshackle huts near the shore. Within a few days Rassam had a message from Theodore saying that he had set up his own camp at Zagé, close to the mouth of the Little Abbai, on the opposite shore of the lake – Rassam could actually see the smoke rising from the camp-fires – and giving an assurance that an escort had gone off to Magdala to collect the captives. The letter was accompanied by the gift of two lion cubs.

By now Rassam had begun to form a fairly clear idea of the nature of the people he had come to rescue. They appeared to number about thirty adults in all, British, French, German, Swiss, and their Ethiopian wives (two of them were the daughters of Bell by a native wife), and twenty-three children, and they were divided into three groups. First there was a team of seven 'artisans' – skilled European workmen, Germans for the most part, who had enlisted in Theodore's service and were not, properly speaking, prisoners at all, since they moved freely about the emperor's camp. Then there were the German missionaries, Mr and Mrs Flad and their three children, together with four more Germans who were on parole and lived in a settlement outside Debra Tabor; and finally there were the people Theodore hated most – Cameron and his European staff of four, and the German missionaries, Mr and Mrs Stern and Mr and Mrs Rosenthal. All these last were in Magdala, and presumably had just been released from their fetters.

One might have supposed that the European colony clung very much together in these dangerous and violent surroundings, but this, Rassam now learned, was very far from being the case; there were constant dissensions and animosities among some of them. One man, a French adventurer named Bardel, who was an artist of sorts, was even suspected of betraying the secrets of his fellow Europeans to the emperor. Nor was it at all clear that they all wanted to leave Ethiopia. The German artisans appeared to be very much attached to Theodore.

For the moment, however, there was nothing for Rassam to do but to wait, to shoot hippopotamuses in the lake and to reply to the stream of flowery messages which Theodore kept dispatching daily from Zagé. Was his beloved friend Rassam happy and contented? Had he everything he wanted? Was he in good health? Yes, Rassam was well enough, but he had the uneasy feeling that things were not quite right, that Theodore was a dangerous man to deal with, and that in some unforeseen way the situation could change in an instant. The present gust of excessive friendship was a little too good to last.

Towards the end of February the missionary Flad arrived at Korata from Debra Tabor, and immediately confirmed these suspicions. He warned Rassam to use great caution and to take nothing for granted as yet. For the moment, however, the signs were favourable. Early in March the artisans came across to the British camp, and they were soon followed by their wives, all Ethiopian girls with the exception of one Frenchwoman. The whole band apparently now wanted to get out of the country. Then on March 10 there was a moving moment when Cameron, haggard with weakness after two years in chains, arrived with the Magdala party and the remainder of Flad's group from Debra Tabor – eighteen of them in all. Rassam deliberately received Cameron rather formally, since he was Theodore's especial enemy, and any great show of warmth towards him might appear to Theodore as bad faith. The European colony was now united at Korata, and all that remained was for the emperor to give the word for them to go.

That word did not arrive. Instead a message of a very different kind was delivered: Theodore demanded that Rassam should hold an inquiry into the misdeeds of Cameron and his companions and let him know the result. A long, confused and wholly bogus list of charges against the captives was given to Rassam to assist him in his inquiry. It was the first hint of the danger ahead, and Rassam, consulting with the others, agreed that it would be foolhardy to oppose Theodore at this moment. After all, they were hundreds of miles from civilization and absolutely helpless in the hands of a man they believed mad. Theodore wanted justification for what he had done before he would let them go, and the only sensible thing to do was to let him have it.

Rassam publicly read out the charges in his tent, went through the form of listening to evidence, and then concocted a solemn letter to Theodore saying that 'all confessed that they had done wrong' and asked forgiveness.

It seemed for the moment that this concession was all that Theodore required. Rassam, Blanc and Prideaux were summoned to Zagé to say good-bye, and they crossed the lake on rafts, changing into their uniforms when they landed. Zagé, then as now, was a wooded promontory jutting out into the lake and famous for its coffee and its pythons (two of them about this time were presented by Theodore to Rassam), and here the royal camp was established a little back from the shore. The British party was received with every show of friendliness; Theodore was waiting for them outside his tent and taking Rassam by the hand he led him into the audience hall. Here they talked amiably for a while, and Theodore with pride displayed the two pistols that Plowden had brought him from Victoria. Yet there was a certain uneasiness in the background, and next day, while they waited in their tents, the British party heard that Theodore had summoned all his chiefs to decide whether or not the captives should be allowed to go. The chiefs apparently were in favour of it, but Theodore kept insisting that he must have some guarantee that once across the border they would not malign him. Still with nothing decided, the British were sent back to Korata the following day.

Rassam in his account of these dealings lays most of the blame for Theodore's prevarications upon Charles Tilstone Beke. There may be something in it. Beke was a London barrister who had set himself up as something of an expert on Ethiopia and the Nile; indeed he had travelled in the Lake Tana area some twenty years before this and had written very sensible papers for the Royal Geographical Society claiming, rightly, that the true source of the river lay at the end of the White Nile, not the Blue. Like many other people in England Beke had grown distrustful of Rassam's ability to get the prisoners out — already there had been a delay of well over a year — and he had volunteered on behalf of the relatives to go out unofficially to Ethiopia and see what he could do. He carried with him letters from the prisoners' wives and families imploring Theodore to let their husbands go. On his journey out from England both the British consul in Cairo and Merewether in Aden pointed out to Beke that he might, by his intervention, very well prejudice Rassam's chances of success, and that he would be much better advised to wait a little longer. But Beke persisted. He sent off the relatives' appeal to Theodore and added that he himself was coming into Ethiopia by way of Tigré to see the emperor. This communication had now arrived at Zagé, and in Rassam's view it made Theodore instantly suspicious. Whom was he supposed to deal with, Beke or Rassam? What was this new man doing entering Ethiopia without permission and by way of the rebel district of Tigré? Was the whole thing an elaborate British plot to get the prisoners out and then invade? (Beke in fact never reached Theodore and returned to England.)

For a few more days he veered to and fro, at one moment inundating Rassam with gifts and promises of his early release, and at the next sending a warning that all the prisoners must prepare to come to him at Zagé to ask for his personal forgiveness. At length, in early April, he brought himself to a decision: the prisoners could go, making their way out of Ethiopia on the Gondar route, and Rassam, Blanc and Prideaux were to come to Zagé to make their last farewells. On Friday, April 13 the two parties set off, Cameron and his people heading north towards the border, and the three members of the mission once more crossing Lake Tana to Zagé.

This time there was no friendly reception for Rassam on the shore. Instead they heard that Theodore had passed the last three days in a drunken debauch, and that now they were to proceed to the audience-hall. On entering they saw no sign of Theodore, but the place was crowded with the leading men about the court. 'Suddenly,' says Rassam, 'three strapping chiefs fell on me, two of whom held my arms and the other the tail of my coat . . . and, on looking behind for my companions, I found that they also had been arrested and were being roughly handled by the soldiers.'

It was now revealed that Theodore was sitting listening behind the door a few feet away, and that the audience-hall had been converted into a court. Charges were read out: Rassam had sent the prisoners away without first reconciling them to the emperor, he had sent letters to the coast without permission – the rigmarole went on and on, and Rassam's every attempt to deny and explain was pushed aside. In the midst of this Theodore suddenly sent a message apologizing to Rassam for what was happening, but also adding the sinister information that Cameron and his party had also been arrested on the other side of the lake and were now being brought into Zagé. Rassam and his companions were then led away under guard to a tent where they spent the night.

On April 15 Cameron and his party were marched into camp, and on the following day all the prisoners were put on trial together. The meeting was held in the open under a hot sun with a thousand Ethiopians in attendance, and Theodore sitting on a sofa in the centre. It was a mad proceeding and it grew madder as it went on. Rassam and his companions were brought in first, and Rassam was given the place of honour at the emperor's side. For an hour Theodore caressed him, reassured him, pledged him his love. Then Cameron and his party were brought forward chained arm to arm in couples. Once more the same old charges were read out and denied. 'Is this your friendship, Mr Rassam,' Theodore demanded, 'that you wish to leave me and take away those who have abused me?' The meeting broke up in the afternoon with nothing decided.

The farce dragged on again next day. This time the proceedings opened with Theodore crying out, 'For Christ's sake forgive me,' and the whole assembly sank to their knees in prayer. This pause seemed to have a clarifying effect on Theodore's mind, for he announced that one of the missionaries, Flad, was to be dispatched at once as an emissary to England. A secretary was sent for, and Theodore dictated a letter to Victoria saying that Cameron and the other prisoners would be allowed to go but that Rassam must remain behind. In a second letter Theodore asked that the Queen should send him a party of skilled workmen to help him modernize his country. Both letters were handed to Flad and he was sent off under escort (but without Mrs Flad) down the track to Metemma. Rassam and the remainder of the prisoners, well knowing that none of them would be released until Flad returned with a reply – if even then – were marched back to their quarters.

The cat and mouse game now captivated Theodore entirely. Most of the prisoners were allowed to walk freely about the camp, and a shower of fresh presents descended upon Rassam and his two assistants, Blanc and Prideaux: saddles inlaid with gold, a special medal 'The Cross and Solomon's Seal', and elaborate silk shirts, the particular sign of the emperor's favour. May 24 was Victoria's birthday, and on hearing this Theodore ordered a twenty-one gun salute and a feast of raw meat. Hoping further to amuse his guests he took them on hunting expeditions along the lake, and one day organized a joust in which he himself, riding furiously, was a leading performer. Meanwhile it was all too painfully evident to the prisoners from the cries they heard by day and night that others of his victims, Ethiopians who had fallen out of favour, were being flogged and tortured to death.

Then, with the beginning of the rains in June, cholera broke out. When a hundred men were dying every day Theodore ordered a general move around the southern end of the lake. On June 7 the whole army with the prisoners in its midst crossed the Blue Nile just below its outlet from the lake and marched on to Rassam's old headquarters at Korata. But still the disease continued to spread, and they went on eastwards towards the higher ground around Debra Tabor, about thirty miles from the unhealthy lake. Here the prisoners were taken to quarters at Gaffat about three miles outside the town. Theodore himself laid the carpets in Rassam's house, and set up his own throne there so that the place would look like a royal residence.

Bewildered, humouring him, calculating every word before he uttered it, Rassam passively went on playing his part as a favourite dog who is alternatively patted and kicked by his master. But things could not continue at this pitch of half-hysterical make-believe for much longer. The prisoners were suddenly brought in from Gaffat and thrust into dark rooms in Debra Tabor. Theodore came to visit them in the middle of the night carrying a lantern and a jug of tej to drink to their friendship. 'I used to hear that I was called a madman for my acts,' he said to Rassam, 'but I never believed it; now, however, after my conduct towards you this afternoon, I have come to the conclusion that I am really so. But as Christians we ought always to be ready to forgive each other.'

This was the last time Rassam spoke to Theodore for a year and nine months. The emperor vanished with his army into the wilderness of the Ethiopian plateau, murdering, torturing, and laying waste the country as he went along. Left behind in the pouring rain at Debra Tabor the prisoners sat, like shipwrecked sailors, in their dismal gaol awaiting rescue from the outside world.

15

No. 1 Army Pigeon

——

Flad reached England in July 1866, and he could scarcely have chosen a worse time to get a hearing. The Earl of Derby, with very tenuous support in the Commons, had only just succeeded in forming a Conservative government, and the riots and disturbances over the Reform Bill engrossed everyone's mind. Then, too, the outbreak of war between Prussia and Austria had been followed by a financial crisis in the City, and a disastrous cattle plague was spreading through England. Compared to these issues the Ethiopian affair was very small beer indeed, and the only satisfactory thing about it from the Conservative point of view was that the Opposition was hardly in a position to taunt the new government, since it was the Liberals who were responsible for failing to answer Theodore's original letter in the first place and for dispatching Rassam later on. Still, something had to be done. Cameron alone might, just conceivably, have been conveniently forgotten for the time being, but it was too much to overlook the detention of Rassam as well. Flad reported that at the time of his departure the prisoners were being treated reasonably well, but within a few weeks of his arrival in England the news of Rassam's imprisonment at Debra Tabor came through, and it was clear that Theodore was going to hold him as a hostage until he was either forced or cajoled into giving him up. Force at the moment, with so many crises impending at home, was impossible, and Derby (or rather his son Stanley, who was at the Foreign Office) naturally opted for diplomacy.

A group of skilled workmen was enlisted, and Flad was instructed to take them back to Ethiopia together with some suitable gifts and a letter from Victoria to Theodore. He was to make sure, however, that Theodore released the prisoners before the workmen or the gifts were handed over. One rather wonders who these skilled workmen were that they should be so willing to put themselves in the lion's mouth, but apparently they were readily obtained.

The letter that Victoria signed at Balmoral on October 4, 1866, was a nice blending of persuasion and dignified reproof. She still addressed Theodore as 'Our Good Friend', she indicated that she had received Flad and heard his news, and she added:

> We will not disguise from your Majesty that we found it difficult to reconcile your assurances with the obstacles which were still opposed to the departure of our servants and the other Europeans from your country but . . . we gave our sanction to the engagement in your Majesty's service of skilled workmen, such as you desired to employ in Abyssinia. These arrangements were made, and Flad was on the point of leaving England to rejoin your Majesty, when intelligence reached us that you had withdrawn from our servant Rassam the favour which you had

hitherto shown him, and had consigned him, together with our servant Cameron and the other Europeans, to prison. We have received no explanations from your Majesty of the grounds of a proceeding so inconsistent with the assurances and professions formerly made by your Majesty, and we have therefore lost no time in allowing Flad to depart, and have given him this letter for your Majesty, not allowing ourselves to doubt that immediately on its receipt you will redeem your promises, and give effect to your professions, by dismissing our servant Rassam, with our servant Cameron and the other Europeans in conformity with the statement made in your letter of the 29th of January.

Your Majesty must be aware that it is the sacred duty of Sovereigns scrupulously to fulfil engagements into which they may have entered; and that the persons of Ambassadors, such as our servant Rassam, and those by whom they are accompanied, are, among all nations assuming to be civilized, invariably held sacred. We have therefore the more difficulty in accounting for your Majesty's hesitation, and we invite your Majesty to prove to the world that you rightly understand your position among Sovereigns. . . . In the uncertainty which we cannot but feel as to your Majesty's intentions, we cannot allow Flad to be the bearer of those tokens of goodwill which we purposed that he should convey to your Majesty. But, in full confidence that the cloud which has darkened the friendship of our relations will pass away on the return of Flad, and desiring that you should as soon as possible thereafter receive the articles which we had proposed to send your Majesty in token of our friendship, we have given orders that those articles should be forthwith sent to Massawa, to be delivered, for conveyance to your Majesty's court, to the officers whom you may depute to conduct our servant Rassam, and our servant Cameron, and the other Europeans, so far on their way to our presence. And so we bid you heartily farewell.

There it was then, the tactful bribe with just a hint of a threat behind it; let Theodore send his prisoners down to the Red Sea coast and he would have his workmen and his gifts, and no harm done.

Flad set off from England in October 1866, and reached Ethiopia in December. Theodore received him at once and was delighted with the letter, but he saw quite clearly what the game was. He did not send a reply but wrote instead to Rassam in prison. 'As Solomon fell at the feet of Hiram,' he wrote, 'so I, under God, fall at the feet of the Queen, and her Government, and her friends. I wish you to get the workmen sent up via Metemma, in order that they may teach me wisdom, and show me clever arts. When this is done, I shall make you glad, and send you away, by the power of God.'

'To have refused the King's request,' Rassam says, 'would have placed all our lives in jeopardy,' and so he sent off a letter to Stanley asking him to agree to Theodore's request. Long before the letter reached England, however, Stanley had decided that it was impossible to bargain any further with Theodore for the moment and the workmen were sent home.

It was one of those dilemmas which are the agony of responsibility. What was the British Government to do? They were unwilling to invade, threats were dangerous and negotiation was leading nowhere. The only alternative was to do nothing and hope that the situation would resolve itself, and this in the end was the policy into which the government drifted. All the spring and early summer of 1867 went by, and in England the Ethiopian affair, like a recurring bad dream, was dissolved in the more pressing events of the day. After all, Ethiopia was very far away.

Meanwhile, Theodore was free to continue with his morbid threatening and tormenting of the prisoners. Early in July 1866 they had been moved under a guard of a hundred men from Debra Tabor to Magdala, some ninety miles away to the east. Cameron and his staff had already been imprisoned there for two years, and now they endured all the weariness and hopelessness of dragging themselves back to their old quarters on the great rock where they had already suffered so much. There was worse to follow. At Magdala fetters were hammered on to their legs once more, and this time Rassam, Blanc and Prideaux were also chained. The chamberlain Samuel accompanied them into captivity. There was no real hope of escape: Magdala was a natural stronghold standing high above the Bashilo River where it runs down to the Blue Nile in central Ethiopia. It was the plug of an extinct volcano, and its plateau of basalt, three-quarters of a mile long by about half a mile wide, was perched a thousand feet above the surrounding plain. There was only one practical path up the precipitous sides of the mountain, and it was blocked at the entrance to the citadel by a formidable gate. Even if the prisoners managed to free themselves from their fetters, even if they obtained scaling ladders or forced the gate, they were still hundreds of miles away from civilization in a country that lived in abject fear of Theodore. It might have been possible for one or two of them to have got away – and indeed Rassam was offered the chance – but then reprisals would certainly have been taken on those left behind, and in any case it was quite impractical to think that so large a party with so many women and small children in it could make its own unaided way out of Ethiopia.

And so they gave up thoughts of escape and made the best of things. Rassam, with a certain fatalism, says that apart from the fetters, none of them could really complain; much the worst part was the mental anxiety that at any moment they could be tortured or flung to death over the precipice, a form of execution Theodore had been fond of using in the past and was to use again. Physically they did rather well. They were accommodated in a group of huts close to the gate, and although these huts were made of branches and straw roofing, and water seeped through the bare floor in the wet season, they were soon made reasonably comfortable. Each hut was furnished with chairs, beds and a table, and had its fireplace in the centre of the floor. The prisoners still possessed their Ethiopian servants and their baggage and European stores, and they were well fed; it was nothing exceptional for them to sit down to a dinner of soup, fish, two or three *entrées*, a joint, pudding, anchovy-toast or cream-cheese. Tej, the Ethiopian mead, arak and coffee were obtainable, they made their own bread, and with seeds sent up from the coast by Merewether grew vegetables, which at this height and so near the Equator developed to a fantastic size: peas five feet high, monstrous potatoes, and tomatoes that bore fruit all round the year. Rassam attracted myriads of the brilliant Ethiopian birds to his garden.

They could not move outside their compound, but, for the rest, it was a fairly loose imprisonment. They could send and receive messages from the coast, and each evening a stream of sympathetic visitors, mostly the wives of Ethiopian nobles, came to see them. They played whist. In the absence of Theodore Magdala was governed by eleven chiefs and they were not unfriendly – they even offered to provide mistresses for the male prisoners, and no reasonable demand of Rassam was ever refused. But for the fear of Theodore the council would gladly have allowed them to escape.

Naturally as time went on and the monotony became oppressive there were disputes among the prisoners, but Rassam was accepted without question as their leader. He, together with Cameron, Blanc, Prideaux, the missionaries Stern and Rosenthal and the Irishman Kerans tended to hang together as a sort of governing committee for the whole group. It was perhaps fortunate that at this stage Bardel, the troublesome Frenchman, and the German artisans were not sent to Magdala; they remained in the royal camp. Flad on his return from England rejoined his wife and Mrs Rosenthal, who had been left behind at Debra Tabor, and also lived in relative freedom.

Magdala all through this time was being built up by Theodore as his principal capital, even though it was in the midst of the territory of the Moslem Gallas, his mortal enemies. It consisted of no more than two or three thousand huts scattered about the plateau, but it had its palace, its round church and a substantial house containing the royal treasure. Without ever appearing himself, Theodore gradually congregated his resources and dependants here, his treasure, his wives and mistresses, and such of his political prisoners whom he had not decided to exterminate as yet. These native prisoners, many of whom had been chained for years, were housed at the opposite end of the plateau to the Europeans, and included the Coptic Patriarch, an elderly Egyptian who, quite groundlessly, had been accused of treachery by Theodore in one of his xenophobic rages. Rassam managed to correspond with all these people, and his messengers kept him well informed about the situation in the rest of central Ethiopia.

This was chaotic. If there is such a thing as an inflationary spiral of tyranny it possessed Ethiopia now; indeed, from the end of 1866 onwards Theodore was less concerned with the government of the Ethiopians than with their extermination. In November of that year he fell on the old capital of Gondar, where some rebels were holding out, and destroyed it utterly, even its Christian churches. Mass killings, the burning of people alive by hundreds, became a commonplace, and the whole of the valley of the Upper Blue Nile was a scene of brutality and terror that not even Bruce, or perhaps anyone in these regions, had ever witnessed. And the more Theodore slaughtered the more rebellions rose up against him. Up to now the bulk of his army, numbering about 100,000, had remained loyal, mainly through the habit of dumb and terrified obedience, but by 1867 desertions had begun and the ranks were diminishing rapidly. The province of Tigré, under a chieftain named Kassai, broke away entirely, and when both Gojjam and Shoa rose as well two more rebel leaders, Menelek, who was of the true royal line, and Wagshum Gobaze, began to form strong centres of resistance. Once for seven weeks Theodore was cut off from Magdala itself.

Rassam, corresponding regularly with Merewether in Aden and the three main rebel chiefs, was well aware of all these upheavals, and in July 1867 Merewether was able to give him a little hope; in England public opinion was beginning to stir itself at last, and the government was coming around – reluctantly, cautiously, but quite definitely – to the notion that it was morally and politically bound to rescue the prisoners if British prestige was to continue to mean anything in Africa and the Near East. In August Derby went the whole way. A peremptory letter was sent to Theodore demanding the release of the prisoners forthwith, and when it remained unanswered orders were given for war.

The village of Adi Woka. From Holland and Hozier's Record of the Expedition to Abyssinia

There has never been in modern times a colonial campaign quite like the British expedition to Ethiopia in 1868. It proceeds from first to last with the decorum and heavy inevitability of a Victorian state banquet, complete with ponderous speeches at the end. And yet it was a fearsome undertaking; for hundreds of years the country had never been invaded, and the savage nature of the terrain alone was enough to promise failure. Unlike Bonaparte's expedition to Egypt, there was no secrecy whatever about this campaign, everyone knew all about it for months in advance, where it was going, what it proposed to do. It was debated at great length in the Press, and although there was general sympathy for the prisoners many people in England were by no means enthusiastic about it. How was the army to get itself across the 4,000-foot ravines in a country where there were no bridges, no roads, no modern appliances of any kind? Who could say that Theodore would not murder the prisoners out of hand once he heard the British had landed? Terrible dangers faced the soldiers; they would be exposed to unknown tropical diseases, adders would get into their blankets at night and fierce wild animals would attack them by day, they would die of thirst, they would die of frostbite, all their mules would succumb to the tsetse fly. One letter of protest followed another in the newspapers, and the insurance companies made a sharp increase in the rates applying to any man who took part in the expedition.

Wisely the government decided that if it was to go into this adventure at all things would have to be done with great thoroughness, whatever the expense. Control of the operations was confided to the Indian Army, since it was experienced in frontier warfare and could be transported without too much difficulty to the Red Sea, and the officer chosen to take command was one of the most promising soldiers of the day. Field-Marshal Lord Napier, whose statue looks down at us in Queen's Gate in London with such a grand air of distant horizons, may seem to the present generation a slightly comic figure, the apotheosis of the spit-and-polish, up-and-at-'em school of Victorian generals. He was, however, a great deal more than this. That battered face contains a strong suggestion of humour and intelligence. 'What do you think the Chinese in their *lingua franca* call the English Bishop?' he once wrote home from China. 'No. 1 Heaven Pigeon: pigeon being the general name for business of all kinds.' By the same token Napier himself might fairly have been described as No. 1 Army Pigeon. More than almost any other British soldier of his time he lived by war, but he did not come to it in the usual way. He was an engineer who for nearly twenty years had toiled up and down India building roads, canals, bridges and encampments before he was given a chance to show what he could do in an active command. When he did enter battle, however, he went in headlong, and at a time when the phrase was not as yet a music-hall joke, twice had his horse shot from under him; and he made no fuss about his wounds. It was the Mutiny that made him. He directed the defence of Lucknow until its second relief, and from there he went on to take command of the British expedition that went to China and entered Pekin in 1860. On his return to India he was given command of the Bombay army, which was now directed to Ethiopia.

He was at this time 57 years of age, and he had recently married, on the death of his first wife, an 18-year-old English girl. She appears to have run his household in Bombay – and it was an entertaining household where good dinners were served and French was spoken – with something of her husband's air of quiet authority.

The statue of Napier in Queen's Gate, London

RECORD

OF THE

EXPEDITION TO ABYSSINIA

COMPILED BY ORDER OF THE

SECRETARY OF STATE FOR WAR

BY

MAJOR TREVENEN J, HOLLAND, C.B. BOMBAY STAFF CORPS

AND

CAPTAIN HENRY M, HOZIER, 3RD DRAGOON GUARDS

VOL. I

UNDER THE DIRECTION OF

COLONEL SIR HENRY JAMES. R.E. F.R.S. M.R.I.A. &c.

DIRECTOR OF THE

TOPOGRAPHICAL AND STATISTICAL DEPARTMENT.

WAR OFFICE.

1870.

Compared with the British generals who in later years were to go to the Nile valley, Napier perhaps lacked something of Gordon's spirit, but he was a nicer, more modest man than Kitchener, and just as competent. It was his smile that the soldiers remembered, and the assurance he seemed to give, like an experienced sailor in a storm, that all would come out right in the end. Perhaps Wavell of the Army of the Nile was his counterpart in the present century.

The methods by which Napier went about directing the huge machine that was now placed under his control were extremely sensible. First, intelligence officers were set to work examining all the records and maps of European explorers in Ethiopia from the time of Bruce onwards. In London Samuel Baker, the ubiquitous Beke, and many other modern travellers and missionaries were consulted. Then while Merewether went off on a reconnaissance along the Red Sea coast to find a landing place, agents were sent inland to contact the dissident tribes.

By mid-August 1867 Napier was able to give the government his estimate of what was required: about 12,000 fighting men with roughly twice as many followers, at least 20,000 mules and other transport animals, artillery of all kinds including heavy mountain guns, and a fleet of 280 ships, both sail and steam, to carry the force to its destination. It was calculated that if the campaign were begun at the start of the dry season in December it could be completed by the following June – about six months in all.

Seventy years had now elapsed since Bonaparte's invasion of Egypt, and it is interesting to see what changes the industrial revolution had forced upon the art of war. The railway, the steamship and the telegraph, all of them unknown in Bonaparte's time, had now immensely extended the speed and scope of operations, and the range and power of guns had given the battlefield a new dimension. And yet there had been a slowing-down process as well: ten times the amount of equipment was required by a modern army in the field, and all the business of the commissariat arrangements – what we would now call logistics – had grown immensely complicated. In the French invasion of Egypt nearly every soldier fought; now at least a dozen non-combatants were needed to support just one man at the front. At the same time warfare had grown much less dangerous: mass killings like those at Borodino and Waterloo had vanished from the world and were not to reappear until the senseless holocaust of the trench fighting on the Western Front in 1914.

It was a fluid moment in military history, and the old methods were intricately, and sometimes absurdly, tied up with the new. The infantry square was still used and so were the brightly coloured uniforms which made such an admirable target on the battlefield. But the army's food was better, the medical services had changed out of recognition, the drill was more efficient, and the soldier was much less of an adventurer and more of a trained professional than he had ever been before. In brief, the army was now planned and managed like some great industrial organization, and it went to war on the momentum of its own routine.

Official military histories do not as a rule make very stimulating reading for later generations, and the two huge volumes (with a case of maps) which were got out in England after the Ethiopian campaign are no exception. But they do reveal the thoroughness and imagination with which this operation was planned, and it is simply staggering. There can hardly

The title-page of the official record of the Abyssinian expedition

have been more paper work done upon the landing of the Allied armies in Normandy in the last world war. It is the intelligence of these arrangements – the intricate dovetailing of things that were astonishingly modern with others that were hopelessly antique – that is so impressive. Thus, for example, forty-four trained elephants were to be sent from India to carry the heavy guns on the march, while hiring commissions were dispatched all over the Mediterranean and the Near East to obtain mules and camels to handle the lighter gear. A railway, complete with locomotives and some twenty miles of track, was to be laid across the coastal plain, and at the landing place large piers, lighthouses and warehouses were to be established. Two condensers to convert salt seawater into fresh were needed, and a telegraph line several hundred miles in length was to maintain communication between the front and the base on the coast. Three hospital ships were to be equipped with Keith's ice-making machines, and among their stock of medicine were 250 dozen of port wine for each vessel. Then there was the question of the Maria Theresa dollars, the only general currency in Ethiopia. Not any dollar would do; only the 1780 minting that Baker described as showing 'a profusion of bust' in the empress's image was acceptable, and a search of the banks and money-lenders in Marseilles, Cairo and Vienna revealed that not nearly enough were available. A contract therefore had to be signed with the imperial mint in Vienna for a new issue of 500,000.

The iron-girder railway bridge over the Kumayli torrent. From Holland and Hozier's Record of the Expedition to Abyssinia

Each white soldier was to have two pairs of boots, an Indian helmet, a flannel cholera belt and a pair of gloves, and the force was to be followed into the field by a horde of native servants, at least two for every officer, one for himself and another for his horse. The rates of pay descended from Napier's 5,833 rupees a month (about £580) to the native soldier's $8\frac{1}{2}$ rupees (about 85p). Chaplains got £50 a month and elephant mahouts £1.

The food situation was greatly complicated by the fact that so many of the men came from different races and sects, each with its own series of taboos, but a basic store was laid down of compressed vegetables, desiccated milk, 50,000 tons each of salt beef and pork and 30,000 gallons of rum.

The force was to be divided into two divisions, each under the command of an experienced Indian Army campaigner, and Merewether's Intelligence Corps contained some interesting people. They included Major James Grant, who with the late John Speke had recently discovered the source of the White Nile in Uganda, missionaries like Johann Krapf, who was the first European to see the snows of Mount Kenya and who had worked in East Africa for many years, and military adventurers like Captain C. Speedy and the Swiss Werner Munzinger, who knew Theodore and who could speak Arabic and Amharic. The British Museum sent a representative, Richard Holmes, who was to carry out archaeological excavations and to bid for the more worthwhile loot which, it was hoped, would be captured in Ethiopia – manuscripts, carvings and the like. A geographer and a zoologist were also added to the strength, and observers were sent by the French, Prussian, Italian, Dutch, Austrian and Spanish armies. Among the war correspondents were Henry Morton Stanley of the *New York Herald*, who was now on the threshold of his tremendous African career, and G. A. Henty, the author of the adventure stories, who represented the London *Standard*.

In the end, as always happens in every expedition, Napier found that he had underestimated the number of men he required, or rather, by a sort of military Parkinson's Law they spontaneously multiplied themselves. He finished up with 32,000 men (which included 13,000 soldiers, of whom 4,000 were Europeans and 9,000 natives) and 55,000 animals. But then this was a most unusual sort of campaign, a struggle against the physical nature of the country rather than against an enemy, a long march rather than a battle, and no naval man could fail to approve of the professionalism with which the whole vast, complicated organization was put into motion. From Calcutta and Bombay, from Liverpool and London, sailing ships and paddle-steamers, vessels that were a combination of steam and sail, converged upon the Red Sea at their appointed times. Half a million pounds was spent in hiring these ships from private firms, and they carried on board every possible contrivance to set up a new temporary civilization in the wilderness, for Napier expected, rightly, that he would find nothing in Ethiopia. The elephant squad alone, a minor piece in the immense jigsaw, required two transports to be specially fitted up. The animals were slung on board without mishap at Bombay and placed in holds with a temporary flooring of stones and shingle. They stood back to back with their heads towards the sides, and a corridor between them to allow the attendants to pass to and fro. A seasick elephant was a formidable thing, and in the Calcutta moorings they had to face a cyclone.

Early in October 1867 Merewether returned from his reconnaissance and reported that he had fixed on Zula as a landing place. This was a derelict village standing on an open plain in Annesley Bay, about thirty miles south of Massawa. Originally it had been a Greek settlement known as Adulis, and from here the caravan route led inland to the ancient city of Axum – the route that Merewether now proposed that they should roughly follow. In the dry season there was a scarcity of water and fodder at Zula, the region possessed no timber or stones for wharves, and the climate was intensely hot. These disadvantages, however, were outweighed, Merewether thought, by the presence of an almost land-locked anchorage, by the closeness of the mountains, only thirteen miles away, and by the fact

Embarking elephants at Bombay

that Zula was in Egyptian territory – and the Moslem Egyptians were ready to give all the help they could in a campaign against their ancient Christian enemies in Ethiopia. The landing therefore would be unopposed. Once the army had crossed the narrow coastal plain they would be faced with a very steep rough climb to the Ethiopian plateau 8,000 feet above, and even more difficult and dangerous passes lay beyond. But there was no avoiding these obstacles; this was the nature of Ethiopia and the explanation why she had never before been invaded as thoroughly as she was to be invaded now. All reports from the interior indicated that Theodore, beset by rebellions, would not contest the British march inland, but would make a stand at Magdala, which was therefore set as the first general objective of the expedition. It lay just under four hundred miles from the coast.

In mid-October 1867, the first advance-guard, mainly engineers, arrived at Zula and began to construct a port. By the end of the month a first pier, 700 yards long, was completed, with a tramway laid along it, and ships and barges were arriving on every tide to discharge their men, animals and stores. A hutted and tented town had sprung up in the billowing dust along the shore and every day it expanded. A labour force of many thousands of Indians, Persians, Egyptians and Ethiopians toiled back and forth between the ships and the shore. By the first week in December a second pier, 900 feet long and 30 feet wide, was

Annesley Bay

finished, the railway was being pushed inland and Zula had become a city; it had its native bazaar, its hospitals and storehouses and its huge compounds for the animals and their drivers. The two condensers fixed at the end of the piers were producing 160 tons of fresh water a day to add to the million tons brought over from Aden.

It was all most impressive, but it contained elements of chaos too. An unknown and unidentified fever had broken out among the horses and mules, and they were dying in hundreds every day. A fearful stench rose from the dead bodies that had been left to rot along the shore. Many of the animals that survived had been landed without attendants, or tethering ropes, and these roamed over the barren plain in search of water. But there was no water. In the appalling heat every well that Merewether had discovered in October went dry, and neither the condensers nor the incoming ships could keep up sufficient supplies to cope with the reinforcements of men and animals that were arriving every day. Frantic mobs of native workers gathered around the water points each night when the ration was doled out, and wildcat strikes were breaking out among the unloading parties. In the anchorage the shipping was getting itself into a serious tangle, and some vessels were left for days or even weeks before they could find a berth. Zula with its perpetual swarms of flies, its fearful heat, its resentful labour gangs and its dead and dying animals was a dismal place.

However, things were going rather better at the front where Merewether and the advance guard had pushed inland to a place called Senafé some forty miles from the sea. They had met no opposition from the inhabitants, but on their way up to the plateau along the dried-up bed of the Kumayli River they had encountered tremendous obstacles. On the Suru Pass, where the Ethiopian plateau rose up in a series of immense scarps and precipices, the track was barely twenty feet wide and strewn with boulders, and engineers were now at work there blasting and ramping a way through to enable the elephants, gun-carriages and carts to follow on. At Senafé itself all was transformed. Great forests of euphorbia, juniper and acacias spread away, water was fresh and abundant, and the temperature fell near freezing point at night. Both men and animals instantly revived once they reached these heights.

Merewether was already in friendly correspondence with Kassai, the rebel leader of Tigré, through whose territory the army was to pass, and messages had come in from the prisoners at Magdala saying that they were all well. He now dispatched Napier's ultimatum to Theodore. It ran as follows:

BELOW *The camp at Zula*

To Theodorus, King of Abyssinia.

I am commanded by Her Majesty the Queen of England to demand that the prisoners whom your Majesty has wrongly detained in captivity shall be immediately released and sent in safety to the British Camp.

Should your Majesty fail to comply with this command, I am further commanded to enter your Majesty's country at the head of an army to enforce it, and nothing will arrest my progress until this object shall have been accomplished.

My Sovereign has no desire to deprive you of any part of your dominions, nor to subvert your authority, although it is obvious that such would in all probability be the result of hostilities.

Your Majesty might avert this danger by immediate surrender of the prisoners. But should they not be delivered safely into my hands, should they suffer a continuance of ill-treatment, or should any injury befall them, your Majesty will be held personally responsible, and no hope of further condonation need be entertained.

R. Napier, Lt-General, Commander-in-Chief, Bombay Army.

It was a fine martial declaration, but it is doubtful if it would have had much influence on Theodore even if it had ever reached him. As things happened it fell into rebel hands and was delivered to Rassam in Magdala, who immediately destroyed it, fearing that it would enrage Theodore against the prisoners. Napier's second communication, a proclamation to the people of Ethiopia also issued about this time, was much more effective:

To the Governors, the Chiefs, the Religious Orders, and the People of Abyssinia.

It is known to you that Theodorus King of Abyssinia detains in captivity the British Consul

OVERLEAF *Watering the transport animals*

The view between Senafé and Rahaguddy. From Holland and Hozier's
Record of the Expedition to Abyssinia

Cameron, the British Envoy Rassam, and many others, in violation of the laws of all civilized nations. All friendly persuasion having failed to obtain their release, my Sovereign has commanded me to lead an army to liberate them.

All who befriend the prisoners or assist in their liberation shall be rewarded, but those who may injure them shall be severely punished.

When the time shall arrive for the march of a British Army through your country, bear in mind, people of Abyssinia, that the Queen of England has no unfriendly feeling towards you, and no design against your country or your liberty. Your religious establishments, your persons and your property shall be carefully protected. All supplies required for my soldiers shall be paid for; no peaceable inhabitants shall be molested.

The sole object for which the British force has been sent to Abyssinia is the liberation of Her Majesty's servants and others unjustly detained as captives, and as soon as that object is effected it will be withdrawn. There is no intention to occupy permanently any portion of the Abyssinian territory, or to interfere with the Government of the country.

Bonaparte's ghost, remembering the Mamelukes and his proclamation to the Egyptians, might have read these words and smiled.

The reconnaissance party now pushed on another thirty-seven miles beyond Senafé to the town of Adigrat in the heart of Kassai's country, and about a quarter of the way to

Magdala. They were met everywhere with friendliness, or at any rate with passivity, and there was still no sign of Theodore or his army.

On the coast meanwhile the situation had greatly improved with the arrival of General Staveley, the second-in-command. He provided Zula with a central strong control which had been lacking before since most of the senior officers had gone inland in the wake of the advance guard. Little by little the unloading programme was sorted out, the town reorganized and cleaned up, and the incoming soldiers were marched off towards the front as they came ashore. By the end of the year most of the fighting force had arrived, and the engineers had succeeded in opening up a rough cart-track all the way to Senafé on the heights above.

On January 2, 1868, Napier himself arrived from Bombay in the steam frigate *Octavia*, with his staff. He disembarked, says the official history, 'in some state'. The *Octavia* fired off all her guns and was given an answering salute from a mountain battery on shore. A guard of redcoats was drawn up on the wharf and the natives of Zula were treated to the strange and wonderful spectacle of a British brass band giving of its best amidst the swirling dust. The commander-in-chief was followed ashore by the first nineteen elephants, and the remaining twenty-five arrived soon afterwards, all of them eating well and apparently ready for the fray ahead. They were possibly the first Indian elephants seen in Africa since the time of Alexander the Great.

Napier, an engineering-general both by training and by the force of the present circumstances, got down briskly to work. He ordered an immediate acceleration of the programme of road and bridge building, of the digging of wells and the extension of the wharfs, and then turned to the organization of his striking force. An *élite* of 5,000 men was to make the final dash to Magdala, while the remainder were to guard the lines of communication to the coast. In order to relieve the burden on the long ant-like stream of mules and camels now on the march into the interior, instructions were given for all personal baggage to be cut down. Three officers henceforward were to share a bell tent and to make do with one mule each for their baggage, and with one mess-servant, one batman and one grass-cutter between them.

For three weeks Napier worked in Zula putting the final touches to his plans. Then on January 25 he went up to the pleasant heights of Senafé to take command in person. On this same day the expedition suffered its first casualty: a Colonel Dunn, V.C., was accidentally killed while shooting partridges in the hills.

16

Appointment at Magdala

——

Theodore first heard of the approach of the British in early December 1867, and he professed to be delighted. 'I long for the day,' he said to some of his German workmen, 'when I shall see a disciplined European army,' and he went on to speak of a legend that a great Ethiopian king and a great European king were destined to meet in Ethiopia and decide the country's future. It was clearly fixed in his mind that he would come to some sort of arrangement with the British, that they would recognize his greatness as an emperor and a man, and treat him accordingly. Whether or not his army was defeated in the field was merely incidental; indeed, he seemed almost eager to see it destroyed by Napier's modern guns.

Yet he proposed to fight. Already in December he had decided to make his stand at Magdala, and with that object he was constructing a road up to the fortress from the Bashilo valley so that his guns and heavy pieces of ordnance would be mounted on the heights. Theodore was not the first or the last paranoid to dream that with the aid of a new and miraculous invention he would put his enemies to flight and save the day at the eleventh hour. His faith was now fixed upon an enormous mortar which his German workmen had made for him. It was an astonishing weapon to have been constructed in these crude surroundings, a solid lump of metal weighing at least seventy tons and shaped like an upended church bell. When filled with pieces of metal and fired by a charge it was expected to produce the loudest and most devastating explosion that had ever been heard in Ethiopia. The mortar was lashed to a heavy wooden gun-carriage, and 500 men were engaged in dragging it yard by yard over the new road to Magdala.

Every week both the army and the road got a little nearer to the fortress, and by January Rassam was receiving a stream of affectionate messages from Theodore. 'How are you, my friend?' he wrote on January 4, 1868. 'The nearer I approach towards you the happier I feel.' And then a little later: 'By the power of God, I am coming to you. Oh my friend, do not think that I bear any hatred towards you. I have placed you in your present position in order that I may come to know the people of your country. . . . God knows I really have no hatred towards you.'

At the end of January Mrs Rosenthal and her child arrived from Debra Tabor together with the German workmen, and they were followed by a new batch of native prisoners who were sent to join the 400 others already chained in Magdala prison. For the Europeans this was an agonizing time. Hardly a day went by without Rassam receiving a message either from Theodore in the Bashilo valley or from Merewether in the British camp, each of them urging him to keep his spirits up – they were approaching as fast as they could. It was just a question as to whether or not he would receive Theodore's maniac embrace before the friendly British guns arrived. And if the British did arrive and proceed to mount their attack against Magdala, what then? Was Theodore going to let the Europeans go? Or was he going to throw them over the precipice?

Nobody in Ethiopia could answer that question at the moment, least of all the British at Senafé, 350 miles away. All that Napier could do was to advance and hope, like Theodore, that, by the power of God, all would be well. At the end of January James Grant was sent on ahead to arrange a meeting between Napier and Kassai, the new ruler of Tigré, and orders were given for a general move forward. It must have been a wonderful sight to see the column go by, nothing but the wild Ethiopian plain around it, the ragged mountains in

The elephant train

the distance, and, just occasionally, on the line of march a tumbledown village where the inhabitants stood like great flocks of birds, chattering, staring and apprehensive.

The cavalry came first, the troopers dressed in crimson caps and green uniforms, and the officers with silver helmets on their heads. Among the infantry that followed on, many of the white men in the Irish regiment wore beards, their cheeks burned a deep brown by the Indian sun, and the native soldiers, the 'Beloochees', marched along dressed in green tunics with red facings and with large green turbans wound round their fezzes. Others were got up in light blue and silver, or in the regulation scarlet jackets and white turbans, while others again among the European officers sported uniforms of their own design. 'One young lordling riding behind Napier,' Stanley says, 'wore kid gloves and a green veil.'

The transport train with the guns and stores came last, and it trailed across the country for seven miles with half the races of India and the Near East marching in its ranks: Turks, Persians, Egyptians, Arabs, Sikhs, Moslems and Hindus. The sight of the elephants with the heavy guns lashed to their backs and the mahouts sitting on their necks filled the

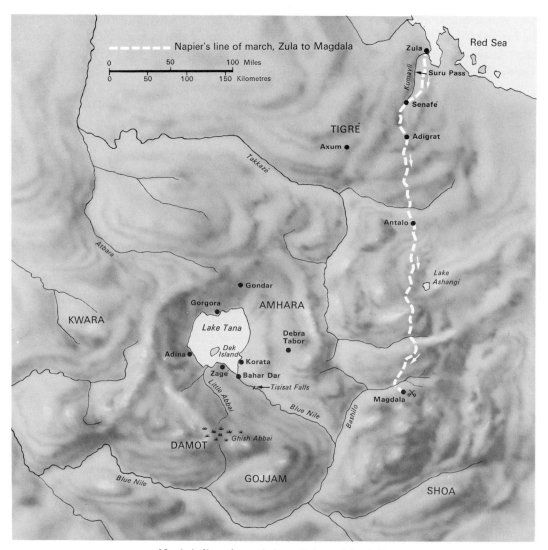

Napier's line of march from Zula to Magdala

Ethiopian villagers with amazement. Here in Africa the elephant was a wild and savage beast. To see it responding to commands and tamely ambling along almost as if it were a cow or an ox – this was a miracle.

Then somewhere in the midst of the vast procession there would be a brass band playing, a crowd of natives swarming round an overturned cart, or a sick protesting camel, a Moslem contingent prostrating itself towards Mecca, and a little group of Parsees riding along with sharp and sober faces, their saddle bags filled with Maria Theresa dollars with which at every halt they bargained with the villagers for food and fodder.

'The column,' Stanley says, 'in spite of its martial air, had something of a piebald look.'

Priests and villagers of Wadela singing the song of Moses for Napier

Yet the discipline was strict. 'No plundering took place,' says the official history of the campaign; and it adds, in one of its rare moments of skittishness, 'No swarthy damsel was subjected to any rude gallantry on the part of the redcoats.' At every village of any consequence Napier received the homage of the local chiefs, and such of the officers who had an interest in antiquities would go off with Richard Holmes, the man from the British Museum, to see the frescoes and manuscripts in the local church.

Each day reveille was sounded half an hour before dawn, and sometimes they were still on the move at nightfall, but naturally it was not a very rapid progress. They were travelling for the most part along a watershed where the headwaters of many small torrents had cut deep ravines into the plain on their way down to join the Nile, hundreds of miles away in the Sudan. To descend for thousands of feet into one of these ravines, to wait while the sappers threw a bridge across the stream and then to climb back to the plateau on the opposite bank – this could be the work of several days. Many of the mules fell sick at this altitude, and the nights were so cold that every man who could got himself under canvas. Napier's tent, at this early stage of the march, was a lavish affair lined with yellow cotton and carpeted with oriental rugs. Here each night the staff would gather to eat an enormous Victorian dinner, and Napier, if we are to believe Stanley, never failed to charm his guests. He loomed over the gathering, stout, blue-eyed, affable and attentive, a symbol of the days when manners and appearance were still compatible with war, and a general's dinner table was something more than a tray in a cafeteria.

These comfortable effects, however, were drastically reduced as the march went on, and the line of mules and oxen toiling back and forth to the base camp on the coast grew steadily longer. Camp followers and servants were sent back to Zula in hundreds, and the officers' baggage was cut down to seventy-five pounds. From now on even the young lordlings, bereft of their batmen, were 'obliged to rely on such assistance as they might obtain from

Kassai

the soldiery'. The soldiers on their side were restricted to twenty-five pounds each, and the rum ration was reduced to one dram a day. In Napier's tent pease pudding and biscuits took the place of the roast with a couple of partridges on the side, and Ethiopian tej circulated instead of port.

Thus lightened the column struck a faster pace. On February 7 Napier was in Adigrat, and a week later the advance guard reached Antalo, some two hundred miles from the coast and half way to Magdala. Here a large staging camp was formed and the column was thinned out again. It was like a growing tree, thick at the base where the railway had now reached the mountains and some twenty thousand animals were plying between one depot and the next, and very thin here at the top where only the fighting men and the engineers and their equipment were allowed to pass through. On the way to Antalo Grant came back with the news that Kassai was approaching with his army, and since Kassai was a valuable ally and this was the first real contact with the Ethiopians Napier halted to receive him with full military honours. The meeting took place on the banks of a small stream where the two commanders, like rival generals conducting a parley in a Shakespearian drama, had each erected a ceremonial tent. Kassai came forward riding on a white mule and with a crimson umbrella held above his head. He was surrounded by about four thousand warriors marching to the sounds of kettle-drums and with banners flying. Simultaneously the British approached, Napier riding on an elephant, with an elephant escort and the redcoats drawn

Captain Speedy

up behind. As Kassai drew near it was seen that he was wearing a lion-skin cape and a silk robe embroidered with large flowers, and his hair was bound up in plaits with a ribbon at the back. He was a man of about 35, dark-olive in complexion, and he looked a little harassed and careworn. Fearing treachery, no doubt, he flinched when the redcoats shot off a salute, but the interpreter, Captain Speedy, reassured him, and the two commanders and their staffs entered the British tent. Napier opened the negotiations by presenting Kassai with an Arab charger, a rifle and some pieces of Bohemian glassware. Port wine, taken from the hospital stores, was then drunk, and Napier took care to be the first to raise his glass to his lips to show that it was not poisoned. The Ethiopians were then treated to a display of British might; the guns were deployed, the infantry skirmished and formed square, and the cavalry in full ceremonial uniform dashed back and forth before the tent.

After this Kassai warmly assured the British that he would do everything in his power to

OVERLEAF *Kassai entertaining Napier*

assist them by providing food and fodder on the line of march, and Napier was now invited to cross with his staff to the Ethiopian tent. Here they were waited upon by Ethiopian girls. Bread and curry were served together with huge bullock horns filled with tej that were instantly replenished when they were emptied. While they ate and drank musicians with long pipes appeared and a minstrel singer, improvising as he went along, welcomed the British to Ethiopia. Napier was then draped with a lion-skin cape, and with a sword, a shield and a spear in his hands was mounted on a grey mule. Thus bedecked he rode back to the British lines under the curious eyes of his own soldiers.

The honours in this game had not altogether gone to the British. In the Ethiopian camp they had been very much struck by Kassai's warriors, their toughness and air of independence, and it was something of a surprise to find that almost every man was equipped with a serviceable rifle. Theodore presumably possessed just such guerrilla fighters as these, and Magdala, with its 1,000-foot precipices, still lay 200 miles away with many dangerous passes in between. Somewhat more cautiously the army pushed on again, and on March 17 Napier and his headquarters, following in the wake of the advance guard, reached Lake Ashangi, 100 miles from Magdala. They were now in a region of 9,000-foot passes, and the tracks up the cliffs were so steep and narrow that if one animal stopped all stopped. Sometimes when the guns were being hauled up and down ravines the whole column was wedged for an hour or more in an immovable traffic block. Tremendous thunderstorms swept the mountains almost every day, and the men were forced to march in sopping clothing with temperatures down to zero.

A further lightening of the baggage was now ordered and this meant that many of the soldiers were obliged to sleep out in the open at night and make do with half the normal rations. Constant rumours of the approach of the enemy passed along the column, but still no shot had been fired, and the sentries posted around the camps at night had nothing more dangerous to contend with than prowling hyenas and an occasional lion roaring over a kill in the darkness. On March 28 the advance guard reached the Takkazé River, forty miles in a direct line from Magdala. The two armies, Theodore in the south on the Bashilo and Napier in the north on the Takkazé, were now rapidly converging on one another, and the tension among the prisoners in Magdala had become extreme.

It was now more than four years since Cameron and his staff had been imprisoned, and all of them had been in chains for nearly two years, since the middle of 1866. During that long time they had learned to live from day to day with a certain fatalism, but this new element of tantalizing hope was difficult to bear. Every messenger from the emperor's camp was closely questioned about Theodore's changing moods, every morning they went to the ramparts hoping to see some sign of the approach of the British. Theodore in his letters to the prisoners continued to be remarkably benign, and on March 5 Rassam was overwhelmed to hear that his fetters were to be removed. 'Now,' Theodore wrote, 'when I, your friend, am brought by God near you, your chains shall be opened; but until I see the intentions of your masters we will watch you, but without chains. . . . Be of good cheer.'

He was as good as his word. 'Some of the chiefs,' Rassam says, 'assisted in striking off my fetters, whilst others placed their fingers between the iron and the flesh to prevent my ankles from being hurt.' He sent off a letter of thanks to Theodore and asked that his

The expedition nearing Lake Ashangi

companions should be released as well. Without precisely agreeing to this, Theodore redoubled his attentions. 'A good day to you, my friend,' he wrote on March 25. 'I am now so near that I can see the top of your house plainly; and if you come out and look down you will see my tent. Our meeting is at hand.'

It was painfully apparent. Two days later Flad arrived with the news that the road up to Magdala was almost complete, and it was plain that Theodore intended to get up to the Magdala heights before the British appeared. During the next few days more of the royal treasure was brought into Magdala, and from the ramparts the prisoners could see the advance guard of the Ethiopian army making camp on the plain of Salamgie, directly below the entrance gate. On March 27 Theodore himself arrived. Surprisingly, he made no attempt to see Rassam or the prisoners; he proceeded directly to the church to worship, and afterwards set himself up on his throne outside his palace. Here he sat for several hours receiving the trembling Magdala chiefs and accusing them of high treason in his absence. In the evening, having assured Rassam by letter that he would send for him shortly, he returned to his camp below the mountain, apparently in a black mood. That night fresh guards were placed on the European prisoners, and they were markedly and ominously hostile. Rassam, who was now in daily communication with the British camp, burnt all the letters he received.

On March 29 (the day on which the British began to cross the Takkazé) Theodore suddenly reappeared in Magdala, and Rassam was handed the following message: 'The reason I have ill-treated you was because I wanted the people of your country to come to me. I am glad they are coming. Whether they beat me or I beat them, I shall always be your friend. I wish to have an interview with you on the plain outside your house, and I want you to appear before me in the same dress in which you used formally to come to me. I will send for you when I am ready.' Rassam sent a submissive reply.

One cannot help wondering a little where one is in all this. Rassam has provided a very full account of all his dealings with Theodore, and yet it leaves one with the feeling that the other prisoners might have had another story to tell. There is something elusive about Rassam. Helpless though they all were in Magdala, he seems at times a little too soft, too compliant, too yielding for his own good. His intimacy with Theodore was certainly not all of his own making, but it is a special sort of intimacy, he submits with a feminine passivity, thinking that he will achieve more by the gentle word at the right moment than by an open show of resistance, and there is not much doubt that he was as strongly drawn to Theodore as Theodore was to him. But was this really the best attitude for the leader of a government mission to take up, even in such extraordinary and dangerous circumstances as these? Might not a less subtle and more downright man have made a stronger impression on Theodore and have brought him to his senses long before this? Theodore clearly saw in Rassam another courtier, a most interesting and valuable one, and it was very flattering to his ego to have in his power this foreign envoy always smiling and humbly submitting, no matter how badly he was treated.

This perhaps is putting Rassam's case in too harsh a light, but still one would have liked a word from Consul Cameron, or from one of the other Europeans, on these matters. Did they all agree with the way Rassam was handling things? Or was it simply that, in their misery and uncertainty, they were prepared to accept any leadership? And since Rassam's policy was patience and submissiveness were they swept along with it from day to day? But we hear nothing from Cameron, and it is interesting to note that Rassam in the book he subsequently wrote has hardly a word of praise or sympathy for the consul. Rassam's theme is, largely, The Emperor and I.

Not too much weight can be placed on Stanley's impressions, since he was an impulsive judge of character and all subtlety was anathema to him, but he too wrote a book on the campaign and his views have to be considered. He thought the prisoners a poor lot, venal, petty and forever quarrelling among themselves; and in particular he never loses an opportunity of making gibes at Rassam. Stanley clearly thought that if the prisoners had had an ounce of courage in them they would have managed to escape long ago.

There is one other aspect that remains something of a mystery. The German artisans seem to have got on very well with Theodore. They were never put in chains; they were not even sent to the Magdala compound. They remained with the emperor in his camp, and Theodore appears never to have mistrusted them as he did the British envoys and the missionaries. Perhaps they were too useful to be maltreated. But it could also be that a tough German stolidity was a more effective foil to Theodore's nervous and frantic mind than all Rassam's soothing diplomacy. It is only fair to add that Rassam thought throughout that he was acting for the best; he behaved towards Theodore as his instincts and his nature impelled him to do, and he was not without courage.

Now, at all events, he got into his blue uniform as soon as he read Theodore's letter, and presently he was summoned by an escort. He was met by an extraordinary sight when he emerged from the prisoners' compound. About two thousand square yards of the open ground had been covered with oriental rugs, and the emperor's ceremonial tent was set up at one end with a great gathering of chiefs around it. Theodore himself was closeted in the tent with his German artisans, but he came forward eagerly to shake hands with Rassam, saying, 'Today we must all be English.' It was nearly two years since they had last met, and Rassam was astonished at his appearance. His hair had gone grey and he looked ten years older. Noticing Rassam's surprise, Theodore said, 'Look at me, and see how grey I have become since we parted.'

'To give the subject a jocular turn,' Rassam says, 'I replied, "It is not to be wondered at that your Majesty has grown grey, considering that you have been enjoying the happiness of wedded life, whereas I am still unencumbered with the trouble and care of a wife." The banter contained in this reply drew a smile from the King, and placing his hands over his face he remarked, "There you hit me hard, my friend Rassam. . . . One day you may see me dead and while you stand by my corpse it may be that you will curse me. You may say then 'This wicked man ought not to be buried; let his remains rot above ground', but I trust in your generosity." ' Rassam begged that he would not mention such a calamity.

For the rest, Rassam goes on, Theodore's 'politeness was extreme, and he was all smiles, except when alluding to Consul Cameron. . . .' He toasted Rassam's health in tej, he roared with laughter at Rassam's jokes, and he instantly agreed that Prideaux and Blanc at least should be released from their fetters. On the subject of the approaching British army he was remarkably complacent: they were aware that he was the descendant of Solomon,

King of Kings, and all would be well. 'I hope, Mr Rassam,' he added, 'that when your people arrive they will not despise me because I am black; God has given us all the same faculties and heart.' With this the interview closed and Theodore descended again to his camp at Salamgie.

Four days later a second meeting took place. Rassam, Blanc and Prideaux were invited to witness the arrival of the great mortar, and on going down the mountain they found Theodore sitting on the edge of a precipice superintending the operations. The mortar was being hauled up a steep patch of the new road at an angle of forty-five degrees, and

Theodore's great mortar 'Sevastopol'. From Rassam's Narrative of the British Mission to Theodore

for a time it looked as though it would break away from its traces and go thundering down the valley. When it reached level ground at last Theodore turned to Rassam and questioned him about the British army – how powerful were their guns, how far could they shoot, how did the soldiers manœuvre? Rassam said he knew nothing of military matters and Theodore went on: 'How can I show these ragged soldiers of mine to your well-dressed troops . . . ? Were I as powerful as I once was, I should certainly have gone down to the coast to meet your people on landing; or I would have sent and asked them what they wanted in my country. As it is, I have lost all Abyssinia but this rock.' The mortar, he added, had been made not to be used against the British but his own countrymen. Then again he returned to his grievances against Cameron and the other prisoners, and it was some time before Rassam could bring him round to a better mood. In the end he agreed that Cameron and all the others who were still in chains should be released, and on returning to the compound in the afternoon Rassam found that the order had already been carried out.

Throughout this meeting Theodore had been rather muted, even a little pathetic, and the prisoners' hopes were further raised that night when a messenger arrived from Merewether saying that the army was now advancing beyond the Takkazé.

During the next six days the prisoners heard very little from Theodore. It was said that he had gone off on a plundering expedition in the Bashilo valley and that, on his return to his camp, he did nothing each day but ascend to the neighbouring height of Selassie with his telescope to scan the horizon for the British troops.

Napier was now making excellent headway. There had been a slight hold-up on April 2 when the advance guard, mistaking some friendly Ethiopian warriors for the enemy, had opened fire, but apologies and gifts had been sent to the local chieftain and the army had pressed on again. On April 5 they reached Theodore's new road on the Chetta River, and at once they began the descent into the Bashilo valley, which was some 3,900 feet below the general level of the country. Magdala, only ten miles away, was now clearly visible, and Napier, on going ahead to reconnoitre, was not reassured. 'Altogether, without taking into account Magdala itself,' he wrote later in his dispatches, 'the formidable character of its outworks exceeded anything which we could possibly have anticipated. . . .' Three flat-topped peaks, each about 9,000 feet in height, rose before them: Fahla on the right, Selassie (whence Theodore was now gazing down on them) on the left, and finally Magdala itself. It seemed to Napier that Fahla, the first peak, and the Aroge plateau below it, dominated the position, and that if he could take these places he could then march on along a saddle to the Salamgie plain where Theodore was now encamped. Whether or not Theodore gave battle either on the Aroge plateau before Fahla, or on the Salamgie plain, Magdala itself would have to be taken by assault. While the main gate was forced by a frontal attack an attempt would have to be made to climb the 1,000-foot cliffs of the fortress with the aid of scaling ladders – one of the most dangerous operations imaginable. That night Napier completed his plans.

About two thousand men were to go into the attack, each carrying in addition to his rifle and ammunition four pounds of rations and a water-bottle which was to be filled in the Bashilo River at the time of the crossing. Sappers and infantry were to lead the way with the guns coming up behind, and the cavalry was to be held in reserve. To prevent Theodore from beating a retreat at the last moment, the Galla tribesmen were to be asked to surround the fortress while the battle was going on – a duty which they were very willing to undertake since Theodore within the past week had utterly ravaged the country around Magdala, and their hatred of him had risen to a frenzy.

Despite his constant communication with Rassam, Napier had difficulty in making any precise estimate of the enemy's strength, but he judged it to be around seven thousand fighting men, most of them equipped with rifles and supported by the mortar and several batteries of guns. If they chose to make a strong stand at Magdala they could certainly inflict heavy casualties and withstand a siege of weeks or even months. For the moment, however, it appeared that Theodore was deploying on the Salamgie plain; from April 5 onwards the British could clearly see his tents and the smoke of his army's cooking fires.

Napier sent off a native messenger with his final ultimatum: 'By the command of the Queen of England I am approaching Magdala with my army, in order to recover from your hands Envoy Rassam, Dr Blanc, Lieutenant Prideaux, and the other Europeans now in your Majesty's power. I request your Majesty to send them to my camp as soon as it is sufficiently near to admit of their coming in safety.'

The final forced marches were particularly severe. Rain and hail storms drenched the men by night, and by day the clear mountain sun was unbearably hot. The elephants were in great distress. They slipped and fell on the wet ground, and for a time some of them refused to go on. When the baggage train fell further and further behind on the narrow tracks many of the men went for thirty-six hours or more without food – and this at the end of an exhausting four-hundred-mile march from the coast. But it was a stimulating thing to see the enemy at last, after three long months in Ethiopia, and the official dispatches are probably not exaggerating when they say that the men, Indians and British alike, went forward with enthusiasm. By the night of April 9 the assault force was congregated on the Bashilo, and on the following morning, Good Friday, they crossed the stream barefooted, stooping to fill their water-bottles on the way. Then, in dead silence, they began climbing the escarpment on the opposite side. They had about five miles to go to reach their first objective, the Aroge plateau.

Theodore meanwhile had posted his mortar and seven guns on the heights of Fahla, while he himself, with the bulk of his men, still remained encamped about a mile and a half further back on the Salamgie plain. At dawn on April 8 Rassam received a message to say that he and all the prisoners, European as well as native, were to descend at once to this camp. They found Theodore dressed in white pantaloons and a robe of Lyons silk worked with gold. 'He looked,' says Rassam, 'more like a harlequin than a sovereign in this novel motley suit'; but his manner was anything but gay. For an hour he talked to the British prisoners, comparing himself to Damocles, but saying that they at least would be safe: he had brought them down from Magdala so as to keep them under his eye. While their own tents and baggage were being fetched they were to lodge themselves in a silk pavilion which he had had specially erected for them, close to his own. The soldiers were then mustered on the plain, and Rassam and his companions looked on while Theodore harangued them from a rock. In a day or two, he said, they were to encounter troops who were far superior to themselves – men who were so rich that their treasure was carried on elephants. 'Are you ready to fight?' he went on, 'and enrich yourselves with the spoils of the white slaves, or will you disgrace me by running away?'

One old man made the expected reply – they would rend the British to pieces – and at once Theodore rounded on him. 'What are you saying, you old fool? Have you ever seen an English soldier? . . . Before you know where you are your belly will be riddled with bullets.' After a few more pleasantries of this kind Theodore dismissed his men, and Rassam now found an opportunity of asking him why he did not enter into negotiations with Napier. 'What is the use of it?' Theodore answered. 'The die is cast. Things must take their course.' He went off then to Selassie with his telescope, and when he returned in the afternoon he told the British prisoners that he had seen a line of elephants laden with baggage coming up the Bashilo valley. He seemed to be in a detached and exalted mood. Nearly 600 native

The Chetta ravine. Watercolour by Frank James

The prisoners released: departure . . .

prisoners had been brought down from Magdala with the Europeans, and in the course of the day most of the women and children, 186 in all, were released, together with 37 chiefs.

The Europeans spent the night in their pavilion, and on the following morning they heard that Theodore had declared a general amnesty. It was a long business, however, getting the fetters opened; by four in the afternoon only ninety-five men had been released, and some of the other prisoners, mostly Gallas, began to complain of the delay. As though he had been waiting for something of this sort to occur, Theodore suddenly went berserk. He rushed out of his tent, sword in hand, and ran with his bodyguard to the huts where the native prisoners were quartered, close to the edge of a precipice. The Europeans were ordered to stay in their tent and did not see the massacre that followed, but they heard the shots being fired and the shouts and screams of the victims. For two hours the prisoners were dragged before Theodore one after another. Hardly any of them had committed any crime more serious than having laughed in Theodore's presence when he was in a black humour or perhaps having failed to hand him a gun or a sword at the right moment. For this they had remained for months, even years, in chains and were now assassinated. He listened, insane with rage, as each wretch was led up to him and the charge was read out, and the verdict was almost always the same: 'Take him away.' The man was then pitched over the precipice, and those that survived the fall were shot dead by riflemen posted in the ravine below. At the height of his fury Theodore himself cut one man through with his sword and shot two others with his pistol. One of the prisoners was a man who had been convicted of interfering with Theodore's concubines, and for a long time had been chained in Magdala along with his two quite innocent sons. The two boys were now led forward and

. . . or death – Theodore's prisoners pitched over the precipice

were instantly ordered to execution, but when the father appeared Theodore, out of some maniac caprice, shouted out, 'Open his chains and let him go.' The killing went on until nightfall before he had had enough; by then 197 bodies lay mangled on the rocks below.

Throughout that night the camp lay still, apprehensive and silent. Theodore slept very little. His servants said later that he ordered arak to be brought to him, and that he passed most of the night drinking and praying. Over and over again he fell on his knees pleading for forgiveness for the massacre he had just committed. In the morning of April 10 the European prisoners were told that Theodore had changed his mind about them: they were to return at once to Magdala, and they were advised to move off without delay since he was still in a savage humour. Rassam, however, made one more effort to get him to open negotiations with Napier. Theodore replied to his letter: 'Do you want me to write to that man? No I will do nothing of the kind since he has been sent here by a woman.'

As the Europeans were leaving the camp Napier's messenger arrived and the ultimatum was handed to Rassam. He at once sent a further note to Theodore asking for permission to bring the messenger before him. Theodore replied by letter, refusing to see either the ultimatum or the messenger. 'If you yourself communicate with the British,' he added, 'my friendship with you will cease and the blood of your messenger will be on your head. Beware.'

On returning to their compound in Magdala the Europeans found the place deserted; many of the civilians had decamped in the night, and barely fifty fighting men were left to defend the fortress. The day had broken grey and sultry, and huge thunderclouds were building up over the mountains.

17

An Easter Death

———

There is a strong atmosphere of fantasy about the Battle of Magdala, and it is not entirely confined to the part played by the Emperor Theodore. In a sense, of course, all battles are fantastic, since they are an abrogation of reason, a deliberate courting of death, but here most of the normal conditions of war seem to be lacking, the pattern is wrong, far too much is being done for too small an object. It is quite unlike Bonaparte's invasion of Egypt or Mohammed Ali's raid on the Sudan; Bonaparte and Mohammed Ali were out for power and possessions, and the Mamelukes and the Sudanese tribesmen fought for their homes and their lives.

But in Ethiopia the British sought no gain of any kind, and they had no quarrel with the Ethiopian people. Once the prisoners had been released they were determined to go away and leave the country to its own dark devices. In other words, the whole vast expensive operation was nothing more nor less than a matter of racial pride; Theodore had affronted a great power and now he was to be punished.

No one could seriously blame the British in all this. They had been extremely patient and reasonable. And yet in an odd way it is Theodore, the arch-criminal himself, who lifts this whole affair out of the ordinary ruck of colonial warfare. Even in the midst of his murderous tantrums he raises issues that are something more than the crude struggle for survival. In his own savage and groping manner he is an elemental figure defying destiny, and he expresses something of the endless conflict between men's sense of guilt and their fundamental discontent with life: their need for a religious certainty. If one can overlook his brutalities for a moment one sees that he was an utterly displaced person, a Caliban with power but none to guide him: he had no place. Napier, with his young wife in the background, his long training and now his peerage in prospect, knew exactly where he was. He was bound on a rational and honoured career; he was placed, he accepted the world. Theodore accepted nothing. He was caught in the African predicament – the imperative need of the intelligent man to emerge from sloth and ignorance – and it was too big for him. All his protests and questionings had merely deranged his mind, so that he saw shadows and treacheries everywhere, and hatred instead of the thing he yearned for – love. He had reached the end, and he knew it and it was intolerable. There remained to him only his pride and a last clutching at dignity.

And so to settle an issue of pride, one man's pride against a nation's, we have now the extraordinary spectacle of two armies advancing against one another high up in this remote eyrie in the Ethiopian mountains. These armies are ignorant beyond dreams; they know nothing of one another's language, politics or way of life. They have no real hatred of one

At dawn on April 11 the British outposts caught sight of a little group approaching, carrying a white flag, and there was a great shout of excitement when it was seen that there was a British uniform (Prideaux's) among them. With cheering soldiers pressing round them the party was quickly passed through to Napier's tent on the further side of the Aroge plateau. They gave the General a verbal message from Theodore saying that he wanted 'a reconciliation', and Napier drafted the following reply:

'Your Majesty has fought like a brave man, and has been overcome by the superior power of the British Army. It is my desire that no more blood may be shed. If, therefore, your Majesty will submit to the Queen of England, and bring all the Europeans now in your Majesty's hands, and deliver them safely, this day, in the British Camp, I guarantee honourable treatment for yourself, and all the members of your Majesty's family.'

This message was buttressed by a threat: the son-in-law, Dejach Alami, was shown the elephants and the heavy guns which had now been brought up, and was told that the weapons which the British had used on the previous day were nothing but playthings to those that would now be employed unless Theodore surrendered. If he tried to escape he would be pursued to the ends of Ethiopia. Dejach Alami was also informed that reprisals would be taken upon him and the other chieftains if they failed to restrain Theodore from further brutalities.

Somewhat shaken by this, Dejach Alami pleaded for a twenty-four hours' delay, which was granted, and Flad and Prideaux, with some misgivings no doubt, returned with him to the emperor's camp. Theodore questioned them very closely about the exact meaning of Napier's letter. What did he mean by honourable treatment? Did they intend to treat him as a prisoner or were they going to assist him in recovering his country from the rebels? And did the British really intend to look after his family? – it was very numerous. He seemed to be in a repressed and dangerous mood again, and Flad noticed a renewed air of belligerence in the Ethiopian camp. It had been feared that at least half Theodore's army had been slaughtered, but now that the night had passed it was seen that the casualties were much fewer than had been supposed. Some of the surviving chiefs were talking of making a further attack on the British that night under the cover of darkness.

Moreover, the reply that Theodore now sent back to Napier was hardly a good augury. He did not mention the prisoners. He did not refer to his own surrender. Instead he declaimed against his own people for their cowardice in battle, their hatred towards him, their irreligion. But then, as though he himself had already passed from the scene, he appealed to Napier, in Biblical language, to look after them:

'In my city there are multitudes whom I have fed: maidens protected and maidens unprotected; women whom yesterday made widows; and aged parents who have no children. God has given you the power. See that you forsake not these people. It is a heathen land. . . .

'Out of what I have done of evil towards my people may God bring good. His will be done. I had intended, if God had so decreed, to conquer the whole world; and it was my desire to die if my purpose could not be fulfilled. Since the day of my birth till now no man has dared to lay hand on me. Whenever my soldiers began to waver in battle, it was for me to arise and rally them. Last night the darkness prevented me from doing so.

'Your people who have passed the night in joy; may God do unto you as he has done to me.

I had hoped, after subduing all my enemies in Ethiopia, to lead my army against Jerusalem, and expel from it the Turks. A warrior who has dandled strong men in his arms like infants will never suffer himself to be dandled in the arms of others.'

This letter, together with the letter Theodore had already received from Napier, was handed to Prideaux and Flad and they were told to return alone to the British camp.

Soon after they had gone Theodore called a council of war, and at this meeting a strong group of his chiefs pressed for the murder of the European prisoners and a renewal of hostilities. Theodore disapproved, saying that if the prisoners were murdered Napier was bound to take reprisals: they must be released. Towards four in the afternoon a group of chiefs were sent to Magdala to bring Rassam and the other Europeans down to the camp.

Throughout these discussions Theodore had seemed relatively calm, but now suddenly, while awaiting the arrival of the prisoners, he flew into a violent spasm of rage. He picked up his double-barrelled pistol, thrust it into his mouth and pulled the trigger. Apparently he had cocked the wrong barrel, for there was no explosion, and one of his men rushed at him and tore the weapon away. In the scuffle the bullet went off and grazing Theodore's ear expended itself harmlessly in the air. Theodore then covered his head with a cloth and laid down on the ground.

Up to this point no one dreamed that Theodore would ever let the prisoners go, and it was now regarded as almost certain that, in his present delirium, he would have them shot when they entered the camp. The prisoners felt this too, and they came down the steep track from Magdala in silence and with the utmost dread. As they were approaching the camp they were told that the emperor had left his tent and was now awaiting them on the road that led down to the British lines. He wanted to see Rassam alone. Leaving the others behind in a group on the roadside, Rassam went forward and found Theodore standing among about twenty of his bodyguard and the German engineers. He was at once beckoned forward, and Theodore asked him how he had passed the day. Then, looking up towards the sun, Theodore said: 'Do you not think it is late for you to go this afternoon to your camp? Would you rather go at once or spend the night with me, and in the morning I will send you straight to your people?'

Rassam answered that he would do whatever Theodore pleased, and Theodore answered, 'Good; you had better go now. But sit down for a moment and let me have a few words with you before you leave.' They sat together on the ground, and Theodore went on, 'You know, Mr Rassam, you and I have always been on good terms. God knows your heart, but as far as I am concerned I have always had a sincere regard for you. It is true that I have behaved badly towards you, but that was because of the behaviour of bad men. However, the past cannot be helped now, and I can only say, God's will be done. I want you to bear this in mind – that unless you befriend me I shall either kill myself or become a monk. Now, good-bye: it's getting late; try and come to see me tomorrow if you can.'

'I then thanked him for his kindness,' Rassam writes, 'and said, "I will come and see your Majesty if possible." He asked again, "Will you come tomorrow?" I replied that it all depended on the orders of the Commander-in-Chief. He then rose, shook hands with me, wept and said, "Farewell; be quick, it is getting late." '

This presented an agonizing difficulty. The rest of the prisoners, including Cameron, whom Theodore hated, were still in a group further up the road. If Rassam walked on alone there was still no guarantee that Theodore might not suddenly order them to be shot down as they went past him. His bodyguard were standing ready with their rifles. Rassam said, 'I thank your Majesty, but my companions are behind.'

'His only answer,' Rassam continues, 'was – and these words were the last I heard from his lips – "You had better go." I was now anxious about my fellow captives, and after

'*The people we came to release*': (standing) *Stern, Rosenthal;* (seated) *Rassam* (in chains), *Mrs Rosenthal, Cameron, and* (far right) *Blanc;* (seated on ground) *Kerans, Prideaux and Pietro, a member of Cameron's staff. Photograph taken by 10th Company, Royal Engineers*

walking on a few paces I stopped. The King was still standing on a rock, surrounded by his musketeers, and holding a double-barrelled rifle in his hands. When he saw me stop and look round, he motioned me with his hand to go on. My fears then began to increase; still, I apprehended that if I said anything we should all be shot down, so I proceeded a few steps farther and stood still, when, to my intense joy, I saw my fellow-captives coming down the hill towards me.'

On their way into the British camp they met Flad and Prideaux, who were returning to Theodore with a message from Napier saying that he could offer no other terms. Since most of the prisoners were now released there was no point in Flad and Prideaux again putting themselves into Theodore's hands that night, and they turned back with the others. The whole party entered the British lines soon after dusk and was received with some emotion in Napier's tent.

Napier was not quite out of his difficulties as yet. Theodore was still at large, Magdala was still in his hands, and even worse, Mrs Flad had been left behind in the fortress since she had been too ill to descend the mountain. Her children were still with her there and a number of other Europeans and their families, mostly Germans, had also remained in Theodore's camp.

The morning of Easter Sunday, however, brought a more encouraging letter from Theodore. He described how 'Satan had come to him in the night' and how he had unsuccessfully tried to commit suicide, and he continued: 'God having thus signified to me that I should not die but live, I sent to you Mr Rassam, that same evening, that your heart might be made easy. Today is Easter; be pleased to let me send a few cows to you. The reason of my returning to you your letter yesterday was that I believed at the time that we should meet one another in heaven, but never on earth.

'I let the night pass without sending for the body of my friend, Gabry, because I thought that after my death we should both be buried together; but since I have lived be pleased to allow him to be buried. You require from me all the Europeans. . . . Well, be it so; they shall go. . . .'

On receipt of this letter Flad set off with a party to bring his wife down from Magdala in a palanquin, and on the way through Theodore's camp they delivered the body of his friend Gabry. That evening, Sunday, April 12, all the remaining Europeans, except the Frenchman Bardel, who was too ill to be moved, were safely brought down to the British. Through the course of the day Theodore sent down 1,000 cows and 500 sheep – all he possessed – to the British camp, and for a time he seems to have been under the impression that they had been accepted. Napier, however, had been informed that, by Ethiopian custom, if he accepted the gift he was morally bound to conclude peace, and the herds were consequently turned back by the pickets.

When on the Sunday evening Theodore heard this news, he exclaimed, 'These people, having got what they want, now seek to kill me,' and in a fury rushed up the path to Magdala calling on his chiefs and soldiers to follow him. He seems to have had some confused idea of escaping on foot by way of a steep path that led down from the ramparts on the eastern side of the fortress, and he planned, he said, to make his way back to Lake Tana and the Blue Nile. About two thousand men followed him at first, but it was a hopeless venture; the Gallas were lying in ambush all round the mountain hoping that just such an attempt would be made, and when his followers began to turn back Theodore himself returned to Magdala. Bitter arguments appear to have continued there through most of the night, Theodore accusing his chiefs of cowardice, and the chiefs replying that he must either surrender or fight: they refused to follow him into retreat since it meant leaving their families and possessions behind. In the end the chiefs agreed among themselves that surrender was the only course, and they decided that if Theodore attempted to carry out any further executions they would seize him and put him in chains. During the night thousands of warriors with their families began to decamp to the British lines.

Plan of the Battle of Magdala

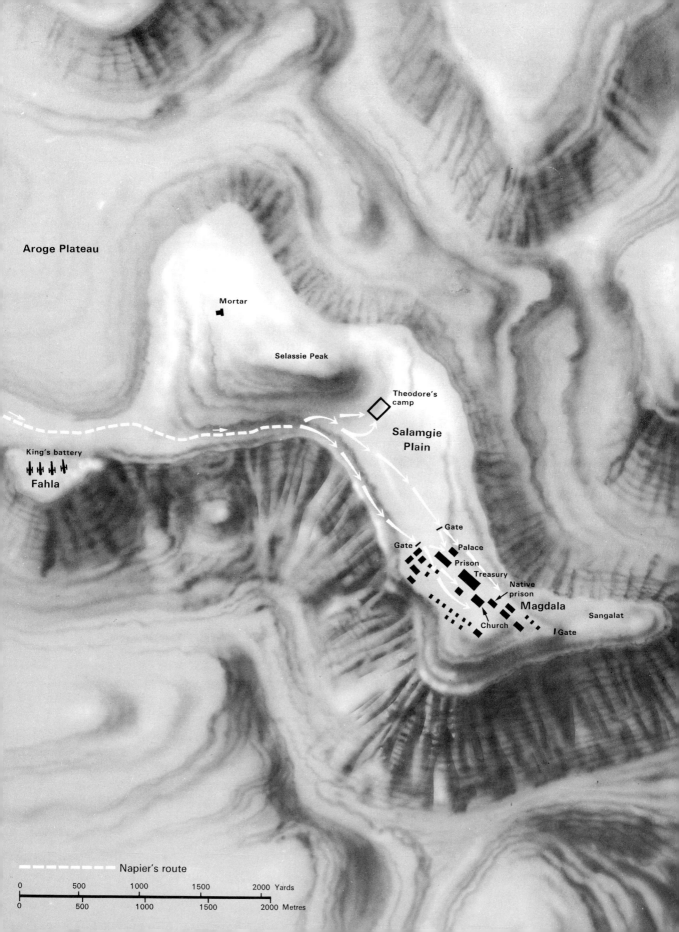

Aroge Plateau

Mortar

Selassie Peak

Theodore's
camp

Salamgie
Plain

King's battery

Fahla

Gate

Gate   Palace
              Prison
              Treasury
                          Native
                          prison

Magdala   Sangalat

Church   Gate

Napier's route

| 0 | 500 | 1000 | 1500 | 2000 Yards |
| 0 | 500 | 1000 | 1500 | 2000 Metres |

The end was now coming very close. Theodore got up at dawn on Monday, April 13, determined that he himself at least would not surrender. He descended the mountain once more to Salamgie with some forty or fifty men who still remained loyal to him, and together they tried to move a battery of heavy guns up the precipitous path to the gate of the fortress. It was an absurd project, and they were interrupted in the midst of it by the appearance of a party of British cavalry. This was too much for Theodore's overburdened mind. He jumped on his horse and began to ride furiously back and forth across the plain, shouting out boasts of his own prowess, firing his rifle in the air, and challenging the British to single combat. When no notice was taken of him he was induced at last by some of his men to retire up the path to Magdala. Here, with a little handful to help him, he set to work piling up huge stones against the entrance gate. They were still engaged on this work at one in the afternoon when the first British shells began to fall.

Napier had decided to give Theodore a little further time to surrender – a little more rope with which to hang himself – but on hearing during the night a rumour that he had escaped he had decided on immediate action. Messages were sent to the Galla tribesmen offering a reward of 50,000 dollars for the capture of the emperor, dead or alive, and in the British camp some three thousand men with artillery support were ordered into the assault. By 8.30 a.m. on April 13 they had covered all the approaches to the Magdala gate, and it was

Storming Magdala on Easter Monday

a little after this that the squadron of cavalry had surprised Theodore on the Salamgie plain. Refugees were now streaming down towards the British lines on every side, and the infantry were obliged to pass through them as they advanced in skirmishing order to the foot of the Magdala cliffs. The first salvoes of rockets were directed on the gate, a pagoda-like affair with a roof and two heavy wooden doors, and the assaulting parties immediately went forward with scaling ladders, some of them using the path, while others scrambled directly up the cliffs towards the ramparts. It was a long climb; rain was falling again, and the noise of thunder combined with the crashing of shells above their heads. Towards 4 p.m. the advance guard reached the gate and here they came under rifle fire while they hacked away at the doors with crowbars. It was not a very heavy fire – only a handful of the enemy were shooting at them from above – but nine of the British went down before they forced their way through. Simultaneously the party that had scaled the ramparts came running in behind the gate from the flank. The little group of defenders now retreated to a second, smaller, gate about seventy yards further up, losing most of their number on the way. This second gate was open, and the British rushed through it on to the Magdala plateau, only to discover that all resistance had collapsed. From every direction Ethiopians came forward to surrender, and presently the watchers on the plain below saw the Union Jack go up on the ramparts. The total British casualties were just fifteen wounded.

On the path leading up to the palace from the second gate a dead man was found lying

The exodus of Theodore's broken army

Theodore, dead

alone on the ground, and no one took much notice of him at first. Yet this was the Emperor Theodore. He had led the resistance at the gate and had gone on firing until it had been broken down. Retreating then through the second gate, he had told his last surviving followers to escape, and had taken his pistol in his hand – one of those same pistols that Plowden had given him so long ago as a gift from Queen Victoria. He had put the muzzle in his mouth, and this time he had not misfired. Rassam, following in the wake of the assault troops, was called to identify the body. Its clothing was already much torn and pulled about by souvenir hunters, and he remembered the voice saying, 'One day you may see me dead and while you stand by my corpse it may be that you will curse me. You may say then "This wicked man ought not to be buried; let his remains rot above ground", but I trust in your generosity.' Rassam had the body taken up and carried to his old quarters in the European compound, where it was covered by a shroud and laid out on a bed.

On the following day Theodore was buried in Magdala church by Coptic priests, and it was, Rassam says, 'an affecting sight to witness the reverence with which the dignitaries of the Church performed these last offices for their departed Sovereign; even in death Theodore had not wholly lost the affection of at least some of his subjects'.

In Magdala meanwhile there was utter confusion. A few of the Ethiopian soldiers had tried to escape by way of the footpath on the eastern side, but they had been immediately confronted by Galla tribesmen who, according to one eye-witness, had cried out to them, 'Come, beloved, come' – at which they had turned back and had joined in the general surrender.

The looting began about 4.30 p.m. with the breaking open of the treasury and the royal palace, and there were some very spectacular things to be had since Theodore had collected here all the remaining ancient treasure of the Ethiopian kings. Stanley speaks of gold chalices, mitres and crowns; of goblets, ornaments studded with precious stones, gifts from foreign monarchs such as Sèvres china and Staffordshire pottery, cases of champagne and other wines, silk tents, carpets, furs, lion capes, ornamented saddles, State umbrellas, swords, embroidered robes, parchments and official papers galore. All these, Stanley says, were tossed about and quarrelled over by soldiers and civilians, and some of the worst of the looters, he asserts, were the European prisoners who had come back to Magdala after the assault. It was not long before the soldiers found the royal stores of tej and arak, and presently the Galla tribesmen who had come rushing in to do murder and join in the general uproar had to be driven off with rifle fire.

The arrival of Napier quietened the worst of these disturbances. A brass band preceded

Some of the treasure of the Ethiopian kings

him, and he marched with his staff and flagbearers through the gate to the strains of 'See, the Conquering Hero Comes!' One of his first acts was to release about 90 Ethiopians who were still manacled in the prison, and to make arrangements for the civilian population. Apart from the 60 Ethiopians who had been killed and the 120 who had been wounded in the fighting, about 4,000 people had been found in the fortress, and it was clear they could not stay where they were. There was an extreme shortage of water on the plateau, and under cover of the drunkenness and looting many private scores were being paid off.

British troops in Magdala

A general evacuation of the fortress was therefore ordered, and in batches the Ethiopian families were escorted down the hill to the British camp where they were safe from the Gallas. Among the first to go were Theodore's family: his beautiful young wife, Teru-Wark and her child Alamayo, his favourite Itamanyo, and various other women. Itamanyo, who was in relatively good spirits, elected to be escorted to her home in Ethiopia, but Teru-Wark said that it had been Theodore's wish that his son should go to England, and that she would willingly follow him there. She was, however, sad, silent and dejected as Rassam took her down the mountain – a thing that struck him as strange since she had never been loved by Theodore, even though it was said that he had become reconciled to her a few days before he died.

There remained now the question of the political succession. Theodore's empire had collapsed entirely, and all northern and central Ethiopia was divided into belligerent tribal camps, all hating one another, all ready for civil war once the British had departed. Wag-shum Gobaze indeed had already gone off on a raid into Theodore's former territory about Lake Tana.

Napier does not appear to have bothered himself too much with the problem; his orders were to rescue the prisoners and then get out of the country as quickly as possible. He had no intention whatever of paying any attention to Theodore's appeal: 'See that you forsake not these people.' Yet there was a strong case here for leaving a British garrison in Ethiopia

Theodore's son, Alamayo

to tide the country over the next few years of political disorder, and when Napier did not put it forward to his superiors in London he automatically condemned the Ethiopians to anarchy.

In the end he simply dodged the issue: the Queen of the Gallas was installed as ruler of Magdala and the surrounding country, and the larger question of Theodore's successor was left hanging in the air. One can only observe that the manner by which the British left Ethiopia did not become them so well as their manner of entering it.

The last act at Magdala was hardly more than a cock-crow of triumph and revenge. By April 16 all the civilians had been evacuated from the fortress, and fifteen of the elephants brought down the loot to the plain below. On the following day engineers blew the breeches of Theodore's guns, and all the larger buildings except the church were mined. At 4 p.m. the great explosion went up. Fire spread rapidly from hut to hut, with shells and cartridges erupting in the flames, and for many miles around soldiers and tribesmen stood in awe as a vast pall of smoke went up. The fires were still burning with a fierce red glow when darkness fell, and in the morning all that was left of the fortress of Magdala was ash.

By this time the homeward march had already begun, but on April 18 there was a pause on the far side of the Bashilo when Napier made a public declaration of thanks to his soldiers and the loot was auctioned. Holmes of the British Museum was one of the biggest bidders – some nine hundred volumes of manuscripts had been saved – and at the end of the sale a total of £5,000 was collected. This was distributed to the soldiers according to rank.

Napier and his staff

All military retreats, whether from victory or defeat, have an air of anticlimax, and this one was no exception; it was simply more colourful than most. The men were very tired, and some of the elephants lay down miserably on the ground, refusing to get up and go on any more. They were shot. It was still an imposing procession, with the bands playing and the flags leading the way, but the army soon learned that they had earned no gratitude in Ethiopia; they were treated as simply another warlike tribe on the move, and now that they were going away like weak and defeated men they were an obvious target for attack.

Tribesmen perched themselves on the heights above the passes and fired down on the weaker parts of the column, hoping for plunder. From time to time forays had to be sent out against them, and food and fodder that was offered for sale on the outward journey now had to be seized by force. Heavy rain followed the army all the way, and when the

ABOVE *Magdala burning*

BELOW *The British departure*

Queen Teru-Wark's funeral procession

baggage animals began to die *en masse* great quantities of stores were either abandoned or blown up.

By the middle of May Napier and his staff were half-way down to the coast at Antalo, and here Queen Teru-Wark collapsed. She had grown steadily weaker since leaving Magdala, and although Rassam and Napier's doctor plied her with port wine and arrowroot she soon refused to eat.

At the height of a night storm at Antalo servants came running to Rassam with the news that she was dead. He had her buried by the local Coptic priests, and the little boy Alamayo continued on with the British under the care of a nurse. He was taken to England on Napier's ship and was subsequently sent to school at Rugby, but he died when he was 19 and was buried at St George's Chapel, Windsor.

At Senafé another halt was called, and Kassai was rewarded for his services by the presentation of a formidable quantity of guns, ammunition and stores. Whether or not there was any political intention behind this is obscure, but its effect on Kassai's fortunes was decisive: he was now the most powerfully armed chieftain in Ethiopia, and no man with arms in these highlands ever failed to use them. It seems hard to believe that Merewether, at least, did not envisage this, and there is a cautious note in the official history of the campaign that throws a little light on the matter.

'The best hope,' it says, 'of Abyssinia enjoying peace lay in the partition of its provinces between at least two distinct rulers. . . . It does not appear likely that Kassai will ever attack Wagshum Gobaze, while it is only too probable that the ambition of Wagshum Gobaze will extend itself to Tigré.' Hence presumably the gift of guns to Kassai so that he could defend himself; after all he had been a good friend to the British expedition and he could well become a valuable ally in the future.

The column was now rolling itself up like an enormous carpet, and although a hundred vessels were already taking off the forward units from Zula there was great need for haste. The rains grew heavier every day, and the dry bed of the Kumayli River was soon submerged by a racing torrent. It carried away seven men and many animals in a cloudburst near the Suru Pass, and for some days the tail of the column was held up.

By June 2, however, they were all through and Napier and his staff reached the coast. Every movable object at Zula was now taken up and loaded on to the ships: the telegraph, the railway lines, the salt-water condensers, the thirty-nine surviving elephants. Except for the wharves and a few locomotives hardly anything remained to show that the British had ever been in Ethiopia. On June 10 Napier embarked on the *Feroze* and sailed direct for Suez and England. Not unnaturally a tumultuous welcome was awaiting him: the thanks of Parliament, a gracious reception by the Queen, a step up in the service and a peerage.

Lord Napier of Magdala was the hero of the day. Nor were his men forgotten. Among the many favours bestowed among them there was a grant of £5,000 for Rassam and £2,000 apiece for Blanc and Prideaux.

It had been a great thing to take part in the Magdala campaign and now that it was all over it could be forgotten. Ethiopia, with her defences breached, her lesson learned and her people abandoned to their natural anarchy, slipped quietly out of the news.

Epilogue

Three abortive cavalry charges against modern firearms had destroyed the isolation of the Nile valley from Lake Tana to the sea. None of these engagements, whether of the Mamelukes against the French at the Battle of the Pyramids, of the Shaiqiya tribesmen against the Turks at Korti, or of the Ethiopians against the British at Magdala, had lasted more than an hour or two, or had involved more than a few thousand men. Yet these were genuine crises: once their defences were breached none of these countries was ever to be the same again. In Ethiopia it was the same as in Egypt and the Sudan; she was now committed to the contemporary world, the jump out of the Middle Ages into the present, and other invaders were soon to follow in the wake of the British. It seems absurd that such momentous consequences should come from three insignificant battles – hardly battles, merely a running of spearsmen against modern guns. We are back at Jericho: the trumpets blow, the walls fall down and an age vanishes in an instant. But perhaps it is in the nature of history to declare itself through apparently small events; certainly such catastrophes as the mass killings on the Somme and at Passchendaele in the First World War decided nothing.

There are some other unusual aspects about this violent awakening. The part played by religion, for example, was very great. This was not a clear-cut issue – there were Coptic Christians in Egypt and Moslems in Ethiopia – but in general the Copts were entrenched in the mountains around the upper reaches of the Blue Nile while the Moslems remained in the desert below. Both peoples were determined to resist the Western invaders, but then they also hated one another, and by nature as well as by religion they were mortal enemies. Of the two racial groups one has to concede that the desert Moslems had developed a much higher civilization than the Ethiopian Christians. Where the Ethiopians had no architecture much beyond a grass-hut, the Moslems had long since produced such masterpieces as the Ibn Tulun mosque in Cairo, and the Koran, whether you believed it or not, was a more cultivated guide than the superstitious dronings of the Ethiopian priests. The Ethiopians were eaters of raw meat, heavy drinkers, uncouth in their manners and given to wild and primitive passions. The Moslems by contrast were ascetics, and in all their arts and crafts and in their pleasure in the refinements of life they were far in advance. They loved the coolness and cleanliness of water, while the Ethiopians on their icy heights huddled together with their cattle at night and seldom washed. And yet the Coptic faith was strong, Theodore and his followers had a Biblical sense of destiny, and they loved their independence more than luxury. The Arab compromised, schemed and bargained, the Ethiopian made rash hysterical gestures to satisfy his pride; and both races, when aroused, were absolutely ruthless.

It might have been thought that the Western Christian influence would have been very great in this troubled scene, since it was backed by Western arms. But such was not the case; none of the Western invaders from Bonaparte's time to this have been able to fix their faith on the river. The Moslem imam and the Coptic priest are still today as firmly entrenched as they ever were. In this sense at least the inhabitants of the Nile have never been conquered.

It is also remarkable that the French, who set in motion the whole nineteenth-century upheaval on the Nile, and who did so much for the exploration of the river, should have had so disproportionate a share in its government and development. Britain, Italy, Belgium and Germany were all destined to found colonies in this part of Africa: never the French. Yet of all the people mentioned in these pages Bonaparte is the one who appears to have had the clearest notion of what was involved in the conquest of the Nile. All the schemes for the regeneration of the river that were eventually carried out – the dams and canals, the land reforms and the local government, even the study of the ancient past – were originally his, and he understood the strategical importance of the Nile better than anyone else. At the pyramids he not only felt that he was being watched by the past; he had a vision of the future centuries as well.

Despite its three million inhabitants and its overlay of skyscrapers and busy traffic, modern Cairo displays its history rather more readily than most big cities. The Mamelukes' tombs are there for all to see, and a part at least of Saladin's great walls and gateways are intact. But one must search with diligence in all this before one discovers relics of the French occupation. Bonaparte's ornamental sword hangs in the national museum, the site of the Battle of the Pyramids remains, and there are, of course, the great archaeological collections through which the French did so much to make ancient Egypt known to the world; but little else has survived. Except for such minor curiosities as the names of Desaix's soldiers carved on the temple at Dendera, time and the desert have obliterated almost all the evidence of their campaign on the river. Not even the landscape is quite the same, since the recently planted eucalyptus groves have greatly changed the appearance of the Lower Nile, and the temples have been cleared of the debris that so impeded Denon in his inquiries.

Beyond Aswan most of the monuments and villages of Nubia are now covered by the waters of the new dam, and it is only through the work of men like Burckhardt that we know anything of their history. As for the great loop in the Nile through the Shaiqiya country and the towns of Dongola and Korti, all this is very much as it was early in the nineteenth century when Ismail hauled his boats up the cataracts. The settlement at Berber is no longer the haunt of roistering traders; for many years now a railway has crossed the stark and terrible desert from Egypt, and although camels still exist the real caravan routes are in the air.

Yet still at Shendy one has a sense of arrivals and departures, and there is a certain excitement in the atmosphere. The market still exists, and it is busier than ever. When the train comes in from Egypt it spills on to the platform, and one is offered for sale splendid pot-bellied baskets which are very much as Burckhardt described them in 1814, and brilliant little cotton flags in red and gold – the symbol of the new Republic of the Sudan.

Shendy is now a military base, and in place of the Leopard King's rusty bodyguard

The market at Shendy

extremely handsome young soldiers walk about in well-pressed uniforms. In the desert beyond, the ruins of Meroë still stand silently in the tremendous heat, and except for occasional parties of archaeologists hardly anyone visits them from one year's end to another.

Khartoum has greatly altered. No one these days would dare to refer to it as vile, filthy or squalid. It is a delightful river town with great avenues of banyan trees growing on the Blue Nile bank, and it contains one of the finest universities in Africa. The cotton trade has done what all the traffic in gold, slaves and ivory failed to do – made the people prosperous; and every year new irrigation works push the desert further back from the river. Mechanical pumps have replaced the waterwheels, and all night electric lights gleam across the Blue Nile where it comes in to join the White.

There is still no road from Khartoum to Sennar. One drives across the open desert and simply chooses a track that leads on southwards along the river. In the dry season it is a surrealist landscape with power lines and telegraph poles vanishing into a vast emptiness, and on these poles sit those same little bright green parrots that Cailliaud observed when he came this way with Ismail in 1821. The country improves as you go south, and presently you are among a network of canals that irrigate the cotton crops. A scrub forest extends along the river bank, and just occasionally you will see a crocodile gleaming like a wet turtle on a sandbank or perhaps a morose-looking marabou stork standing motionless in the shallows. Modern Sennar is a dusty township with wide streets and a tumbledown bazaar, and the Blue Nile here is blocked by a huge dam with a railway running across it. In recent years engineers have been working there all day and all night on a new electrical undertaking. Of old Sennar there is little or nothing to be seen, but the heat at times is every bit as oppressive as Bruce described it, and the Dinka tribesmen living with their cattle in the great plains beyond are almost as naked, as primitive and as unresponsive to the healthy dreariness of modern civilization as they ever were. Theirs is a world of mosquitoes, of smoking cow-dung fires, and of cattle-worship so extreme that a man will spend all day with a favourite cow, caressing it, crooning to it, absorbing its cow-ness into his being. One even hears of boys gazing at their reflections in puddles of water in the hope that they will discover some way of decorating their faces so that they will resemble the animal they adore. These people do not want to change.

South again from Sennar one enters the rain forest: fever trees with bright ochre trunks and sage-coloured leaves, baobabs which are all trunk, bulging to an enormous size, and a scrub that is of a ghostly whiteness and deadness until the rains arrive. Mongooses scuttle across the track, and the hornbills swoop in thousands. On the river itself there is very little life in the way of boats or villages, but it is much fresher and less spoiled than the White Nile, and it continues to be very grand, a quarter of a mile from bank to bank, and there is a clear sparkling movement in the water. And thus at the end of a long day from Sennar one reaches Roseires. This is an enchanting place. Neame trees and banyans cast a green shade along the river, and the little town perches itself among broken hills. The British during their long occupation of the Sudan, from 1898 to 1956, put an indelible stamp on these settlements along the Blue Nile, and no one who has been to India will fail to recognize it: the district commissioner's house with its rose-red bricks and its netted verandas, the servants in turbans and white gowns and the gardeners running little canals of water through the flowering shrubs, the native bazaar with its whitewashed shops and its tinkers and its muleteers sitting in the dust, the smell of heavy tropical flowers and the thin drone of pipes, the crowds wandering through a wall of heat, the goats and still more goats. All this sits queerly on a world which was a savage wilderness when the Turks broke into it in 1821.

There is no bridge on the Blue Nile between Sennar and the Debra Markos road in Ethiopia – a distance of some five hundred miles – but the traveller can cross the river with his truck at Roseires by calling out the convicts from the prison. They push the vehicle aboard a barge and, like the Volga boatmen, tow it upstream for a little way, singing in chorus as they haul on the rope. Then with a shove from the bank you are away into the current and a steady paddling brings the barge to the opposite shore. Now, on the left bank, one can explore the country where Ismail went slave-raiding and Cailliaud made his search for gold. It cannot have altered very much. Huge granite outcrops dot the plain, and at their bases the inhabitants have made their villages beside the water-holes. They are a handsome, smiling people, the men with head-dresses made of feathers, and the women with complicated strings of coloured beads criss-crossed between their breasts. On the Ethiopian border, south of the Yabus River, the people grow still more primitive, and one sees again the women that Cailliaud saw, plastered from head to foot with red ochre until they shine like Chinese lacquer, and the tribesmen who, with their well-made spears and throwing-sticks, range the scrub in search of game. The resistance of these people to the teaching of Christian missionaries is very great, but in the townships like Kurmuk Islam is strong; it is a familiar sight to see the elders, mostly Arab traders and officials and their followers, standing in line in the square, turbaned and white-gowned, in readiness for the evening prayer. The night falls quickly; a little after four there is a first breath of cool air and before six it is dark.

Between Roseires and the Ethiopian frontier near Fazughli there is still very little habitation on the Blue Nile. The water slips smoothly over black granite rocks, and at the end of a rough five hours' drive from Roseires one looks up and sees with delight the first foothills of the Ethiopian mountains. This place, for all its wildness and solitariness, is still something of a cross-roads, and there are many slight but definite evidences of the past. Gold is still found – the people will show you nuggets that they have washed out of the *khors* or streams – and Fazughli with its ancient mines is still a synonym for gold. Here, too, in this unlikely spot, a caravan of *West* Africans making the pilgrimage to Mecca halted at some time in the remote past and got no further. These people tilled the ground, intermarried with the local natives, and so, like lotus-eaters, they have let the years go by and end in nothing but the slow routine of simply keeping alive under a hot sun. Their women descend to the river each evening with gourds on their heads, the earth is scratched up with wooden hoes, the drums sound for a marriage or a feast, and Mecca is still a thousand miles away. The river here, on making its final disappearance from the plains, is unbelievably beautiful, a conjunction of the green hills and the unspoiled rushing stream. In the dry season it turns and twists between many little uninhabited islands, and droves of tropical birds keep crossing between these islands and the shore. There is a nightjar which is fantastic. In the last red light of the sunset it hovers with its four wings – two of them merely black tufts at the end of a long thin quill – about thirty feet above the ground, hunting for insects. It is as fragile and delicate as a Chinese print.

The traveller here proceeds no further on his way. The Blue Nile gorge which begins a few miles beyond the frontier is still as implacable as ever, and the Shifta tribesmen who inhabit this lower end have a reputation for waylaying unarmed strangers. If he wishes to explore the upper reaches of the river he must travel into central Ethiopia either by air from Khartoum or by taking a truck or mules up the rough pass that leads from Metemma to Lake Tana – the route that Rassam took. Either way this is a journey that reveals very quickly how it is that the Blue Nile in Ethiopia has remained for so long a virtually un-known river. The great edge of the plateau rises up crag on crag for eight thousand feet or more, and much of the plateau itself is still uninhabited.

All through these years with which we have been dealing – 1798 to 1868 – exploration was going on, and in 1862 the Englishman Speke had actually got to the source of the White Nile in Uganda. Speke, like Bruce, had to wait twenty years or more before his discovery was acknowledged, yet it was a solid achievement, and it led people to believe that the whole pattern of the river was now explained. But this was not so at all: the Blue Nile had still not been explored. Since Bruce's time the course of the river had been marked on all the maps, but no one in fact had penetrated into that immense ravine that ran for more than three hundred miles from Lake Tana to the Sudanese border. Rassam, when he first reached Theodore, had seen something of the source and the extreme upper reaches, and the British at Magdala had perched for a day or two on one of the principal tributaries, the Bashilo; but they had gone no further. Nor was there any attempt to explore this vital stretch of the river – the stretch that provided the Sudan and Egypt with most of their water – for the next thirty-four years.

W. N. Macmillan, a wealthy American big-game hunter, was the first man to try his hand. In 1902 he engaged a Norwegian explorer named B. H. Jessen, and at much expense a number of boats were constructed and transported to the river. They arranged to tackle the gorge from two directions at once: while Jessen came up with a launch from Khartoum the other boats were to sail downstream from the vicinity of Lake Tana. Nothing whatever was achieved. Jessen found himself blocked by rapids at Famaka in the Sudan, before he ever got to the Ethiopian border, and all Macmillan's boats were wrecked as soon as they were launched in the headlong current. In 1905 Macmillan encouraged Jessen to try again. This time Jessen set off with a mule caravan from Khartoum, and he entered the gorge from the Sudan. But he was defeated when he was still three hundred miles away from Lake Tana. After this there was another long silence on the river until Colonel R. E. Cheesman arrived in 1925 as British consul in north-west Ethiopia. 'The latest maps,' Cheesman wrote, 'showed the course of the Blue Nile as a series of dotted lines. . . . It seemed almost unbelievable that such a famous river, and one on which Egypt had depended for its prosperity throughout the ages, could have been so long neglected. . . . The course of the Blue Nile,' he added, 'might be considered as offering the only bit of pioneering exploration left in Africa.'

For the next eight years Cheesman devoted himself to this work whenever he could get away from his consular duties. He soon realized that there was no question of following the river bed either by boat or on foot – the course had to be mapped from above – but he penetrated down into the gorge whenever he could to check his bearings, and he travelled in all some five thousand miles by mule over country never before seen by a European. In addition he was the first man to circumnavigate Lake Tana. It was a formidable achievement and Cheesman must be regarded as the first true geographer of the Blue Nile.

Cheesman wrote a book about his adventures and when he returned to England he had the galling experience of losing his manuscript. It was stolen from his car and an appeal to the thieves brought no response: all had to be done again. However, the rewritten book, *Lake Tana and the Blue Nile*, is an absorbing document. On the lake Cheesman visited Korata and Zagé and all the other places Rassam and the prisoners had known so well; at the source of the Little Abbai he stood where Bruce had stood, and he followed his path down to the Tisisat Falls. For the first time the world now learned what life was like at the bottom of the gorge. Cheesman found very few inhabitants there – it was too hot and malarial – but there was an abundance of wild life that had been driven off the plateau above, the greater kudu and many other antelopes, hippopotamuses and crocodiles, an occasional pride of lions. Among the groves of white oleander and tamarisks growing on the banks he saw the wonderful Ethiopian birds in myriads: spur-winged geese, crowned cranes, yellow-billed ducks, ibises, herons and pelicans. When grass fires started up on shelves of level ground carmine bee-eaters dived through the smoke for insects, and looked like 'glowing red embers' in the sky. Stage by stage he descended from the country of the Coptic Christians to that of the Gallas, and finally to that of the pagan Negroes and the Arabs; and the river, he discovered, grew steadily wilder as he went along. It rushed by at twelve miles an hour and when finally it emerged into the Sudan it had dropped four thousand five hundred feet from Lake Tana. Here in the plains it plunged over its last cataracts and widened out to three hundred yards or more. At night tribesmen came out with lights on their boats to spear the fish. Already in those days there was a track beside the river leading to the township of Roseires, and when two cars appeared on it Cheesman's mules bolted into the forest; like most of the human inhabitants of Ethiopia they had never seen a car before.

The Italians, after their conquest of Ethiopia in 1935, had an imaginative notion for blocking the present outlet of the Blue Nile from Lake Tana. They planned instead to drain the lake into the fertile plains on the west by means of a tunnel thirty kilometres long. But the Italians were only six years in Ethiopia and nothing came of this.

Then in 1941 the river was roused once again by the appearance of the Emperor Haile Selassie and a British army coming upstream from the Sudan. All the old Ethiopia hands were involved in this: Daniel Arthur Sandford, a colleague of Cheesman's, perched himself in secret in the Lake Tana district and made contact with the rebels, while Cheesman ran the Ethiopian intelligence in Khartoum. Meanwhile Haile Selassie, with Wingate, the leader of the expedition, marched upstream with the main column from Roseires. Camels, not elephants, were used on this expedition – some twenty thousand of them, all destined to die in the cold of the mountains – and they chose a route that kept them above the gorge. For reasons that have never been quite explained Wingate insisted on avoiding the beaten tracks, and instead obliged his soldiers to hack their way across country through heavy

ABOVE *Camels loaded with stores and ammunition were taken through 200 miles of jungle. Photograph taken in January 1941*

BELOW *The Emperor Haile Selassie with Orde Wingate on his left, in January 1941*

scrub. But then Wingate was a strange man. 'His narrow blue eyes,' says William Allen in his admirable book on the campaign, 'narrow set, burned with an insatiable glare. His spare bony figure with its crouching gait had the hang of an animal run by hunting, yet hungry for the next night's prey. Some demon chased Wingate over the Gojjam highlands. . . .' One marvels a little at the reversals of history here – the British, still with their eye on the Red Sea route from India, returning after seventy years, not to destroy an emperor, but to reinstate Theodore's successor. One is even tempted to speculate how things would have turned out if it had not been Rassam but Wingate, an eccentric if there ever was one, who had been sent to Theodore so long ago. Now at all events they made their way across the old battlefields and river crossings, scattering the Italians as they went along, and at the end of 1941 Haile Selassie was installed once more at his new capital of Addis Ababa, a town that did not even exist in Theodore's time. From Magdala, now a half-forgotten village, there was nothing but silence.

The 1940s drifted into the 1950s and still very little apart from Cheesman's account was known about the Blue Nile gorge. The planners and the road builders avoided it where they could, and the Ethiopians, even with the aid of DDT to fight malaria, had no desire to go down into those depths which had always had a name for superstition and evil. There was still talk from time to time of how Ethiopia might ruin Egypt and the Sudan by throwing a series of dams across the gorge, or even by poisoning the stream, and the matter was raised again in 1956 when the British were invading Egypt. It was still nonsense, of course, there was enough water in the Blue Nile flood to overwhelm any artificial obstruction; but by the 1960s the westernization of Ethiopia had reached a point where it had become necessary to investigate the resources of the river. An American survey team was brought in, and now for the first time the gorge was studied in detail; engineers in helicopters were able to fly down to the most hidden corners.

The writer was fortunate in being able to spend a day on one of these excursions, and it was a revelation of a kind, rather like that moment when one first put on a diving mask and explored the bottom of the sea. We took off early one morning from Addis Ababa and flew directly to the river, one hundred miles away. The helicopter, skimming along only ten yards above the ground, was a madly strange thing in these regions, and the villagers uncovered their heads and bowed to us as we went by. All around them the undulating plateau spread away, dotted with eucalyptus groves, and a hundred little streams and waterfalls rushed down to the great curving valley of the river nearly a mile below. Coming up to the edge of this valley one sank, as in an elevator, into the gorge itself, down and down, past scattered forests and cliffs of glaring black rock and gravel.

As we descended the walls of the gorge came steadily closer and the sky above contracted into a narrow arch of light. Finally we hovered over the river itself, and it was full of movement: it coursed along only one hundred feet across at the narrower places, greenish-grey in colour, and at every bend in its winding course it broke into eddies and whirlpools that would have been very difficult to negotiate in a boat. This was in January, when the river is low, but by the end of the wet season in July it would be another thirty feet higher and the current twice as fast. Except where a tributary came in and stained the clear water with a murky grey the banks presented an unbroken cliff-face not too steep for a man to clamber along perhaps, but impossible for a mule. For a while we shot upstream, and it was an exhilarating thing to sit there in our absurd transparent box, seeing everything with an eagle's eye, and being too absorbed to be afraid. At first no human beings anywhere appeared, but there was a good deal of wild game on the sandbanks and occasional flat ledges of ground: storks and other wading birds among the reeds, waterhogs, blacker even than this black sand, kneeling to drink, small herds of antelopes, a hippopotamus or two mooning in the deeper pools and crocodiles everywhere. Our roaring engine was an incomprehensible intrusion.

All these creatures scattered and vanished as we flew over them, but it did not seem to be the automatic fear that overtakes herds that are regularly hunted. It was, rather, a bewildered and dumbfounded panic, the sort of reaction human beings have when confronted by some sudden and monstrous reversal in nature, such as an earthquake or a tornado rushing out of a clear sky. At all events these animals soon got over their fright: directly the hellish and inexplicable noise had gone by they emerged again and began feeding as though nothing had happened.

Presently we reached a place where an electronic device had been set up to gauge the speed and the rise and fall of the current, and here we put down on a pocket handkerchief of level ground beside the river. The helicopter blades ran to a stop as we stepped out, and at once one was absorbed into the silence and the immensity of the gorge. The air was thick and hot, and the surrounding bush growing up the steep sides of the cliffs had that curious stillness and completeness that rest on places that have never been disturbed by man. Down in the Sudan and Egypt one fears the diseases in the broad and placid water of the Nile – bilharzia and the guinea worm, the danger of blindness – but here, in this untouched racing stream, we were able to bathe and drink, and provided one avoided the pools there was no real reason to worry about the crocodiles. And so all day from the point where the Guder River comes in to the Nile we buzzed upstream like a gadfly, dropping down on sandbanks where there was something interesting to see, and then on again over hidden bends in the river where the valley widened out and where an occasional village, cut off from all the world, scraped a living from a threadbare crop of maize.

It was not exactly claustrophobic in the gorge – at many places its sides at the top were ten or fifteen miles apart – but it created a certain dullness and uneasiness in the mind, a feeling that it was not natural for one to be there, that one had somehow got oneself involved in one of Conan Doyle's stories of lost worlds, of nameless, unknown swamps and valleys inhabited by the pterodactyl and the dinosaur. A sort of timelessness was in the air, and one looked up occasionally to the clear sky above with a sense of relief.

When eventually the suspension bridge on the Debra Markos road came into view – this one sign of man in so many hundreds of miles of primitive wilderness – it was a slight shock, an anticlimax such as one sometimes experiences on emerging from a dark room into the clear prosaic light of day. We turned up a tributary then until we were confronted by a waterfall that descended in almost vertical cascades from the heights above. Rising up in front of the white rush of spray we regained the plateau and flew back uneventfully to Addis Ababa. It had been a superficial glimpse, of course, but in this one day we had seen things which had taken Colonel Cheesman eight years of journeying to reach.

Many strange matters are coming to light in the Blue Nile valley as the American survey goes on. Once near Magdala the engineers were shown a cave where some twenty or thirty mummies wrapped in a coarse brown canvas were strewn about. The cave appeared to have no end, but a second opening kept it fresh and dry with a current of air, and so the mummies were well preserved; but how long they had been there, and who these people were, no one could say. Other relics of past generations are being revealed as the aerial photographing of the river goes on. Thus, for example, an immense ditch too wide for a horse to jump across has been discovered, and it winds away over valleys and hills for hundreds of miles. Is this the ancient boundary between two tribes, the earthworks of some forgotten Theodore? Then again, a member of the survey team has taken specimens of the Blue Nile silt – that famous silt upon which the fertility of Egypt is supposed to depend – and he has been quite unable to make anything grow in it. Dry or wet the soil is sterile. Can it then be that the Blue Nile is only a water-supplier? – and that the Egyptian delta, which rises several inches every century with the intake of this Ethiopian silt, is really dependent upon the thick slime-filled ooze of the White Nile to manure its crops? This is an entirely new idea. In the end perhaps someone will have to take a boat down the Blue Nile and actually live at the bottom of the gorge before this and many other questions are answered.

As for the inhabitants of Ethiopia, it is already difficult to recognize in them the descendants of Theodore's tribesmen. They are a thin and nervous people with a curious mixture of darting quickness and gravity in their manners. One feels the emotional warmth of Africa here, the lingering handshake, the cool, smooth black hand in yours, inert, idle, unwilling to let go; and one observes the greetings and farewells among the Ethiopians themselves – the way the men very rapidly kiss one another alternately on either cheek, bobbing and ducking all the while. They repeat this process five or six times or more. And all this on an airfield where the planes come roaring in, and the passengers, in the demon depths of the concrete reception buildings, walk gravely to the booking offices in jodhpurs and cloaks, coloured umbrellas and fly-whisks in their hands, while the loudspeakers blare out Amharic announcements over their heads. Once in the air the planes pass over country as solitary as the ocean.

These things are very strange, and they are made stranger still by a certain feeling of hysteria in the atmosphere, an almost palpable tension. One feels that at any moment all this affection might turn into hate and violence. Europeans in Addis Ababa like to go down to the hot plains for their holidays, and there, they say, their nerves are calmer.

Lake Tana and the source of the Blue Nile can be visited without much difficulty. One flies on a little country air-service from Addis Ababa to the village of Bahar Dar on the southern shore of Lake Tana, and thence one can be paddled out on a raft to the place where the river debouches from the lake. With mules and guides one can also follow Bruce's route up to the source of the Little Abbai, where the water still oozes out of a bog precisely as he saw it; and with a little persistence – a mule with a wooden saddle is an uncompromising seat for a novice – one can reach the Tisisat Falls in a day's steady riding from Bahar Dar. It is a rewarding journey. Towards evening one sees in the distance the glimmering cloud of spray rising over the falls, and then, by swimming the mules across to the left bank, one can proceed directly into the wet jungle that lies around the falls themselves. At one vantage point the whole roaring overflow can be seen, and it is pleasant to stand there speculating as to whether or not Father Lobo could really have found a perch beneath the deluge, and knowing that little or nothing has altered here since his or Bruce's time. The spray that falls like gentle rain, wetting one to the skin, falls forever – two centuries and more ago on Lobo and Bruce, now on oneself, and still upon any traveller who chances to be at that beautiful place at this present moment. Sometimes a log, borne along by the current, teeters for a moment at the lip of the vast abyss, and then plunges downward on its long journey to Egypt and the sea.

Select Bibliography

Baker, Sir Samuel W. *The Nile Tributaries of Abyssinia*. London, 1867

Browne, W. G. *Travels in Africa, Egypt and Syria from the year 1792 to 1798*, 2nd ed. London, 1806

Bruce, James. *Travels to Discover the Sources of the Nile, in the Years 1768, 1769, 1770, 1771, 1772 and 1773*. London, 1804

Burckhardt, John Lewis. *Travels in Nubia*, 2nd ed. London, 1822

Cailliaud, Frédéric. *Voyage à Méroé, au Fleuve Blanc, au-delà de Fâzoql dans le midi du royaume de Sennâr*. Paris, 1826

Charles-Roux, François. *Bonaparte: Governor of Egypt*. Trans. E. W. Dickes. London, 1937

Cheesman, Col. R. E. *Lake Tana and the Blue Nile*. London, 1936

Crawford, O. G. S. *The Fung Kingdom of Sennar*. Gloucester, 1951

Cumming, D. C. 'The History of Kassala', *Sudan Notes and Records*, Vol. XXX, 1937, and Vol. XXXIII, 1940

De Cosson, E. A. *The Cradle of the Blue Nile*. London, 1877

Denon, Dominique Vivant. *Voyage dans la Basse et la Haute Égypte pendant les campagnes du général Bonaparte*. London, 1809

Description de l'Égypte. Paris, 1809–25

Dodwell, Henry. *The Founder of Modern Egypt*. London, 1931

Elgood, P. G. *Bonaparte's Adventure in Egypt*. London, 1931

English, George Bethune. *A Narrative of the Expedition to Dongola and Sennaar, under the command of Ismael Pasha*. Boston, Mass., 1823

Ghorbal, Shafik. *The Beginnings of the Egyptian Question and the Rise of Mehemet Ali*. London, 1928

Gordon, Lady Lucie Duff. *Letters from Egypt, 1863–1865*. Ed. Sarah Austin. London, 1865

Head, Major F. B. *The Life of Bruce, the African Traveller*, 2nd ed. London, 1836

Hill, Richard. *Biographical Dictionary of the Anglo-Egyptian Sudan*. Oxford, 1951

—*Egypt in the Sudan 1820–81*. London, 1959

Holland, Major T. J., and Hozier, Capt. H. M. *Record of the Expedition to Abyssinia*. London, 1870

Holt, P. M. *A Modern History of the Sudan*. London, 1961

Jollois, Jean Baptiste Prosper. *Journal d'un Ingénieur attaché à l'Expédition d'Égypte 1798–1802*. Paris, 1904

La Jonquière, Clément de. *L'Expédition d'Égypte 1798–1801*. Paris, 1902–4

Lane, Edward William. *Manners and Customs of the Modern Egyptians*, reprinted from 3rd ed. London, 1890

Legh, Thomas. *Narrative of a Journey in Egypt and in the Country beyond the Cataracts*. London, 1816

Lobo, J. *A Voyage to Abyssinia by Father Jerome Lobo*. Trans. and abridged from Joachim le Grand's French version by Samuel Johnson. London, 1735

Madelin, Louis. *L'Ascension de Bonaparte.* (Vol. 2 of *Histoire du Consulat et de l'Empire.* Paris, 1937–54)

Martha-Beker, Félix, Comte de Mons. *Le Général Desaix, étude historique.* Paris, 1852

Melly, George. *Khartoum and the Blue and White Niles.* London, 1851

Napier, Lt-Col. the Hon. H. D. *Field Marshal Lord Napier of Magdala.* London, 1927

Napoleon I. *Mémoires pour servir à l'histoire de France sous Napoléon, écrits à Sainte Hélène, par les généraux qui ont partagé sa captivité, et publiés sur les manuscrits entièrement corrigés de la main de Napoléon,* 2nd ed. Paris, 1830

Parkyns, Mansfield. *Life in Abyssinia: being Notes collected during three years Residence and Travels in that Country.* London, 1853

Pinkerton, John. *A General Collection of the Best and Most Interesting Voyages and Travels in All Parts of the World.* London, 1808–14

Plowden, Walter Chicele. *Travels in Abyssinia and the Galla Country.* Ed. T. C. Plowden. London, 1868

Rassam, Hormuzd. *Narrative of the British Mission to Theodore, King of Abyssinia.* London, 1869

Robinson, A. E. 'The Conquest of the Sudan by the Wali of Egypt Muhammad Ali Pasha 1820–1824', *Journal of the African Society,* Vol. XXV, 1925–6

Sauzet, Armand. *Desaix, le 'Sultan Juste'.* Paris, 1954

Stanley, H. M. *Coomassie and Magdala: the Story of two British Campaigns in Africa.* London, 1874

Steegmuller, F., ed. and trans. *The Selected Letters of Gustave Flaubert.* New York, 1957

Telles, Balthazar. *Travels of the Jesuits in Ethiopia.* (In *A New Collection of Travels and Voyages.* Ed. John Stevens. London, 1708–10)

Waddington, G., and the Rev. Barnard Hanbury. *Journal of a Visit to Some Parts of Ethiopia.* London, 1822

Note. The quotation from Samuel Johnson in Chapter 3 is from *A Voyage to Abyssinia,* his translation of Lobo's account; the note on Bruce's treatment of Latrobe comes from Crawford's *The Fung Kingdom of Sennar.* The quotation from Professor Arnold Toynbee in Chapter 5 is taken from his preface to Ghorbal's *Beginnings of the Egyptian Question.* Abdul-Rahman al-Jabarti's description of reaction in Cairo to the French invasion and occupation, quoted in Chapter 6, was reprinted in Napoleon's *Mémoires.*

Illustration Acknowledgments

COLOUR PLATES

JACKET Musée de Versailles. Photo: Cliché des Musées Nationaux

1 Stephen Harrison
2 Rodney Searight. Photo: John Freeman Ltd
3 Musée de Versailles. Photo: Cliché des Musées Nationaux
4 Victoria and Albert Museum, London. From *Egypt and Nubia* by David Roberts
5 Rodney Searight. Photo: John Freeman Ltd
6 Guildhall Library and Art Gallery, London
7 Musée de Versailles. Photo: Cliché des Musées Nationaux
8 Musée de Versailles. Photo: Cliché des Musées Nationaux
9 ABOVE Houghton Library, Harvard University, Cambridge, Mass. BELOW Rodney Searight, Photo: John Freeman Ltd
10 Rodney Searight. Photo: John Freeman Ltd
11 Rodney Searight. From *Researches in Egypt and Nubia* by G. B. Belzoni, London, 1820. Photo: John Freeman Ltd
12 National Army Museum, London
13 From *Reisen in Nord-Ost-Afrika* by Theodor von Heuglin. Gotha, 1857. Photos: Derrick Witty
14 By permission of the Chief Royal Engineer. Photo: E. H. & B. E. Snell

MONOCHROME

Frontispiece A waterwheel.
Victoria and Albert Museum,
London. From *Egypt and
Nubia* by David Roberts.
Photo: John Freeman Ltd

15 From *Voyage sur la côte
orientale de la Mer Rouge dans
le pays d' Adel et le royaume
de Choa* by François Xavier.
Paris, 1841. Photos: John
Freeman Ltd

18–19 UNESCO. Photo: Keating

19 J. Allan Cash

20 UNESCO. Photo: Annemiek
Veldman

22 From *Travels in Egypt and
Nubia* by Frederick Lewis
Norden. London, 1757.
Photo: John Freeman Ltd

23 From *Travels in Egypt and
Nubia* by Frederick Lewis
Norden. London, 1757.
Photo: John Freeman Ltd

26 Royal Geographical Society.
From *Voyages and Travels* by
Lord Valentia. Photo: John
Freeman Ltd

28 From *Voyage to Abyssinia* by
Henry Salt. London, 1814.
Photo: John Freeman Ltd

29 Rodney Searight. Photo: John
Freeman Ltd

31 From *Travels to Discover the
Sources of the Nile* by James
Bruce. London, 1804

35 From *Travels to Discover the
Sources of the Nile* (2nd ed.)
by James Bruce. Edinburgh,
1805. Photo: John Freeman
Ltd

37 Reproduced by courtesy of
the Trustees of the British
Museum (B.M. Orient 533)

38 From *Reisen in Europa, Asien
und Afrika* by Joseph
Russegger. Stuttgart, 1842.
Photo: John Freeman Ltd

41 Reproduced by courtesy of
The Earl of Elgin. Photo:
Tom Scott

43 Reproduced by Gracious
Permission of Her Majesty
The Queen

45 Royal Commission on Ancient
Monuments, Scotland. From
*Ancient Castles and Mansions
of the Stirling Nobility* by
J. S. Fleming. Edinburgh,
1902. Photo: Crown Copyright

47 Radio Times Hulton Picture
Library

49 From *Travels to Discover the
Sources of the Nile* by James
Bruce. London, 1804

50 Bibliothèque Nationale, Paris

55 Private Collection

56 Musée Carnavalet, Paris.
Photo: Bulloz

57 LEFT Musée Carnavalet, Paris.
Photo: Giraudon
RIGHT Bibliothèque Nationale,
Paris

58 ABOVE LEFT Musée de
Versailles. Photo: Cliché des
Musées Nationaux
ABOVE RIGHT From
Luninski's *Napoleon*
BELOW Musée de Versailles.
Photo: Cliché des Musées
Nationaux

59 ABOVE LEFT Bibliothèque
Nationale, Paris
ABOVE RIGHT Collection
Viollet, Paris
BELOW Musée de Versailles.
Photo: Cliché des Musées
Nationaux

60–1 Musée de la Marine, Paris

63 Bibliothèque Nationale, Paris

66 Archives de la Guerre, Paris

67 Bibliothèque Nationale, Paris

68 Bibliothèque Nationale, Paris

70 From *Description de l'Égypte*.
Paris, 1809–25

71 From *Description de l'Égypt*.
Paris, 1809–25

74–5 From *Description de
l'Égypte*. Paris, 1809–25.
Photos: John Freeman Ltd
RIGHT From *Social Life in
Egypt* by Stanley Lane-Poole.
London, 1884. Photo: John
Freeman Ltd

77 From *Social Life in Egypt* by
Stanley Lane-Poole. London,
1884. Photo: John Freeman
Ltd

78–9 From *Description de
l'Égypte*. Paris, 1809–25.

80–1 Bibliothèque Nationale,
Paris

83 From *Social Life in Egypt* by
Stanley Lane-Poole. London.
1884

84 From *Description de l'Égypte*.
Paris, 1809–25. Photo: John
Freeman Ltd

86 From *Description de l'Égypte*.
Paris, 1809–25. Photo: John
Freeman Ltd

88–9 From *Description de
l'Égypte*. Paris, 1809–25

90–1 From *Recueil complet des
costumes autorités civiles et
militaires* by J. Grasse.
Saint Sauveur, 1796

92 From *Description de l'Égypte*.
Paris, 1809–25. Photo: John
Freeman Ltd

95 ABOVE From *Description de
l'Égypte*. Paris, 1809–25.
Photo: John Freeman Ltd
BELOW Rodney Searight. From
Researches in Egypt and Nubia
by G. B. Belzoni. London, 1820

96 Bibliothèque Nationale, Paris

100–101 Bibliothèque Nationale,
Paris. Photo: Bulloz

103 Musée de Versailles. Photo:
Cliché des Musées Nationaux

107 Collection Viollet

108 Bibliothèque Nationale, Paris.
Photo: Collection Viollet

115 Bibliothèque Nationale, Paris.
Photo: Harlingue Viollet

118 From an engraving by
Dominique Vivant Denon

119 From *Description de l'Égypte*.
Paris, 1809–25. Photo: John
Freeman Ltd.

122–3 Rodney Searight. From
*Voyage dans la Basse et la
Haute Égypte* by Dominique
Vivant Denon. London, 1809

125 Bibliothèque Nationale, Paris

126–7 Bibliothèque Nationale,
Paris

131 Victoria and Albert Museum,
London. *Egypt and Nubia* by
David Roberts. Photo: John
Freeman Ltd

132 Victoria and Albert Museum,
London. From *Egypt and
Nubia* by David Roberts.
Photo: John Freeman Ltd

135 Photo: Bulloz

138 Bibliothèque Nationale, Paris

140 Rodney Searight

141 Rodney Searight

142 Reproduced by courtesy of
the Trustees of the British
Museum

147 From *Social Life in Egypt* by
Stanley Lane-Poole. London,
1884. Photos: John Freeman
Ltd

151 Bibliothèque Nationale, Paris

152 Rodney Searight

154 Rodney Searight

157 Victoria and Albert Museum,
London. From *Egypt and
Nubia* by David Roberts.
Photo: John Freeman Ltd

158 From *Travels in Ethiopia,
above the Second Cataract of
the Nile* by G. A. Hoskins.
London, 1835. Photo: John
Freeman Ltd

165 From *Voyage to Abyssinia* by
Henry Salt. London, 1814.
Photo: John Freeman Ltd

166 From *Narrative of Travel in
North Africa* by G. F. Lyon.
London, 1821. Photo: John
Freeman Ltd

168 Hoskins MSS. II 76. Photo:
Ashmolean Museum, Oxford

170 From *Reise in das Gebiet des
Weissen Nil 1862–64* by
Theodor von Heuglin. Leipzig
and Heidelberg, 1869. Photo:
John Freeman Ltd

173 Reproduced by courtesy of the
Trustees of the British
Museum. From Krump's
Hoher und Feuchtbahrer

Palm-Baum desz Heiligen Evangelik, 1710
176 Dean and Chapter of Durham
178 Rodney Searight
179 From a sketch by Frédéric Cailliaud in *Voyage à Méroé.* Paris, 1826
180 From *Voyage sur la côte orientale de la Mer Rouge dans le pays d'Adel et le royaume de Choa* by François Xavier. Paris, 1841. Photo: John Freeman Ltd
181 Rodney Searight
184–5 Rodney Searight
186 Ashmolean Museum, Oxford
188 From *Voyage à Méroé* by Frédéric Cailliaud. Paris, 1826
190 From *Voyage sur la côte orientale de la Mer Rouge dans le pays d'Adel et le royaume de Choa* by François Xavier. Paris, 1841. Photo: John Freeman Ltd
192 From *Life in Abyssinia* (2nd ed.) by Mansfield Parkyns. London. 1868. Photo: John Freeman Ltd
193 From *Social Life in Egypt* by Stanley Lane-Poole. London, 1884. Photo: John Freeman Ltd
195 LEFT Archives Photographiques, Paris. Photo: Harlingue-Viollet RIGHT Collection Viollet
196 Victoria and Albert Museum, London. From *Egypt and Nubia* by David Roberts. Photo: John Freeman Ltd
197 Victoria and Albert Museum, London. From *Egypt and Nubia* by David Roberts. Photo: John Freeman Ltd
198–9 Victoria and Albert Museum, London. From *Egypt and Nubia* by David Roberts. Photo: John Freeman Ltd
200–201 Victoria and Albert Museum, London. From *Egypt and Nubia* by David

Roberts. Photo: John Freeman Ltd
203 From *The Nile Tributaries of Abyssinia* by Sir Samuel Baker. London, 1867. Photo: John Freeman Ltd
204–5 From *The Nile Tributaries of Abyssinia* by Sir Samuel Baker. London, 1867. Photo: John Freeman Ltd
210 From *Théodore II* by Guillaume Le Jean. Paris, 1865
213 Radio Times Hulton Picture Library
216 LEFT Hans Tasiemka. Photo: John Freeman Ltd RIGHT From the *Illustrated London News* of August 1, 1868
217 From *Coomassie and Magdala* by Henry M. Stanley. London, 1874. Photo: John Freeman Ltd
219 From *Record of the Expedition to Abyssinia* by T. J. Holland and H. M. Hozier. London, 1870. Photo: John Freeman Ltd
228 From *Record of the Expedition to Abyssinia* by T. J. Holland and H. M. Hozier. London, 1870. Photo: John Freeman Ltd
231 Dept of the Environment. Photo: Crown Copyright
232 From *Record of the Expedition to Abyssinia* by T. J. Holland and H. M. Hozier. London, 1870. Photo: John Freeman Ltd
234 From *Record of the Expedition to Abyssinia* by T. J. Holland and H. M. Hozier. London, 1870
236 From the *Illustrated London News* of January 11, 1868
237 Mansell Collection
238–9 National Army Museum, London
240 From the *Illustrated London News* of May 9, 1868
242 From *Record of the Expedition to Abyssinia* by T. J. Holland and H. M. Hozier. London,

1870. Photo: John Freeman Ltd
245 From the *Illustrated London News* of August 1, 1868
247 From the *Illustrated London News* of June 6, 1868,
248 From the *Illustrated London News* of July 11, 1868
249 Radio Times Hulton Picture Library
250–51 Mansell Collection
253 From the *Illustrated London News* of May 9, 1868
256 From a sketch by Whynper in *Narrative of the British Mission to Theodore* by H. Rassam. London, 1869
259 National Army Museum, London
260 From the *Illustrated London News* of June 6, 1868
261 Mansell Collection
264–5 From the *Illustrated London News* of June 6, 1868
269 Radio Times Hulton Picture Library
272 From the *Illustrated London News* of June 6, 1868
273 From the *Illustrated London News* of June 13, 1868
274 Mansell Collection
275 From the *Illustrated London News* of June 23, 1868
276 Radio Times Hulton Picture Library
277 From the *Illustrated London News,* 1868
278 From a lithograph by Ferguson in *Record of the Expedition to Abyssinia* by T. J. Holland and H. M. Hozier. London, 1870
279 ABOVE From the *Illustrated London News* of June 13, 1868 BELOW From the *Illustrated London News* of July 4, 1868
280 From the *Illustrated London News* of June 27, 1868
284 LIFE © Time Inc. Photo: Eliot Elisofon
289 Imperial War Museum, London

Index